REFLECTIVE PARENTING

Following on from her acclaimed first book, *Reflective Parenting*, Sheila Redfern brings a fresh look at parenting young children in today's world.

In this revised edition, Dr Redfern uses her extensive experience of working with children and their families to help parents adopt an approach to their children that ensures their long-term security, resilience and well-being in the face of life's challenges. Using everyday examples, this book provides you with practical strategies to develop a reflective style of parenting that supports your child's development, enhances their relationships – with you and with their friends and siblings – and reach their full potential. *Reflective Parenting* shows us that there are no quick fixes to difficult behaviours or emotions and that the best route to managing children's behaviour is to help guide them in how they manage their emotions. Crucially, it shows us that parents are the key to their children's long-term emotional and behavioural well-being and that adopting a reflective parenting stance can vastly improve your relationship with your child.

Reflective Parenting is an informative and enriching read for parents, written to help parents form a better relationship with their children and to help support their healthy emotional development in today's challenging world. It is also an essential resource for clinicians working with children, young people and families to support them in managing the dynamics of the child–parent relationship.

Sheila Redfern, PhD, is a consultant clinical child and adolescent psychologist and the Director of Redfern Psychology. She has worked with children, adolescents and their caregivers in mental health settings for 30 years. She is a parent to three boys.

"Sheila Redfern's *Reflective Parenting* is a masterful blend of clinical rigour and compassionate wisdom. Drawing on decades of practice, Redfern translates the best of developmental research into clear, practical guidance that invites adults to look inward as they nurture the children in their care. Every insight is grounded in evidence, yet delivered with a warmth that makes complex ideas accessible and immediately useful. Ten years on, this new updated book feels even more relevant: it empowers parents, carers, teachers and therapists alike to understand the emotional worlds of children—and their own—so they can respond with attuned, confident compassion. This anniversary edition is not just a reprint; it is a vital companion for anyone committed to fostering secure, healthy relationships across the generations."

Julia Samuel, *MBE, psychotherapist, author, podcaster*

"Reflective parenting is turning out to be a key to mental health. This book really helps us understand what it involves in practice."

Sue Gerhardt, *author of Why Love Matters and The Selfish Society*

"If you want your kids to mentally flourish and be able to have a great life in a world that's gone insane then this book will tell you everything you need to know. It's the ultimate guide on how to be the parents you wished you had."

Ruby Wax

REFLECTIVE PARENTING

RAISING EMOTIONALLY HEALTHY CHILDREN

Second Edition

Sheila Redfern

Routledge
Taylor & Francis Group

LONDON AND NEW YORK

Designed cover image: ©Kiriko Kubo

First published 2026
by Routledge
4 Park Square, Milton Park, Abingdon, Oxon OX14 4RN

and by Routledge
605 Third Avenue, New York, NY 10158

*Routledge is an imprint of the Taylor & Francis Group,
an informa business*

© 2026 Sheila Redfern

For Product Safety Concerns and Information please contact our EU representative GPSR@taylorandfrancis.com. Taylor & Francis Verlag GmbH, Kaufingerstraße 24, 80331 München, Germany.

Trademark notice: Product or corporate names may be trademarks or registered trademarks, and are used only for identification and explanation without intent to infringe.

First edition published by Routledge 2016

British Library Cataloguing-in-Publication Data
A catalogue record for this book is available from the British Library

ISBN: 9781032775678 (hbk)
ISBN: 9781032775630 (pbk)
ISBN: 9781003483762 (ebk)

DOI: 10.4324/9781003483762

Typeset in Sabon
by codeMantra

CONTENTS

CONTENTS

FOREWORD

It doesn't happen to me often that I feel worthwhile. Most days I do what I feel I have to do, and if I have done 50% of what I needed to, I feel good. The outcome I aim for is just to have coped. In reading Sheila Redfern's book, I briefly stepped into a different world. Here was the application of ideas and research findings from two decades of work suddenly being turned into something worthwhile. For this I am immensely grateful.

The conceptual framework and empirical findings concerning reflective function or mentalizing have been influential in research and have found their way into some aspects of social work practice. What I did not realise could happen is for these findings to have the power to influence the way parents bring up their children. Of course, this was exactly what we had in mind originally when thinking about the transmission of secure attachment patterns across the generations and how this could be mediated by the extent to which parents are able to think about the thoughts, feelings, beliefs, wishes and desires in their child's mind as they responded to the child's actions. But few of us dared to hope that the translation from theory to practice could *actually* be achieved. In the real world, ideas are easy: we can all have them. The tougher task is to make something real out of abstract concepts. The author is generous in her attribution to those whose research initiated the work she has undertaken; yet truly it is in her application of these ideas to working with parents where the real creativity lies.

This book is one of the best I have read in terms of providing a coherent and eminently practical framework within which the quality of the social environment that the family creates for the child can be genuinely improved. This book is not just practical in the sense of being easy to implement while providing firm direction as to what needs to be implemented; as the time-honoured quip goes, 'there is nothing as practical as a good theory.' In using ideas on reflective function to create a guide to Reflective Parenting, Sheila Redfern also implicitly develops the theory she works with. She integrates parenting with the notion of emotion regulation; she brings in a number of behavioural and cognitive-behavioural principles in line with the mentalizing model; and most intriguingly, she extends the model to cover systemic theorising. What is extraordinary is that she achieves all this high-level integration while remaining 100% in touch with the people she is working with – children and their parents. While this book is aimed at parents, it is just as important for professionals working with parents to read. The author offers sound advice throughout and does so in an entertaining and perhaps even gripping style. There is a 'page-turner' quality to the book, which comes from the application of a key principle of Reflective Parenting: she arouses curiosity in the reader. You read and you want to find out what happens next. The curiosity is hopefully infectious – in the sense that curiosity about what is going on in a child's mind is what Reflective Parenting is all about. It is this natural wish to find out that is so often lost among the competing priorities of modern living, where it is so much easier to take a shortcut, even if this entails making massive assumptions about another person's thoughts and feelings. Yet, at least as far as our children are concerned, we so rarely bother to find out if we were right or wrong. The curiosity also works in another way: the parent's curiosity about what is on the child's mind should – and in my experience, does – create curiosity in the child's psyche about his or her parents. There is nothing like feeling that someone is interested in you to make you curious about what might be going on in that person's mind. This is perhaps the single most important reason why reflectiveness generates a secure bond and a good child-parent relationship.

Quality of parenting remains an important predictor of most outcomes we value in our children. One particular finding I am fond of sharing concerns the likelihood of persistent aggression and violence across childhood. We know that children are at their most violent at around two years of age. They do not have sufficient verbal skills to be persuasive, so physical aggression has an adaptive, if slightly asocial, role. Not all children are like this, of course; temperament plays an important part. But most children, thankfully, desist from this violent behaviour during the ensuing few years. Sadly, 5–10%

do not, and these can develop serious conduct problems. It will not surprise anyone to find out that those children who desist are twice as likely to have positive interactions with their parents, to receive consistent parenting and to have parents who appear less hostile and more effective. These findings come from a Canadian study which looked at over 10,000 children (1). The reason I am mentioning this is because of the striking power of these observations. The likelihood that these observations were due to chance is less than one in a billion billion! The parents have an important role to play, and that role has become increasingly important as family size decreased from ancient times, when it was genuinely a village who raised a child, to modern times, when the task falls on just one or two adults. The pressure sometimes can be almost unbearable. Humans did not evolve to be sole carers of their children; our genes dictate that there should be grandparents, aunts and uncles, cousins – an extended family network. The increased mobility linked originally to the industrial revolution has made parenting harder, and the time that reflection requires more precious than ever. What we know about child development suggests that children require quality rather than quantity: that is to say, the occasional experience of the true presence of a parent is more important than his or her constant physical, but unreflective, presence. By 'true presence' I mean being there for the child, having the child's mind in mind, thinking about the child's thoughts, feeling the child's feelings. It is this capacity that engenders the capacity to think and feel in the young human. It is this capacity that is the foundation for our humanity. It is this capacity that this book attempts and succeeds in making just that little bit more accessible to all of us. I wish I had had this book when I was bringing up my children!

by Peter Fonagy FMedSci FBA OBE.
Professor and Head, Research Department of Clinical,
Educational and Health Psychology, University College London

Reference

1. Cote, S.M., Vaillancourt, T., LeBlanc, J.C., Nagin, D.S., & Tremblay, R.E. (2006). The development of physical aggression from toddlerhood to pre-adolescence: A nationwide longitudinal study of Canadian children. *Journal of Abnormal Child Psychology, 34* (1), 71–85. doi: 10.1007/s10802-005-9001-z

ACKNOWLEDGEMENTS

I am mostly indebted to my parents, Marian and Dick Redfern, who both influenced me so massively in both my personal and professional life. They raised me to be curious about others and the world around me, and instilled in me a strong sense of social justice that I carried into my work with children and families. My mum, Marian, a sociology lecturer who left school at 16 because she just wanted to buy earrings and go dancing, returned to education, gaining a degree while I was at junior school, and is still the most inspirational woman I've ever known. Through her warm and loving parenting, she gave me the confidence and security to believe in myself and to trust others.

I am hugely grateful to Claire Cross for her editorial input and reflective comments on the content and structure of this book. In between writing and editing, we have had so much fun doing pottery together. I want to thank Kiriko Kubo for her wonderful and original cartoons. I am indebted to the wonderful researchers, academics and clinicians, whose work has inspired and underpins this book: without them this book would not have been possible.

I would like to thank Peter Fonagy and Judy Dunn for providing the inspiration for this work, for their original work in so many fields and for making it make sense. The real inspiration for continuing to develop this research in clinical practice comes from the parents, caregivers, children and young people who have shown such determination to improve their relationships and understand themselves. My biggest thanks go to my brilliant and wonderful boys; Gabriel, Joseph and William – the people who have taught me the most about what it means to hold another person's mind in mind, and who are my whole world. Finally, love and thanks go to my husband, Richard, without whom none of this would be possible.

PROLOGUE

The following fictitious families are described throughout this book. Some of their everyday struggles and family scenarios I hope will be familiar to you.

Family One

Finn (38) and Lisa (36) have two children, Charlie (6) and Ella (4). Finn works in local government and gets very stressed by his work. He has a group of friends outside of work that he likes to meet up with regularly to take his mind off work and to have time out from his family. Lisa also works part time for a travel company. She likes to be organised and get things done on time but finds the commitment of a job and two young children makes it hard to always be as organised as she would like. Lisa does the majority of the childcare and at times this can cause tension. Finn sometimes takes over the care of the children when Lisa has work commitments, and enjoys this, but finds it also conflicts with the demands of his stressful job. Finn has both his parents who can help with childcare from time to time. Lisa's parents are no longer alive. Charlie is a boisterous six-year-old and likes to be active and physical as much as possible. He and his younger sister Ella can play well together, but often get into battles, vying for their mum and dad's attention. Charlie likes the fact that he is the eldest child.

Family Two

Karen (41) and Tom (44) have three children, Maddy (12), Sam (10) and Molly (2). Tom works for a finance company and has a critical boss. He would like to change jobs to something he enjoys more, but the family depends on his income to support them, and so he feels stuck. He is a keen cyclist and will sometimes go away for long cycling trips on his own or with a group of friends. Karen supports his interest but wishes she had something similar so that she could have more of a break from the children. Karen also works part time as a receptionist in a health clinic. Her job is poorly paid for the hours she works but is very busy. Karen's parents are divorced and she had a difficult childhood with her parents arguing much of the time. Her mother is involved with the children and offered childcare when the children were little, but as her mother gets older, Karen is finding she needs to care for both her mother and her three children, which puts a strain on her and the family. Her relationship with her mother is quite tense. Tom's parents are both still alive but live overseas and so are much less involved with the children.

Family Three

Rachel (32) and Matt (31) have three children, twins Grace and Lilly (7) and nine-month-old baby Jack. When Jack was three months old, Rachel and Matt, who were not married, separated and are now living apart. Matt sees the children on alternate weekends, but because Jack is still a baby, he does not have them to stay overnight at his house yet. He finds it hard being separated from the children and enjoys taking them out when it is his weekend to spend time with them. Matt works as a furniture maker and has his own small business, which means he does not always have work. Rachel is unable to work because it is too expensive for childcare for the baby and after-school care for the twins. She has mixed feelings about being a stay-at-home mum. She enjoys the one-to-one time with Jack but finds the responsibility of three children on her own much of the time very difficult. Rachel has a wide circle of friends on whom she depends. Her parents are both alive and help out whenever she asks, although Rachel finds it hard to ask for help sometimes and would like to show that she can manage on her own. Matt's parents live locally to him and are involved with the children. They would like Matt to try to resolve his relationship with Rachel.

INTRODUCTION

'Parenting style can significantly influence a child's mental health'

This news headline appeared in April 2023 on the US Network ABC News, reporting on a study conducted in Ireland of 7,500 children under the age of 9 (1). As I write this revised introduction for the second edition, I'm reflecting on how much has changed in the short period of time since the publication of the first edition in 2016. The need for Reflective Parenting in today's climate feels even more important, as there are increasing societal pressures bearing down on both parents and children and young people – from the prevalence of social media and the impact of Covid-19 and the cost of living crisis to mounting worry about the impact of climate change. In 2016, one in nine children and young people were recorded as having a mental health difficulty; by 2020 this had risen to one in six. The most recent report – The Mental Health of Children and Young People in England, 2023, published by NHS England, surveying 2,370 children aged 8 to 25 showed about one in six children and young people in England aged 8 to 25 had a probable mental health disorder. Add to this the huge demand for mental health services that far outweighs the actual capacity of those services to support children's mental health needs and this might feel like an overwhelming place to start a book for parents. I hope by reading this book, you will feel quite the opposite. My aim is to hold your hand metaphorically throughout this book and guide you through the steps involved in supporting your child's development and protecting their mental health.

DOI: 10.4324/9781003483762-1

The power of Reflective Parenting

Once you have read the book you can consider the above headline again. Hopefully then, it will be self-evident that your relationship with your baby or young child has a huge impact on their mental health and helps them build resilience. My sincere hope is that with more understanding of how your parenting style can not only influence your child's mental health, but also act as a buffer against the inevitable challenges they will face in today's world, you will adopt a stance that will promote your child's overall well-being and robust mental health.

The focus in this book is on children from newborn infants up to 12 years old. If you have an older child, you will find my second book, *How Do You Hug a Cactus?*, where I speak to parents of young teenagers and young adults about the specific issues facing them today, more relevant. The parenting model is largely the same, but the application of Reflective Parenting to babies, young children and preteens is somewhat different from the application of the Reflective Parenting model to teenagers and young adults. It is well documented and well evidenced that the first two years are crucial in terms of children's development, both emotional and behavioural, and what is commonly referred to as the first 1001 days of a child's development is known to be absolutely essential to later outcomes. This refers to the time from conception to a child's second birthday. However, clinical experience has taught me that even when there are difficulties in the first few years of life, or if you are a parent picking up this book when your child is more than two years old, taking a Reflective Parenting approach at any time during your child's development is hugely beneficial. Being a reflective parent can help you develop a closer connection with your child, whatever your child's age or stage, leading to better regulated emotions in both you and your child. Let's consider the following scenario:

It is early on a Monday morning after a stressful family breakfast. Everyone is busy preparing for the start of the week. Karen, the mum, is getting the children ready for school and nursery, but Molly, her two-year-old daughter, is being defiant and oppositional, saying 'No' to just about everything and running around the front room, still in her pyjamas, refusing to put on her clothes. Both parents are running late for work and Tom, the dad, is scrolling through his email messages on his phone with an angry and tired expression on his face. Maddy, their 12-year-old daughter is also looking through her phone, despite the family rule of 'no phones at the table.' In addition, the previous night they had an argument about finances and whether they could afford for Tom to switch careers. Consequently, tempers are running high; threats of sanctions seem to be inflaming the situation and bribing with treats offers no resolution. Both parents are trying simultaneously to ignore Molly and each other. Karen then changes tack and tries to find a way to praise Molly for eating her breakfast but with little success; after having tried all week during half-term to get Molly to follow a routine. Tom gets up from the table and pretends that he has to get something important from upstairs for work. Suddenly, Karen takes a moment to step back and reflect on Molly's behaviour. She takes Molly to one side and asks in a kind voice, 'What's going on today? Why do things seem so different this morning? Are you worried about going back to nursery after a lovely half term at home? I feel the same; it's been nice being together all week.' Molly's body instantly relaxes; her head turns to the floor as she confirms with a nod that she is worried. After a brief chat about her worry about being away from home again and what might help (in this instance taking a toy in her bag to remind her of home) they set off to school, leaving Tom in a curious state wondering what had just happened and how a simple question could have such a powerful effect.

As he drives to work, Tom wonders just what was making his daughter so worried about going to nursery and why and how this had affected her behaviour. He feels guilty for hiding from the family on his phone, but he's also feeling exhausted, from work and family life combined.

> *Looking back on the situation a day or two later, it became clear to Tom and Karen that Molly was anxious. At the time Tom had no space in his mind to think about anything other than that his youngest daughter was being difficult and making him late for work. A build-up of stress over half term, with its relentless chores and Molly's non-compliant behaviour, meant that he had found it hard to reflect in that moment on what might be going on inside Molly's mind. He had no clear sense of Molly's thoughts or feelings in that moment. Instead he was simply absorbed in his own experience, overwhelmed by feeling helpless, irritated and distracted by his own thoughts about work and what he had on that day, and was exasperated with Molly running around, so he absented himself and went upstairs. He is left wondering how just a few words from Karen had made such a difference to Molly's mood and behaviour.*

What just happened in this situation and what helped? Karen's effectiveness was not solely down to the fact that she took charge of the situation, or because Molly realised her mum had the authority; rather, it had very much to do with *how* Karen approached the situation, and how Molly experienced her. First, she did not approach the situation as a problem, but simply a normal, everyday interaction. Second, and importantly, she did not focus on the behaviour itself, but was more interested in why the behaviour was there; she focused on the meaning of Molly's behaviour and *her* experience. And finally, she did not become overly frustrated and managed to keep her emotions in check throughout the interaction. Here lie the effective ingredients in managing these everyday challenging interactions, and they relate to the style of parenting I developed called Reflective Parenting. The two ingredients that are especially important in this approach are:

1. How sensitive a parent is to the mind of their child (the ability to mentalize/reflect on your child).
2. How sensitive the parent is to their own mind (the ability to mentalize/reflect on yourself).

Why practice Reflective Parenting?

So, why did I develop the model of Reflective Parenting based on my own clinical and academic research in the field of attachment and mentalization and what makes me so convinced that this is the way forward if you really want to enjoy the best possible relationship with your child, or simply improve your relationship? As a clinical psychologist working with struggling families and a parent of three boys, often peddling hard to keep everything running smoothly, I know something of how hard it is to manage family dynamics plus my own emotional and work life. After training in clinical psychology, I was immediately drawn to working with children and young people who were referred to the NHS's Child and Adolescent Mental Health services. After over 30 years of working with babies, young children, adolescents and their families in the NHS and the charity sector, I became increasingly interested in the impact and influence of early attachment relationships – the relationship children have with their parents in the first weeks and months of life – on how children develop socially and cope with emotional challenges later on in their childhood and into adolescence. So it never felt sufficient to look simply at the problematic behaviour that children were referred with. Instead, helping parents to improve their relationship with their child, and to think about what was going on inside their child's mind, often led to the most positive changes in their behaviour and a more harmonious relationship. The theories underpinning this book are also concerned with helping you as a parent to promote a feeling of security in your child and build their resilience. Resilience and a sense of security are essential for children's overall development and how they make their way in the world. Children who have been parented in a reflective way are better able to navigate their way through the joys and difficulties encountered in life and relationships. How you interact with your child will determine, to a great degree, how they will grow up and interact with other people. With this in mind, there are two central questions:

1. What exactly is Reflective Parenting?
2. How can you as a parent become more reflective in your parenting?

The core purpose of this book is to answer these two questions. Without wishing to bombard you with too much scientific research, but equally wanting to answer the valid question of whether this model has any hard evidence and research behind it, I will briefly outline the ideas behind Reflective Parenting. If you've picked up this book, I'm assuming you have a curious mind that is keen to understand your child a little better, and that you are also eager to find a method of parenting based on solid research and clinical evidence to support your child's development. After all, you wouldn't go to the doctor with a medical problem if you didn't trust they had the best advice, grounded in evidence, would you? I will also look at the new context in which we are all parenting today – post the Covid-19 pandemic, and in a politically and environmentally challenging time.

Reflective functioning

The term 'reflective parent' links closely to the established concept within the field of research on parent–child relationships known as reflective functioning. The construct of reflective functioning was introduced by Peter Fonagy, Miriam Steele, Howard Steele and Mary Target nearly 30 years ago (2,3). Through his research, clinical psychologist and psychoanalyst Peter Fonagy found that parents who have high 'reflective functioning,' that is, who are able to consider what is going on in their child's mind as well as being aware of their own thoughts and feelings, bring clear benefits to their children, including promoting secure attachment (see below), good social skills and the ability to 'read' others, as well as an ability to manage, or regulate, their own emotions, sometimes in difficult and challenging situations or interactions. So when I use the term 'Reflective Parenting,' I'm referring to a style of relating and responding to your child that has characteristics associated with parents who have high reflective functioning. I believe it is important that all parents are able to benefit from the research on Reflective Parenting, and it is this belief that motivated me to write this book.

Reflective parents do not focus solely on the external behaviour of their child, but also keep a focus on their child as an individual with their own mind. The term 'he has a mind of his own' is often used in a slightly derogatory way to describe a wilful and oppositional child. However, reflective parents more often than not would see that their child does indeed have their own mind that is a rich tapestry of interwoven thoughts, ideas and motivations, and they wish to understand the workings of this mind. At the same time, they realise their child's experience can be very different from their own – that is, their interpretation of an event could be quite different from their child's experience of it. Reflective parents can frequently see that their child often does things for reasons that are linked to how they are thinking or feeling – that there is an inside story. Parents can then respond to that inside story of thoughts and feelings, rather than just reacting to the behaviour. Reflective parents are also more likely to be in touch with their own thoughts and feelings when interacting with their child, and to have some understanding of how their own emotions might affect moments with their child and the actual outcome of situations. The foundations of Reflective Parenting are found in the concepts of attachment theory and mentalization, discussed below.

Attachment theory

Attachment theory was first discussed by British psychiatrist and psychoanalyst John Bowlby (4) and his work has had an incredibly powerful impact on how we understand parent-infant relationships. Bowlby proposed that all infants have an innate motivational and behavioural system that drives them to seek proximity with their primary caregiver – usually the mother. In an evolutionary context, this desire to stay close to the mother would have ensured protection when a child was in danger or threatened by danger. The most important aspect of attachment theory in relation to understanding parent-child relationships is that every infant needs to develop a relationship with one important primary caregiver for their social and emotional development, and more specifically for learning how to regulate, or control, their feelings. In other words, when an infant enjoys a good attachment early in life, this relationship gives them the security to explore their world and works as a template for future successful relationships. Developmental psychologist Mary Ainsworth, who joined Bowlby at the Tavistock Clinic in London researching the effects of maternal separation on child development and worked extensively in the area of parent-child development, devised a famous experiment where she established four classifications of attachment (5). She found that most people had experienced 'secure' attachment as a baby, having enjoyed a responsive and close attachment to a parent. The experiment found that when children in this group are separated from their primary caregivers, they experience distress, but are quickly comforted upon reunion. The classification of attachment is made on the basis of the relationship between an infant and his main, primary caregiver. In most cases, this is the mother, but obviously not in all, and not across all cultures. The 'secure' infant uses their primary caregiver as a safe base from which to explore the world. Parents who consistently (or at least most of the time) respond sensitively to their infant's needs will have children who are securely attached. These children will learn that when they are distressed, their parents will comfort and soothe them, and so they grow up with the expectation that other people are also available to help and support them. Importantly, these children develop a complementary model of themselves as worthy and deserving of that love and comfort. Secure attachment underpins the development of good 'mentalization'. The theory of mentalization, grows from the fertile soil of attachment theory – they are, in essence, part of the same family.

What is mentalizing?

The term mentalization, first used by Peter Fonagy in 1989 (6), describes the ability to reflect on the mental states, that is the thoughts and feelings, of others. The ability to understand another person's mental state is strongly linked to whether an individual was securely attached to their primary caregiver as an infant. One important study (in the theory of attachment) looked at how a pregnant woman's own attachment as an infant could predict whether her own baby would be securely attached and found that the most significant predictive factor was whether the mother was able to mentalize her relationship with her own parents, that is, whether she was able to think about and reflect on her parents' behaviour, emotions and states of mind. The parents who could do this were said to be high in reflective functioning (see below).

When we 'mentalize' this means that not only do we recognise that others have emotions but we also understand and respond to these emotions. The ability to mentalize is thought to be rooted in our early relationships and whether our primary caregivers were able to reflect accurately on our own thoughts and feelings, and, crucially, were able to show by their corresponding actions and words that they understood and could interpret our mental states. When parents are able to reflect on the mental states (internal thoughts and feelings) of their child, the child in turn becomes better able to control their own emotions. This process occurs because when parents 'mirror' back to the child (through the way they speak to, look at and behave with the child) how the child is feeling, the child begins to understand, and eventually to control, their own emotions. Without a parent who can reflect back, infants don't know how to make

sense of what they are feeling. The parent becomes a trainer to the infant in learning to understand himself and his feelings.

Parents as the regulators of emotion

If you are still wondering why this concept known as mentalizing is so important to your parenting, consider this question: what do you think causes behavioural problems in children? Are some children just 'born naughty' or out to make your life difficult, or do you think their behaviour only appears to be challenging when you are struggling and they haven't managed to control their emotions? A child who throws a toy across the room, slams a door, screams in a tantrum as they stamp their feet or rolls around isn't able to regulate their feelings in that particular moment. Of course, all children have moments like this throughout their childhood and it would be quite odd even if they never did, because everyone loses the capacity to regulate their emotions all the time, including adults. However, the more a child is taught how to manage, or regulate, their emotions, the less likely will be their tendency to act out these unregulated or dysregulated emotions. Teaching a child emotion regulation begins with modelling the ability to regulate your own. The small, every-day interactions that take place between a primary caregiver (often but not always or exclusively the mother) and infant, where the mother mirrors her infant and shows him with her face and voice that she has an understanding (or at least is trying to imagine) what he's thinking and feeling, form the foundations of learning to men-talize. I will describe this in more detail in Chapter 1, but to put this concept into an everyday context, imagine the following scenario where mum Karen is taking her two-year-old child, Molly, to nurs-ery and running late:

> Karen and her two-year-old daughter, Molly, are rush-ing to nursery so Karen can drop her off and get to work where she has a meeting she's been worrying about over the weekend. It's a relatively short walk from their home to the nursery, but Molly delights in stopping regularly to look at the berries on the bushes at the edge of the park and notices a spider's web on one of the fences. Each time she spots something new and interesting, she stops to look at it, and each time Karen sighs heavily and pulls her by the hand, urging her to 'get a move on, we're going to be late.' The more Karen rushes her and pulls her along, the more Molly starts to protest until, eventually, Molly sits down on the pavement and says 'not moving, staying here.' Karen gets even more exasperated and, realising she's probably going to be both late for nursery drop off and late for work, she explodes and shouts at Molly, 'Why are you trying to make me late? You seem to want to wind me up this morning and I haven't got time for it.' Seeing her mum's angry face, Molly bursts into tears and cries all the way to nursery as her mum drags her along. She is even more upset at the nursery door and Karen forgets to kiss her, feeling preoccupied now by how late she is. Molly cries even harder and shouts 'Mummy, don't leave!' as Karen walks away. When Karen gets on the train to go to work, she feels overwhelmed with feelings of regret, annoyance and anxiety. She takes out her phone and texts her hus-band, Tom, to let off some steam.

In this scenario, it's clear that the interaction is less than ideal or connected between Karen and Molly. While we might empathise with Karen in her rush to get to work and her irritation that her daughter wants to go at a slow pace first thing in the morning, we can also understand that Molly is fascinated by what she sees on the way and wants her mummy to stop and look with her. Karen resorted to authoritarian, controlling behaviour, pulling her daughter physically into the nursery and reprimanding her for 'making' her late. She is in no frame of mind to mentalize her young daughter as she is becoming overwhelmed by her own state of mind, which is full of anxiety about her meeting and being late. The feeling is so strong that Karen can't think at all (I would call this a failure to mentalize) and this makes it impossible to see any meaning to her daughter's behaviour. Instead of reflecting, all she can do is lose control herself and lash out verbally at her daughter.

I imagine that many of you reading this scenario might relate to it. After all, haven't we all blamed other people, including our children, when we've felt stressed about something ourselves? These failures, or lapses, in mentalizing are extremely common and we all do this when our emotions are running high. Learning to mentalize, especially in relation to parenting, means developing the ability to understand our own thoughts and feelings first, as parents. This in turn allows us to be regulated enough to start to reflect on (or mentalize) our children's behaviour, becoming curious about what it means. Ironically, what initially appears to be the quickest way to get her child to nursery actually turns out to be the long route as the more Karen loses control of her own emotions, the more emotionally dysregulated Molly becomes. If we imagine an alternative scenario, in which Karen had stopped perhaps briefly once or twice to notice what Molly found so interesting on the way, commenting on how interested she was while adding that she wished she had more time to look longer, but has to get to work, we can imagine a different outcome. What is likely to have happened instead is Molly feels her mum is interested in what she finds interesting (and therefore interested in *her*) which would help Molly to stay well regulated emotionally. Although Karen might plan to set off a little earlier next time, these small changes to how she parents during these everyday moments would lead to better regulation of emotions in her daughter and a change (or reduction) in Molly's defiant behaviour. In Chapter 4, I will outline a tool parents can use to help them apply this mentalizing approach to their child. Before you can begin to do this, it's important to learn how to reflect on your own state of mind and regulate yourself; I will go through these simple steps in Chapter 2.

Changing pressures on young people today

Every generation's parents remark on the differences between their own childhoods and their children's. When I was a child, my parents would say things like, 'Don't watch too much television, it will rot your brain.' Like most of my peers, this probably only fuelled my enthusiasm! Today's parents have arguably more to feel anxious about, given that the influence of some things feels even further beyond their understanding. You might feel out of your depth with these issues – particularly as influences such as social media seem omnipresent, without any time to switch off from them, how do these factors influence your parenting and relationships? Let's look at a few of the more significant issues in today's landscape.

• **Social media and phones**
  Recall the scenario at the start of this chapter, where Karen and husband Tom are trying to get their children ready for the return to school and nursery after a break. In this scenario, you will probably have noticed both dad and eldest daughter, Maddy, are on their phones during the morning rush. Mobile phone use is almost universal and can be a common bone of contention between parents and their children, as well as between couples. Children access the majority of their information not from their parents or the daily TV news bulletins, as many parents used to, but from the constant stream of news they access via social media platforms. Such is the accessibility of this information, it's likely that, as parents, you might receive news via your own children first, rather than from a report you read or hear yourselves. In this social media-saturated world, it's impossible to shield children from world events and this access to negative or frightening information can feel beyond your control. Even when individual parents limit their child's access to social media, unless the whole cohort of their child's peers' parents do the same, the chances are that your child still has access to a lot of information about global events that are either frightening and true or unchecked 'facts.'
  Today, young children can compare themselves not just to the children they see at school in their year group but also to the millions of people on the planet they come into virtual contact with on their phones. It's hardly surprising that children's anxiety has risen, partly as a result of this constant comparison, for who wouldn't fall short if they were comparing themselves to

12

Taylor Swift or a top sporting idol. Moreover, mobile phones themselves are changing children's development. Speech and language therapists have noted a deterioration in young children's language development as a result of a lack of face-to-face contact with parents; and school teachers comment on the increase in children's behavioural problems and a general increase in the prevalence of global developmental delay in young children. An excessive amount of screen time means children miss out on developing key motor skills as they become more sedentary, less focused on longer tasks and less engaged in conversations where they would ordinarily practice their language skills. While I can't claim to have the answers to the problems created by excessive time spent on phones and devices, there is a lot parents can do to support their children's development and play away from phones; I look at this in some detail in Chapter 9 (Mentalizing Good Times). Professor of psychology Jonathan Haidt's impactful book *The Anxious Generation* sets out the rise in anxiety in our children, beginning with a sharp increase around the 2010 period, as he concludes that rates of mental illness (particularly rates of depression and anxiety) went up between 2010 and 2015 among Generation Z (classified as children born between 1997 and 2012). He concludes that this is the first generation to have gone through puberty with mobile phones.

I have had my own battles with my children over how much time they spend on devices, and I know it is a common cause of concern among many parents. Concerns range from the amount of time children spend on devices, to the type of activity they are engaged in. While it's true that the majority of parents I know and work with clinically would say they don't want their child to be on a device and would prefer them to play with friends face to face or get outdoor exercise, they also claim to feel 'powerless' or 'trapped' by the digital world their child inhabits. The message is usually a very strong, 'There's nothing I can do about it; it's how the world is today.' And while I would include myself among those parents who would prefer her children to spend less time staring at a screen, I don't agree that parents are powerless. Children still take their cue from their parents from the day they are born. They mimic our actions, our moods and our behaviour, and in the first two years at least, this is how they learn about the world and their relationships in it. If they enter the world observing the people who are most important to them, staring at their screens and communicating with others via text or online

video platforms, then clearly this teaches them that these are the means of communication, not play or face-to-face contact, but one-step-removed communication. We can, and should, set a different environment from the moment they are born.

- **The impact of Covid-19**
  How did Covid-19 impact you and your family? If you have a child under the age of 5, then perhaps you were pregnant during a lockdown. In fact, every parent reading this will have a child who has been impacted in some way. My own children missed proms, A-level exams, end of school parties, school journeys, time playing with their classmates. Perhaps your child relished the time at home with you and became anxious about going back to school and being in large groups again, or perhaps they missed their friends and in-person connections. Any, or all, of these scenarios may apply to you, but it is irrefutable that the pandemic has had an impact on children's development and on parent-child relationships, and we are only now beginning to see that impact. In my clinical team, we continued to work with some families who were in extremely dire circumstances, but we always felt that many of the children and young people we work with would struggle more when the pandemic was over, and that has turned out to be true, sadly.

  The evidence indicates that levels of mental health difficulties steadily increased over the initial couple of years of the COVID-19 pandemic. However, the pattern was somewhat different for children aged 7–16 years: where one in nine were likely to have a mental health difficulty in 2016; this rose to one in six in 2020 but then remained stable in 2021 and 2022. Data published in 2024 revealed that the prevalence of mental health difficulties in children is now one in five. Another large study estimated that had the pandemic *not* occurred, 6% fewer children and young people would have experienced higher levels of depression (5). Moreover, there are particular groups of children who had a really tough time during Covid – over and above the difficulties experienced by their school friends. Children in care; those from families on very low or no incomes; young people who identify as LGBTQ+; children with special educational needs; children with existing mental health difficulties (particularly anxiety) and other culturally minoritised children and young people, all had significantly more difficulties during the Covid pandemic and its associated lockdowns.

The majority of you reading this book will have children under 12 and we know from the research data that the main impact of Covid-19 on young children has been on their behaviour. The pandemic had a disproportionate impact on young children (aged five and under) because of its duration and restrictions taking up a greater part of children's lives in comparison to adults or even older children, their inherent vulnerability, and because it occurred at a highly sensitive time in their development. For the youngest children, the pandemic happened at a key time for their development, a time where they would normally rely on extended family and friends and access a range of services regularly such as soft play areas and parent-toddler classes. Curtailing access to a wider community, support and services may have a lasting and ongoing impact on young children and their families. Research by the Parent Infant Foundation and Institute of Health Visiting (6) found that in 2022, more babies and young children experienced stresses and adversity, while they also had less access to positive activities than before the pandemic. It has also been shown that more generally, the youngest children have been most affected by pandemic measures, both in relation to early learning, language and numeracy skills and in their social and emotional development. In England 2020/2021, the proportion of children who gained a good level of social and emotional development at the end of their Reception year was 13% smaller than in 2018/2019, although for 2021/2022, it has picked up to almost pre-pandemic levels for the same age cohort. Child development outcomes for two to two-and-a-half-year-olds for 2021/2022 in England, however, are lower than pre-pandemic levels by almost one percentage point.

In England, 'children looked after' is the collective term for children under state care for example, foster care, residential care or secure homes (for children with significant mental health needs). You may be a foster carer who cared for young children during the pandemic. If so, you will be familiar with the statistic that children in care experience higher levels of mental health difficulties than children in the general population, with one meta-analysis estimating levels to be nearly four times higher in these children (7). In England, the mental health of children in state care is routinely assessed using a resource called *The Strengths and Difficulties Questionnaire*. This shows that the proportion of children with elevated levels of mental health difficulties remained relatively consistent – at between 49 and 52% – between 2018 and 2022.

The Reflective Parenting approach applies to *all* caregivers, but in Chapter 7, I specifically address the ways in which the approach can be applied to children in care and children who have developmental differences, in particular Autistic Spectrum Disorder (ASD) and/or a history of traumatic relationships where there has been either neglect or maltreatment. Regardless of the type of carer you are, the Covid pandemic will have had some impact on your child's development and their view of the world. When we reflect on children's thoughts and feelings generally, and more specifically think about what's going on in their minds in the here and now, we need to take into account how this global event has impacted their view of the world and their relationships within it.

- **Impact of the cost of living crisis on parents**
  Back in the 1950s, psychologist Abraham Maslow developed a 'hierarchy of need,' which became known as Maslow's Hierarchy and it still has relevance today. In his model, Maslow set out the importance of people's basic needs for food and shelter being met before they could begin to work on their mental health. According to Maslow (8) in the hierarchy of human needs, physiological needs are at the bottom of the pyramid, being the fundamental and most important needs, and the more creative and intellectually oriented needs are at the top. It seems obvious to us now that these fundamental human needs have to

be met before addressing other concerns and yet support pro-grammes for children, young people and families that address their physical and psychological needs collectively are rare.

Many of the families I've worked with over the years in children's mental health services have had the additional pressure of struggling to meet their child's basic need for food and shelter. In one clinic, I recall having to wait until families had passed through our waiting room to get our lunch out for fear that the smell and sight of food would be too triggering for them when they had so little food in their cupboards at home. Of course, we offered some snacks to the children in these sessions, but it was painful to witness children and parents struggling to maintain their mental health while hungry.

Even for families who do have food in their cupboards, the pressure of rising food and fuel prices has a significant impact on their ability to regulate their own emotions so they can be emotionally available to their young children. When working on parent-child relationships and children's mental health, I feel strongly that it is vital to take into account the financial pressures on parents that include the pressure to provide presents for celebrations and family holidays during the summer. Any parent who is preoccupied with the basics of life will understandably struggle to engage with their child's psychological needs; the Reflective Parenting approach takes this into account (see Parent MAP, Chapter 1) and helps parents to reflect on the relevance of these pressures when thinking about how they parent. It is inappropriate to expect a parent to mentalize themselves or their child when there are more urgent, pressing matters.

* **An escalating climate crisis**
  In my work with children and young people, I'm struck by the number of very young children who are aware of the impact of climate change on their lives. A young boy I worked with recently, who had a keen interest in frogs and wildlife, was so upset by the way he saw nature being affected by the changing climate that he organised a cake sale to raise money for an environmental charity. One of my own children commented a couple of years ago that he didn't see himself living to a very old age. I felt so sad about this and asked him why he thought that way; he responded, 'Because it will probably be too hot on the planet by then, Mum.' While these are anecdotal examples of children's growing concerns, robust research provides strong

evidence that our children and young people are extremely anxious about their futures.

A large scale study of 10,000 children and young people (aged 16–25) in ten countries (Australia, Brazil, Finland, France, India, Nigeria, Philippines, Portugal, the UK and the USA; 1,000 participants per country), published in the respected medical journal The Lancet in 2021, indicated that for more than 50% of children and young people, concern about global warming significantly impacted their mood (9).

Respondents across all the countries were worried about climate change (59% were very or extremely worried and 84% were at least moderately worried). More than 50% reported each of the following emotions: sadness, anxiety, anger, powerlessness, helplessness and guilt. More than 45% of respondents said their feelings about climate change negatively affected their daily life and functioning, and many reported a high number of negative thoughts, with, for example, 75% reporting that they often think the future is frightening and 83% having frequent thoughts that people have failed to take care of the planet.

Reduced risk-taking and protective parenting practices

It might sound odd, but one of the biggest risks to children and young people today isn't the type of risky behaviours your parents might have worried about you getting involved in, such as having an accident on your bike or getting lost, walking home from school alone, and for teenagers, excessive partying, teenage pregnancy, dangerous or reckless driving and so on, but more the *lack* of risks they take, which can increase their chances of facing the biggest risk to today's children: *struggling with their mental health*. According to research, today's generation of young people aged 11–26 are the *least likely* to take risks such as smoking, drinking alcohol or having underage sex. Instead, today's children have parents who are more likely to protect them from these risks; as a result, children are more likely to be anxious about taking even small risks and are generally more conservative in their outlook. This avoidance of risk even extends to how children play, for example in more monitored places with soft surfaces, or indoors, rather than in open spaces. It's tempting to resort to the old cliché of, 'In my day, we climbed trees and played in rivers' when thinking about generational differences, but there *is* something significant about how parenting practices, specifically in relation to risk management, have shifted and are influencing young children's development today.

The importance of play and risk-taking for development

In 1959, the United Nations General Assembly adopted the Declaration of the Rights of the Child (UNDRC), which recognises, among other rights, children's rights to education, play, a supportive environment and healthcare. This declaration recognises the right of children to play and enjoy recreational time and states that society and public authorities should promote this right. The UNDRC also states that the best interests of the child should be the guiding principle of those responsible for their education. Given how vital play and an environment that supports this right to play is it feels important to look at how we can create the sort of conditions where children can play freely.

A 2013 study, interviewing children about their play habits, revealed that primary school children in England have less freedom compared to kids 40 years ago. One major difference in parenting practices across the last couple of generations is in how children travel to and from school. In the early 1970s, almost nine out of ten primary school-aged children did this journey without an adult. The report compared school children in England to those in Germany, where three quarters were allowed to travel to and from school by themselves. The research highlighted that some children's mental health charities think children should be given more freedom because this is an essential part of growing up. The researchers asked the children in their study if they go to school by themselves or with an adult. The findings revealed that some parents drive their kids to school because they fear they could be abducted or hit by a car while walking to school. But is this a reasonable explanation for why parents have changed their behaviour over the past few decades, when the statistics behind these particular risks haven't changed significantly over the years? There aren't more children at risk of abduction today than there were 50 years ago, so what is this overprotection of children all about, and how is it impacting children's development?

For a very long time, it has been well established in both child development and educational fields that the basis of all development in children is play. Children first learn to walk through play and trial and error, including falling down and picking themselves up. They learn to take turns through playing alongside parents, and then with siblings and peers at playgroups and nurseries. Then they learn to chase each other, play hide-and-seek and pretend games, usually involving multiple players. Through this play, with its inherent rules, children learn that they sometimes make mistakes, get left out, come last, win approval and so on. In other words, this type of play, what we could call 'free play,' is an extremely fertile context for learning about the self and the world, and for developing the type of skills and relationships that are essential for being an independent and competent individual in the world. Peter Gray, a developmental psychologist and researcher on play at Boston University said, 'Play requires suppression of the desire to dominate and enables the formation of long-lasting cooperative bonds.' Play is also the context in which children make small mistakes that don't cost them much; for example, they learn to tolerate small injuries they might sustain during a physical activity, or they learn to resolve an argument over who was the best at the game Stuck in the Mud in the school playground. They also learn how to relate to their peers, understand other people's thoughts and feelings and to see things from another person's perspective – all essential components of mentalizing or of having a 'Theory of Mind,' which means being able to appreciate that someone else can hold a belief that is different from your own.

In his book *The Anxious Generation*, Jonathan Haidt sets out the premise that a play-based childhood is highly preferable for children's development – specifically for their mental health – compared with a 'phone-based childhood' (10). A phone-based childhood is the opposite of a play-based – specifically free-play-based –childhood, as activities on a phone or device are engaged with largely alone, or in a virtual group, where the participants can suddenly elect to leave. Phone-based activities involve social comparison and have a strong focus on likeability: how many 'likes' will I get for my post or comment? The dependence on mass approval from complete strangers, as opposed to the approval and friendly criticism of an in-real-life peer group, is a major factor in children's heightened anxiety today. Increased anxiety leads to a decrease in risk-taking and, as young people take fewer risks and parents become more protective and risk-averse on behalf of their children, we are seeing some very negative consequences for children's outcomes in the mental health field.

What would you consider a normal risk for your ten-year-old to take? Does walking home from school with a friend, without any parent, seem too risky? How about walking or cycling to the local shop to pick up some bread? Where do you draw the line on what feels like a small, but developmentally helpful, risks and what feels like a reckless or irresponsible bit of parenting? It is hard to make a unilateral decision about these things without considering the judgemental attention this might attract. A recent story in the United Kingdom highlighted the 'negligent' parenting of a TV presenter who allowed her son to go inter-railing with his friends at 16 years old, while a similar story in the *New York Times* spoke of a parent who received widespread judgement from other parents for allowing her 15-year-old son to travel home from school by subway, rather than be collected in person by his parents (in a car, presumably).

I flag up these stories only to illustrate how much risk-taking is discouraged in today's society and to highlight how this is a contributing factor in older children's growing levels of anxiety. For if you don't take any risks then you might never fail, and if you never fail, how will you cope with one day not succeeding in, say, a job interview or a relationship? I can't emphasise enough the rise in anxiety and behavioural problems in older and younger children, respectively. The combination of world events, the rise of social media and changes in parenting practices are inevitably contributing factors. For you as a parent, taking responsibility for supporting your child in managing their emotions, expecting sometimes to take risks that result in failure, and considering other people's perspectives on the same event – all essential components of increased resilience and good mental health – will be hugely beneficial for your child.

How can Reflective Parenting help me and my child?

Reading all of the above, it wouldn't be surprising if you were left feeling powerless, wondering what on earth can you do about the global economy, climate crisis, social media and their impact on your child? You might also be wondering why your child seems *so* anxious a lot of the time. After all, it's not as if previous generations haven't lived through economic crises, threats to the environment and even world wars. However, the major difference today is the *visibility* of these issues, and the lack of social cooperation among groups of children, young people and adults to come together to do something about the anxiety-provoking events in today's world. Moreover, events are amplified via social media/phones and so you might also be experiencing higher levels of anxiety, and showing this to your child. You might even be relieved they take fewer risks in this difficult world. In this book, I want to focus almost entirely on **what you can do** to help your child. It might be a surprise to learn that, actually, there is a lot you can do. Reflective Parenting helps you to regulate your emotions, as you'll discover in the book, which in turn helps your child to feel more secure.

When, as a parent, you are able to regulate your emotions well, your child is likely to feel more secure, happy and able to manage their own emotions, too. If your child learns to understand their own emotions and other people's, they are much less likely to struggle with their behaviour, in their relationships and, importantly, much more likely to have good mental health – even in the face of seemingly overwhelming global and social events. It all comes down to the concept of secure attachment, discussed at the start of this introduction.

Causes of emotion dysregulation

I have set out a number of changes in our society and the world as a whole that have impacted children. While it is likely that your most pressing, everyday concerns are much more focused on your child's daily routines, health and behaviour, it is nevertheless important to consider other influences, external to your family, which impact you, your child and your relationship. The individual and collective impact of all of these crises in our environment and social networks is the dysregulation of emotions which in turn leads to dysregulated behaviour. In other words, children and parents become stressed, anxious and unable to control their emotions and this leads to behaviours such as couples shouting and arguing with each other; parents exerting control over their children; parents shouting at young children and sometimes even physical aggression between family members. All of this leads to an escalation in the general levels of anxiety and upset within and between family members.

Since writing the first edition of *Reflective Parenting*, I've come to think more about not just the parent-child relationship but this relationship in the context of wider stresses. It seems more important than ever that we turn our focus from these world events, which can often feel out of our control, onto the controllable and the more personal aspects of our lives and consider how our most important relationships with our children and close family members can not only protect children from some of the impact of these global events but also build their resilience to the inevitable impact on mental health of living in such challenging times.

So, if emotion regulation is one of the key factors in managing mental health, behaviour and relationships, how do we achieve emotion regulation? It's long established that secure attachment within relationships and having a good understanding of our own emotions help us to regulate how we're feeling, so the key mechanism for emotion regulation is our first, and most important, relationship: that with our primary caregiver. How else can we learn about our own experiences? Babies aren't born understanding the difference between anger and frustration, or boredom and loneliness, but when caregivers, usually (but not exclusively) mothers, put words to those feelings and experiences, babies understand not only how *they* feel but they also learn that someone else understands them. This is how emotional regulation starts and how even understanding the self begins.

An extreme example is of a baby who has not experienced their own emotions being mirrored by their primary caregiver, and we can see that this leads to a child, and then adult, who struggles to understand their own, and other people's, feelings and intentions. Let's take the following example of a young toddler playing with a toy, when they accidentally knock themselves with the hard edge of a wooden play brick.

> *The toddler starts to cry and looks, first at the brick and then up at their mum, who has been half watching from the sofa. The mum starts to laugh and says, 'You clumsy clot, hitting yourself with a brick! Are you trying to beat yourself up?'*
>
> *The toddler, seeing his mum's face, tries to smile, seeing this is apparently the 'right' emotion, but as he's in pain from the toy block, this emotion is incongruent with how he's actually feeling. He curls up into a ball, adopting a position of shame, while his mum continues to giggle and says, 'Come on, get up now, brave little soldiers don't cry.'*

This small interaction between a toddler and his mum is extremely confusing for his emotional development. The incongruence between his internal feeling and his mum's response leaves him confused about what he's really feeling and also about how his mum feels about him. If this is just a one-off experience, it's unlikely it would have much impact on his development, but if this is repeated multiple times in different ways, the toddler will grow up unsure of what he's really feeling, and unsure about other people's feelings and their understanding of him. As an older child and eventually young adult, the boy finds it hard to understand his internal states and also other people's emotions. This can manifest in someone who misinterprets other people and gets into conflict, or who experiences such dysregulated emotions that they have to resort to other means of regulation, such as substance misuse, self-harm or aggressive behaviour.

I firmly believe – and evidence from my long career in mental health bears this out – that helping infants and children to regulate their emotions is at the heart of every important aspect of their development: from a baby's sleep habits to a 12-year-old's use of social media, to longer term mental health outcomes.

Throughout this book, I promote the idea that children's behaviour has meaning and intention – it is rarely random. I will look at how Reflective Parenting helps you to think about your child's 'inside story' as well as your own. Recognising this and taking an interested stance towards why your child does what they do is at the heart of Reflective Parenting. Some parents seem to guess intuitively much of the time why their child is behaving in a particular way. Often, though, parents can find it hard to focus on the *why* – the feelings and thoughts underlying their child's behaviour. And we are all capable of making snap judgements about why our children are behaving in a certain way, which often are based more on what's going on in our own minds than what's going on in our child's (just like the example of Karen and Molly on their way to the nursery).

In reality, all parents fluctuate on a scale in their ability to relate to their child in a reflective way, depending on internal and external influences. This is entirely normal, as studies show that on average we only mentalize around 30% of the time and the rest of the time we are acting more instinctively or reactively. As you go through the book, it's important to hold this statistic in mind and to understand that it is entirely normal not to be reflecting for the majority of the time. Most of the time we are more involved with *acting or doing* than reflecting, but the importance of adopting a Reflective Parenting stance is to see how even short bursts of active and intentional mentalizing can have a powerful effect on your connection with your child.

I will talk you through how to develop skills that will enhance your relationship with your child and increase their confidence and self-esteem, as well as help you to feel more successful in your parenting. Essentially, I will invite you to observe yourself from the outside more, to imagine how you may come across to your child, and I will encourage you to see your child from the inside more, to consider what their experiences, thoughts and feelings (their mental states) might be in certain situations – both extremely important concepts. To help you achieve this, I begin by helping you, as a parent, to think first about your own feelings, as the ability to do this is vital before you can start to think about your child's mind.

Of course, it is virtually impossible to do this all of the time in your relationships, but the chapters will help you develop and enhance your awareness of and ability to practice Reflective Parenting, knowing that it will help your child develop greater resilience and support their mental health. My aim is that you will be able to use the book as a guide to steer you through the difficult parenting experiences that we all face, almost daily. I also hope that taking a Reflective Parenting stance will ensure there are fewer misunderstandings between you and your child that behavioural problems will be resolved more easily and that you enjoy greater harmony in your relationship.

1

THE ORIGINS OF
REFLECTIVE PARENTING

In this chapter, I take a closer look at the main ideas behind Reflective Parenting, and how important these are in helping you and your baby or child to enjoy a positive and harmonious relationship. I will explain briefly the research behind the ideas presented to you in this book to help you understand the foundation for this approach. Reflective Parenting has many benefits for children. With its roots in secure attachment, Reflective Parenting leads to happier, confident, successful and resilient children, who are also more able to understand the thoughts and feelings of other people (1). We have already considered the growing challenges to children's mental health and it feels more pressing than ever to understand how vital your relationship is with your child to their longer term well-being.

The rest of the book will take you step by step through the techniques you need for becoming a more reflective parent, increasing the skills you require to achieve this, as well as looking at problem areas where it can feel especially hard to see things from your child's point of view. I will give you some tools and strategies and introduce you to the concept of the 'Parent APP,' a guide to the essential qualities needed for truly Reflective Parenting, explained in Chapter 4, which you can refer to when you find yourself stuck for ways to manage your relationship with your child, or where you feel you have tried absolutely everything to manage a difficult behaviour and you need a new approach. First, though, let's look at where the ideas on Reflective Parenting come from, and what it is about this approach that will be so helpful to both your baby or young child's development and your relationship with him.

The research on babies and children shows that we are motivated to understand what the actions of other people mean, and it seems that this motivation is present almost as soon as we are born. From the minute babies are born, they have in mind the concept

     DOI: 10.4324/9781003483762-2

of another person; they are hardwired if you like to interact. More importantly, babies are supersensitive to adults who show them attention and act in ways that match their own emotional states – who seek to engage with them in a way that mirrors how they are feeling and what they are doing. When you respond to your baby in this sensitive way, your baby is very capable of holding their attention so that they can interact with you. They can take part in an ongoing 'conversation' over the course of their early childhood, which, if all goes well, continues as they grow up. In this way, your baby's mind begins to form, be built and moulded as they purposefully interact with you.

You are your child's relationship trainer

Your baby is totally dependent on you from the minute they are born . . . to feed them, change them, keep them warm, protect them, touch them and make them feel safe. Your baby's relationship with you is incredibly important, as it is through this relationship and the way in which you respond to them that you can help them develop the skills they will need to bounce back from adversity throughout their childhood, adolescence and into adulthood. Think of the relationship your child has with you as a training opportunity. With you, they can practice and experience what it's like to be in a relationship, and this training prepares them for interacting with the world of people beyond their family. Teaching them about how other people work, through your everyday relationship and exchanges with them, and through what they observe of your own relationships, will be one of the most important lessons of their life. Within your relationship with your baby and child, you can help them to develop emotionally by taking a particular interest in how they think, how they feel and why they do things. And by talking about all of these things with them, you will help them learn about their inner world of thoughts and feelings and how people interact with them. The more you can learn to think about your relationship with your child and to help them understand their emotions as well as how you are feeling, the happier your relationship will be.

Let me start by setting the scene for how babies learn to interact with the world around them, and centrally their parents. For your baby, this 'training programme' for relationships throughout their life, with you, their parents, starts early – in fact, even before they are born. Studies have shown that the sound of a mother's voice it is calming, both in the womb and when you finally get to meet them as a newborn. Scientists have recorded that unborn babies clearly respond to different vibrations and sounds with changes in their heart rate or movement patterns and are particularly responsive to the sound of their mother's voice (2,3). This has led them to conclude that your unborn baby learns to recognise and remember your voice during your pregnancy. This means the conversations that you have with your bump in the third trimester are laying the foundations for their social and emotional development, as well as their language skills and memory. Your voice is already shaping their understanding of the world.

When your baby comes into the world, the way that they look, act, interact etc. will have already have been influenced by their genetic history and temperament. There is a large body of important research around these areas. I want to acknowledge these influences and briefly explain them, but my focus is going to be much more on your relationship from the moment your baby is born and what you can each bring to this relationship.

Influences on. your baby's development

There are many factors that influence the unique emotional makeup that babies are born with. Every baby has an innate temperament which then interacts with the experiences the baby has with the important people and events in their world. This might include being cuddled, feeling criticised, receiving attention or being ignored. Think of temperament as tension in a tennis racket. The tighter the tension, the more reactive the racket might be to an approaching tennis ball. In this way, some babies react more to experiences in their environment, whatever they might be.

Maternal hormones influence the baby's development in the womb, and the emotions a woman feels during pregnancy can affect her hormones, so this in turn can have a big impact on the baby's development, particularly on brain development. The most compelling link is between maternal stress and a baby's development in the womb. The hormone cortisol, released during stressful situations, is particularly influential, and studies show that where mothers are very highly stressed, babies tend to be more fussy and irritable when born. It's believed that this is due to the negative impact of an 'overdose' of cortisol during pregnancy, which affects the baby's developing brain. On the flip side, the impact of affection and love when the baby is born has far-reaching positive effects (4), including helping babies to develop what is known in the research as a 'social brain' (5,6). We now know from neuroscience research that the baby's developing brain is designed to be moulded by the environment it encounters (7). In this way, a brain can begin to understand the thoughts, feelings and intentions of other people. This ability, known as 'mentalizing' (8), is going to be a word I refer to quite a bit throughout the book, and which I outlined in the Introduction. To remind you, what it means, essentially, is the ability to make sense of one's own actions, and also the actions of other people, with reference to beliefs, desires and feelings – to see yourself from the outside and your baby from the inside. When things are going well, your baby needs to experience a relationship that has a mind which keeps their mind in mind. I will help you throughout this book to understand why this skill of mentalizing is not only important, but quite simple to start doing in your everyday interactions. And you are probably doing a lot of it already, without even knowing it.

There may also be developmental factors that can make it more difficult to interact in a reflective and sensitive way with some babies. Babies born blind or on the autistic spectrum, for example, will send out a different set of signals to their parents than babies without these developmental issues, and so as a parent you may have a baby who needs a different level of sensitivity, or different cues from you, in order to maximise the closeness and security they feel in their relationship with you. That said, you can absolutely still create a secure attachment and a mentalizing relationship with your baby, whatever their developmental issues.

Reflective Parenting helps to buffer children from the negative effects of some of these early influences. Growing evidence demonstrates that where babies have reflective parents, these children grow up to develop the means of being able to understand and be more in control of their feelings (self-regulation) and develop the skills they need for establishing and maintaining relationships.

The origins of children learning to manage feelings

The origins of how your baby learns how to manage feelings, and to be able to regulate them, lie in the first few weeks and months of their relationship with you. Your baby's brain makes them respond to things that happen before they have any understanding of what these feelings and experiences mean. Your baby can be easily overwhelmed by unfamiliar things in their environment, such as smells, noises and separations from a parent. For example, baby

Jack is lying in his cot, squirming around and grizzling. He gets more uncomfortable and starts to cry. Inside his mind and body, his brain and nervous system are trying to manage this unpleasant feeling. Before his mum Rachel comes to him, he lacks any reference point from this inside feeling to what happens on the outside. It is as if his feelings inside just happen almost randomly without any anchor of an outside event to hang it on. So what would help Jack to manage this feeling? Fortunately, Jack can rely heavily on an external manager of his feelings, which is his mum.

Your baby's emotional development is a complex process and almost entirely dependent on you, their parents, and others close to them. Luckily, much of the time you will be naturally supporting this process without necessarily even realising. You need first to notice and then to understand your baby's emotional states (what's inside their mind) and then to link these emotions in your mind to a triggering event or action (what's outside their mind), such as in Jack's case an uncomfortable sensation from a wet nappy. In practical terms, this could be as mundane as a mind-minded comment from his mum when Jack cries that helps him connect his feeling of discomfort and distress with his wet nappy, such as 'Ah, does Mummy need to change your wet nappy? It's not very comfy is it?' In this simple statement, Jack's mum is telling him that she understands that he has a mind that contains thoughts and feelings, which are not only separate from her own, but that she can tell him about. Each time you link what your baby is feeling to the physical world, your baby begins to understand how things connect and work together. When you state out loud what you feel is going on inside your baby's mind, you are really helping them to understand their thoughts and feelings, you and the outside world. And all of this can be done in typical everyday relationships. Moreover, you can start to make these mind-minded statements from the point of first discovering you are pregnant.

> Have you noticed times when you do this? Try asking yourself the question: 'What might be going on in my child's mind right now?'

These kinds of mind-minded statements can be made directly *to* your child or *about* your child to a partner or family member. Research has shown that 'tuning in' to what your baby is thinking and feeling – in other words, being more mind-minded – means that your child is more likely to be securely attached, have better language and play abilities at age 2, and have better understanding of other people's thoughts and feelings when they start school (9). **Being mind-minded when your child is a baby also means that your child will be less likely to have behaviour problems in the preschool years.** Using mind-minded statements beyond this age is enormously helpful for helping your child to understand other people, manage their own emotions and help them stay connected to you.

When you are making these mind-minded comments, your attunement with your baby's feeling will naturally change your facial expression to match their feelings. This is known as marked-mirroring. The mums on the front cover, and in the picture below are mirroring their children. Your baby would see their feelings reflected back at them in your facial expressions or tone of voice.

When your baby sees your facial expressions in response to their own feelings, they can start to link and connect emotions, and your response begins to make sense. In essence, the way you look tells your baby how they feel inside. This is the beginning of your child learning about *how they* feel, and crucially this is the start of them learning to manage their feelings so that they don't overwhelm them. The way that you can do this is basically to respond to their emotions in a way that shows them that you can both understand how they are feeling and do something about it. For example, Jack's mum might say, 'Let me change that wet nappy for you into a nice warm dry one,' whilst her facial expression would be warm and comforting. Jack sees his mum as the regulator of how he is feeling. In other words, the supportive and in-tune presence of his mother is what helps him to first put a name to his feeling, then manage his feeling of distress, which over time as he grows, teaches him that feelings can be managed. As he gets older, he will be able to increasingly do this for himself, as if this ability gets passed from his mum to him. If something has upset you, connected with your own life, and your baby cries out in distress, it might take extra effort to match your tone and expression to how your baby feels, and so you might bring your own (quite separate) state of mind into the interaction. This is perfectly understandable and normal, but it does usually mean that it takes longer for the baby to regulate how they are feeling, as they need your help to do this. In this situation, it would be best to take a few moments yourself to manage your own feelings, and then you will be in a better frame of mind to be reflective with how your baby feels. I've developed a special tool called the Parent Map to help you do this, and I'll go over this in Chapter 2.

Marked-mirroring

As your baby grows from a determined, busy toddler to an increasingly independent child, continuing to be alert to what they are thinking or feeling is still incredibly valid and helpful. Reflective Parenting – developing a greater awareness of your own emotions and then thinking about what is going on inside your child's mind – has been shown to be a key influence on children's emotional development. The more often you can be reflective in your daily normal exchanges with your child, the more you will be helping them to understand their own feelings. Children don't just grow out of difficult behaviour of their own accord; they need you to show them how to grapple with emotions, which then impacts on misbehaviour. You might find that over the course of their childhood they will need your help more as their feelings about events in their life become more powerful. This kind of challenging behaviour is a natural part of childhood, just like growing physically. If children don't get this kind of help from you, then these emotions can become more exaggerated as they make greater efforts to get a response from you.

Do babies have relationship skills?

When Rachel's ex-partner Matt was at a play zone with his nine-month-old son Jack and talked to two other dads about their views of the first year of their children's lives, there was disagreement about how much, if anything of interest, happened when their children were babies. One parent thought that being a father with a young baby was a little boring as they did not seem to do much, but then after about a year things improved markedly. Another found the first year fascinating, if a little daunting. The experiences of having a baby for mothers and fathers can differ enormously, but as the Reflective Parenting model is all about different perspectives, these different experiences are equally valid and often equally helpful to your child. So, whether you are a father or a mother, or caregiver, is there more to babies and how we relate to them that could make this experience a great deal more interesting, both for the parent and the baby?

What did you feel like when your baby was born? When you looked at them, what did you imagine was going on inside their head? Did you even think about that? And what was going on inside yours? What did you imagine they were capable of doing? And did you think you had any direct influence on this? Maybe you remember your own son or daughter, newly born, staring in wonder at the chaos of light, noise and smell, and then looking at you? Your baby had a preference for you, their parent, and preferred the smell of you, the sight of you and the sound of your voice to anything or anyone else – they were born with an innate desire to interact with you. You might have found yourself so focused on keeping this little person alive, you gave little or no thought to what was actually going on inside them.

What must it be like to be a newborn baby, a little person who knows nothing about the world? It is easy to assume that a baby is unable to understand anything either inside their mind or in the outside world: that babies come into the world a completely blank slate. Indeed, until the start of the twentieth century, many researchers believed just this: that babies had no awareness of either themselves or other people around them. If you think back to those first few days and weeks of your baby's life, what was your main focus? Wondering what was going on inside them, what kind of person they were going to be? Or making sure that you had their temperature just right at night time and that they weren't getting a nappy rash and was feeding well? We now understand that babies can hear and respond to their mothers' voices in utero and I wonder when you started to think about your baby as a person with a mind? It might be that you weren't even aware you were doing this, but many women make comments to their baby well before they are born, saying things like, 'oh, you're very lively today' when their baby kicks.

Sometimes it seems though that this view of a baby's limited abilities is still around today, with some parenting books focusing only on programmes for managing feeding, sleeping and toileting routines, instead of on your relationship with each other. While these are all important and essential to your baby's survival, I believe it is also helpful, and indeed vitally important, to start thinking at an early stage about what else might be going on in your baby's mind. It can be hard to make this your focus, as understandably you are taken up with thoughts about how to keep this new life fed and warm, and most importantly alive. However, by doing this, you will be better able to manage difficult behaviour later on, and to iron out difficulties in your relationship with your child. You will also be supporting the development of their relationship skills with other people, such as friends at school and in their adult life. The research tells us that starting to think about what's going on inside your baby, and importantly, showing them this through your communication with them, is a great way of helping your baby to both think about and manage how they feel.

The tide of thinking started to change in the 1970s when developmental psychologists, such as Trevarthen (10), spent a lot of time observing infants and their parents. By watching babies, he found that when they were feeling calm and comfortable they seemed to move in purposeful ways, as if a baby has an idea of what they want to do before they do it. The research showed that babies were not always randomly kicking and moving or making sounds with no awareness of their parents, but often moved and made noises in interaction with them. Research on newborn babies (11) showed that, just hours after birth, newborn babies could move their fingers when they saw other people moving their fingers. Babies also got better at copying over time, showing their potential for learning and improving the coordination of their actions. What all of this tells us is that from the minute they are born, babies already have a strong inclination to think about and interact with an 'other.' And the most important other is most certainly you.

Babies are immediately skilled at communicating with others and make a great effort to do so. And as a baby gets older, they become really interested in experiencing how other people see him. Think of a nine-month-old baby, holding up a toy for others to see. For a young baby, it is fun discovering new things, but it becomes much more fun when you find out that you can share these things with other people who can take delight in joining in your fun. For your baby, even objects become intrinsically more interesting when they see that another person is interested in them. This is worth remembering for later on, as you will see that in your play with your baby, and later in childhood, showing your own interest in something that they have focused on will make it immediately more appealing and interesting for them. This can be a very useful tool that you might not have realised you even had. Or imagine when you find yourself standing at the checkout in the supermarket and a baby in the buggy in front of you looks at you with wide eyes and grins, your instinct is most likely going to be to widen your eyes and grin back. Babies automatically seek out and respond back to positive, expressive communication from other people. Also babies can draw interested attentive adults into a pattern of interacting and conversing that grows over the weeks and months in an almost ritualistic fashion. Think about how expressive a baby's face is. When you notice and take delight in your baby's expressions and movements, such as frowns, pouts, grimacing or furrowing of their brow, or turning their head or kicking their feet, you motivate them to repeat these actions. Your baby learns that by using expressions and actions, they trigger a response from the adults around them, and so when you react in this way, you are helping your baby to engage in communication. Babies begin to anticipate their parents' responses and take enjoyment from them, and crucially learn that they can have an effect on other people.

Have you ever said to a friend or relative who is interacting with your baby, 'They are so interested in you' or 'They like you doing that'? If so, you had accurately guessed that your baby has a mind of their own and had already begun working out what they like and don't like. You would have also noticed that they are interested in interacting with other people. A baby is not just someone who needs their physical needs met and to have consistency and routines. They also need you to interact with them and to enter into a relationship with them. This may sound obvious, but it's striking how many of us can get so wrapped up in the daily care of our baby's physical needs that we forget to find the time to turn our attention to what's actually going on inside our babies' heads.

Babies have a preference for whom they interact with

Even though a baby is interested in people generally, they are much more interested in interacting with people who reciprocate this interest. Babies naturally respond better to people who are sensitive to them. They like it when people make good eye contact, raise their eyebrows at them in an expressive way, take turns and wait

35

for a response, and can match how they are feeling through their tone of voice and facial expressions. Babies love people who show these verbal and non-verbal signs of interest; expressive, interested faces are definitely more appealing and immediately engaging for a baby than blank or hostile faces. This makes sense for us adults too. A sales person has a much better chance of selling us something if they make an effort to engage with us and understand what we want. However, the sales pitch cannot be over the top – it needs to be matched to our feelings and intentions at that moment; an over-eager salesperson is almost as bad as a disinterested one. Researchers (12) showed that babies at 14 months old are much more likely to pick up an object that the researcher has shown an interest in and give it to the researcher if that person had spent time engaging with them first. Babies seemed to be more motivated to connect with one object over another if the adult they are interacting with authentically connected with them and shared a dialogue. When babies get a sense that 'you have noticed and understood what it is like to be me,' they are more able to learn about the world and explore. They feel listened to, which builds trust.

Am I boring you? Having a mind that is interested in yours

If babies have a set of skills to bring to their relationship with you, what do you think *you* bring to the relationship? In an ideal world, when we interact with our children, it would be similar to an improvisation between two musicians. The improvisation would be based on what was going on in the moment, like musicians responding to each other unhindered by old musical scores or patterns. Over time, hopefully a nice tune would start to emerge and the musicians would be in synch with each other. In our parenting, we would bounce off our children's ideas and they would bounce off ours, unhindered by other influences. This would allow us to be fully attentive to what our children are doing or saying and we would be able to follow their lead. This is certainly an aspect of Reflective Parenting. This doesn't always happen though in our interactions with others.

Have you ever been with someone where you feel you aren't being interesting enough for them? You're chatting away about something that happened to you, telling the person what you thought was a funny story about a friend, and you notice that they seem distracted, checking their watch for the time and then perhaps even starting to text someone on their mobile. What's that feeling like? Does it make you want to try harder to hold their attention? Tell a funny story? Even perform a bit more? Or do you withdraw? Start to feel a bit inadequate and go quiet, resolving that next time you might not bother coming out for the evening, as you're better off being on your own if that's the kind of disinterested reaction you get? You start to wonder if maybe you're just a bit boring. Now imagine yourself as a young baby or child, feeling that you aren't interesting to your mum or dad. You might engage in any one, or in turn all, of the attention-seeking strategies described earlier – or you might simply withdraw.

Rewind to the evening out with your friend, and this time you sense that the person you're with is interested in what you have to say, and how you feel about it all and is giving you their full attention, both in their facial expression and the way they ask questions and listen to you. Immediately, you feel not only closer to them but in some way also better about yourself, and the conversation flows. This is the same for children because when the person they are closest to listens to what they are saying and feeling, and then responds to them in a way that supports what they are feeling, they feel interesting and of value. And when your baby or child feels that you are there just for them and interested in their thoughts and feelings, they make themselves wide open to learning about not just their own mind, but yours as well. Just as you experience a more enjoyable evening with your friends if they are paying attention to you and showing interest, so it is that a baby experiences a feeling of being valued if you show that you see something of value in them.

The important thing here is the difference between someone not only noticing your mind but also being able to respond to it, in a way that fits with how you are feeling, and moreover, being curious about how your mind works. Compared with being with someone who not only doesn't appear interested in what's going on in your mind but also maybe hasn't even noticed its very existence.

Now imagine Rachel waiting at a bus stop in the rain with baby Jack. There are several ways of dealing with this everyday mundane situation, but the subtle differences between how Rachel might handle it can make a big difference to how both she and Jack might feel by the time they get home. If Rachel is able to interact with Jack in a way that draws him in, by being both interested in him and showing him the world around him, there will almost certainly be a different experience for both baby and parent. For example, imagine if Rachel pulls funny faces or starts to show an interest in the raindrops, smiling as the rain hits her hand and showing her wet hand to Jack to pass the time. Jack can engage with this, particularly if he sees his mother's expressive face showing her own interest, and he is likely to respond with interest and excitement himself. However, if Rachel feels a bit bored is a little preoccupied with worries about money and her ex-husband, and only shows irritation at waiting at a bus stop in the rain, then interacting with Jack may not even come into her mind. Rachel feels impatient about the bus not arriving and ignores Jack; Jack begins to get bored and frustrated at the lack of interaction and attention and starts to cry. Parent and baby get on the bus feeling irritable and less willing to interact with each other, and, in a worst-case scenario, the journey home involves a screaming baby on a full bus and a very irritable or angry mother. It is important to note that acting otherwise can sometimes feel impossible, and it is something you have to make a conscious effort to do at first. What this example shows us is how the behaviour and emotional states of the parent affect the behaviour and emotional states of the child and vice versa.

What do you bring to the relationship?

In your everyday moments with your child, I would imagine that there are many times when you haven't acted exactly how you had thought you should have, with hindsight. Maybe later you felt a sense of shame or disappointment in how you acted? It could be you felt drawn into an interaction and gave a response that seemed over the top or overly negative? For example, a simple question from your child has you snapping back and feeling extremely irritated. Have you ever wondered why this happens? There are many factors that interfere with how we respond and react to our children, but there are two factors in particular that influence us and make it extremely difficult to enjoy a free, unhindered improvisation with our children a lot of the time. These factors are the impact of the parenting you received as a child and being influenced by strong emotions when you are relating to your child.

The influence of how you were parented

Everyone sees situations differently. We might react to certain situations more than others, whereas some things we might not even notice. For example, Karen walked into a shop to buy something and heard the shop assistant sigh after she had asked him a question.

She reacted in an extreme way to this, perceiving his sigh as a personal slight and thinking that the shop assistant was showing her a lack of respect and shouted as she walked out of the shop. In the same situation, some people may not have noticed the sigh, while others may have assumed that the sigh was probably due to the shop assistant having had being a long tough day at work and nothing to do with them. However, if we found out more about Karen and learned that she had a history of critical and rejecting parenting, it would be easier to understand why she was so hypersensitive to perceived rejection. Past experiences can have a really strong influence on the present. This is quite an extreme example, but you may be able to think of examples from your own life where you have found yourself, for example, sensitive to criticism and feeling extremely hurt; perhaps at work, or in the local Parent Teacher Association meeting, you didn't feel your ideas were listened to, and this may connect back to feeling undervalued or unheard when you were much younger. It is helpful to be aware of these influences, and to know that we all look at the world and our relationships through a different lens, depending on our past influences. Sometimes, it can be hard to turn down the volume on our own parents' voices in our heads and think clearly.

The same is true of how we notice and interpret our children's behaviour – we all do this differently. How we see and interact with our children is influenced by our experiences of our own parents when we were young. Your parents and the home environment were all you knew during your most vulnerable and impressionable stages in life. Whether this was when you cried when you were a baby or were a child anxious about going to school, your parents reacted in particular ways to everything you did. The way you were raised as a child has an impact on the rest of your life. Even if you are not aware of it, the imprint of your own parents' responses remains inside your head, influencing your parenting. And how you deal with this influence could be much more important to how you handle your relationship with your own child than you might already realise. Your early experiences form your view of the world and can impact on how you parent your children. An interesting study (13) found that when pregnant mothers were interviewed about their own childhood experiences of being parented, it was possible to predict from these histories the type of relationship they would have with their future child. For example, a secure parent went on to have a secure attachment with her own child. Notably, the important factor in linking the past with future parenting styles was not what the parent had experienced in her early childhood so much as how she talked about it and reflected on it, telling a coherent story. This is important to how we understand and think about how you can become reflective in your current approach to parenting. The next two chapters will particularly focus on this.

If in your own childhood a parent, or caregiver, was able to recognise and comment on what was going on in your mind as a baby, then it is highly likely that you will have felt secure in this relationship and experienced being understood. Achieving this level of understanding with your child may sound difficult, but it's actually quite easy as most of this commentary takes place during the most mundane of everyday exchanges, such as during a nappy change, a feed or a bedtime routine. This would look something like this: as you lean over to change your baby's nappy you might say, 'ooh, poor baby, are you feeling a bit wet and cold? Shall mummy change you into a nice clean snuggly nappy?' And as you do this, your expression would reflect both the baby's current discomfort, and then your expression would change to offer comfort and soothing. So, being reflective promotes security, but what can you do if your own childhood didn't have this type of attachment, but you want to try to achieve this now with your own baby? Can it be done? Even if you had a really difficult experience in your childhood, I will take you through ways in which you can take on a reflective stance and develop a more secure relationship with your baby.

It's important to realise then that all interactions with your child are impressionistic, that is you are interpreting and making sense of situations rather than responding to them in a factual way that is totally correct. We all do this in different ways, and they are real for us. What is important is to start to think about how you can separate your own experience from what you feel now with your child.

For example, when Karen's two-year-old daughter Molly said 'No!' to her mother's request to go to bed, Karen experienced strong feelings of rejection, based on her own history of being rejected frequently by her own parents. In this present interaction, her reaction was based on a strong sense that her own daughter was also rejecting her and she felt compelled to withdraw from Molly as she did her own parents. Obviously, if this continued over time, the worry would be that Karen's negative reaction to her two-year-old's behaviour would result in Molly feeling rejected and unsafe, possibly leading to further rejection of her mother in a negative cycle of rejection.

So one of the important steps towards learning to become a more reflective parent with your own child is recognising the part that your own history plays in this relationship. If Karen in this example was able to begin to separate her own past childhood experiences from this present scenario, she would be more able to reflect on her child's behaviour with curiosity and interest. This just starts with Karen noticing that she has a strong reaction to Molly and is especially sensitive to Molly saying 'no' to her. She might also be able to see Molly's reaction as a developmental stage, or realise that the response related to her daughter feeling upset that her mum missed out on her bath time. Karen's understanding would promote a feeling of security in her child and would enable a more positive interaction to evolve, as her daughter would start to experience her mum as someone who was able to comment on what was going on in her mind. This is another example of mind-mindedness: the ability of parents to talk about what they think is going on in their child's mind. It's interesting to note that where parents are able to comment accurately on what they think is going on in their child's mind, these children then go on to be able to understand other people better. An example of how this would look would be for Karen to say, 'I think you're a bit fed up that I didn't get home in time to spend enough time playing with you before bed time tonight. It doesn't feel fair, does it?'

The influence of strong emotions when relating to your child

You can be influenced by strong emotions that arise from situations both outside of and within your relationship with your child. Try to think back to a recent difficult moment with your child, and ask yourself whether the level of your emotional reaction fitted the situation. Was your reaction disproportionate, and what do you think may have contributed to you reacting in this way? How might a friend have experienced you in this situation, what would they have seen? Can you link your reaction in this situation to previous situations?

Here's an example:

> Lisa returned home, stressed from other events from earlier in the day. Although she wasn't aware of how she was feeling, too many demands and having to meet other people's needs had led to her feeling irritated and resentful.

Consequently, when her daughter Ella asked for ketchup, a drink and complained that her brother Charlie had more chips than her at the table before she had even sat down, she overreacted and responded angrily, throwing her plate hard down on the table and storming off into the kitchen, muttering expletives to herself.

These kinds of moments can happen in every family and it can be helpful to check back to what happened before these incidents, to rewind and reflect, so you can be more aware of the impact of events leading up to difficult moments. Being aware of strong emotions experienced within the parent-child relationship is important. For example, feeling stressed out is likely to influence how you respond to a scream from an overtired baby. It may change your interpretation from a need for comfort or food to an intention to torment you when you feel the need to be left alone. Take this example from a bedtime routine with Lisa and her four-year-old daughter, Ella.

The routine starts well, with Lisa taking Ella up the stairs. A fun bath-time is followed by two stories in bed and a kiss goodnight, after which mum starts to make her way downstairs. She is feeling close to her little girl and happy that they have enjoyed a lovely shared moment of intimacy, where both felt loved and secure.

Suddenly as she's halfway down the stairs she shouts out, 'I'm still hungry. I need a snack.' Lisa calls back, 'It's too late for snacks now, you've had your dinner. Just go to sleep my love.' Ella calls back, 'I don't like it in my bedroom. Can I have a little lie on your bed please Mummy?' Lisa calls back, a little snappier now, 'Time for sleep now, Mummy's very tired.' This conversation goes back and forth until Lisa gets angry and starts muttering to herself, 'I've had a really long day myself, when do I get to sit down and have a minute's peace myself?' Ella becomes distressed and before long both are upset and close to tears.

So how has this relationship switched from feeling intimate to antagonistic so quickly? Lisa has clearly reached the point where she lost the capacity to think about another person. The impact on her child was to feel upset and not thought about, and both lost the ability to feel concerned and close to each other. So how can you handle this sort of situation in a way that doesn't lead to a tantrum of your own?

Being misunderstood is highly aversive and so when both parent and child are feeling this at the same time, it's a toxic dynamic that both parties will feel keen to get away from. Lisa was feeling misunderstood by her four-year-old. The sort of question running through her mind at this point was 'Why can't she understand that I've had a really tiring day, and can't give any more to anyone else right now?' On the other hand, the thoughts running through her four-year-old's mind might have been something like, 'I haven't seen my Mummy all day while she's been at work. I want a bit more time of just me and her and another story.' In this example, it is difficult for the mother to respond to her child's needs because of the strength of her emotions in the relationship at that moment. This strong emotion then dictates how she reacts to and interprets her daughter's behaviour. When we misunderstand a situation, we tend to act on a false assumption. So in this example, Lisa may begin to feel that Ella is 'getting at her' or even intentionally provoking her. Ella may feel abandoned, neglected, maybe even unloved or unvalued.

What Reflective Parenting feels like for children

When your one-year-old daughter grins at you, wide-eyed with excitement at her first birthday party as she eats a piece of chocolate cake really too big for her own mouth, imagine the impact on her of the following three reactions from you:

A. You grin back at her, your own eyes widening and say 'Wow! That chocolate cake is absolutely yummy, isn't it? It's bigger than your mouth, but you can still just about get it in!' Then you laugh.

B. You scowl at her, eyes narrowing and say, 'You're making a big mess with that all over your face. If you try to eat a piece that big, you'll probably be sick and I'll be the one who has to clear it all up!'

C. You look at her momentarily, but your face is blank, not smiling or scowling. You're trying to remember if you ever had a cake on your birthday and are suddenly struck by an image of your parents arguing; you can't remember how old you were at the time.

43

These three different reactions have the following different effects on your one-year-old, not consciously thought, of course, but experienced in a very real way:

A. Mum can see that I love my cake and I'm feeling happy at my party. She's happy that I'm happy and she is really interested in me feeling this way.
B. This cake tastes good, but I'm not sure I'm enjoying myself. Mum looks angry, I feel a bit bad inside, and I'm not sure why. Maybe it's not really very nice eating cake.
C. I don't know what I feel right now. I don't know if I even have a mind / who or what I am.

The experience for the one year old in example A is one of feelings that the parent has really joined her in her experience of her delicious chocolate cake. What the mother does in this example is to open up her mind totally to the experience of her young child, in a way that is receptive to the child's state of mind. Her mum's reflections on the 'yummy-ness' of the cake and statement that 'It's bigger than your mouth, but you can still just about get it in!' says 'I know what you are feeling and thinking about that cake and this whole experience.' Her laughter afterwards is a moment of shared pleasure in the experience. The mother is of course smiling at her own enjoyment at seeing her one year old having such a great time, but the smile is also her reflection of her young child's state of mind. This moment of sharing the same feelings with each other is a moment of simple, but intense, shared enjoyment for both mother and child.

Experiencing great pleasure in something, and seeing this reflected back at you in the face and voice of your parent, is about as good as it gets for a baby. The feeling that not only does this feel good for me but it also looks like you are enjoying showing me how good it feels for both me and you mum, makes that experience of eating the chocolate birthday cake like a black-and-white photo going into bright technicolour for your baby. Nothing feels quite as good.

Conclusion

When you reflect back at your baby what is going on in their mind, they learn that they have a mind that is separate from yours, and one that is interpretable and makes sense. Reflective Parenting is driven by an accurate mirroring of what the parent infers is going on in her baby's mind. In reflecting back your own thoughts and feelings, you are also helping your baby to understand that other people have their own thoughts and intentions. When you start to talk to your baby and child about what you think is going on in their mind, you are doing what is referred to as mentalizing, that is helping to show them that you understand they have thoughts, feelings and wishes that are separate and different from your own, as well as that you can understand these and reflect them back to them. Even more importantly, your baby can't learn this without you teaching them. The good news is that teaching your child about thoughts and emotions is actually pretty simple, and you're undoubtedly doing a lot of this already without even knowing it, in the everyday exchanges you have between you and your child. With some help, you can start to notice when you are doing this well (when you are mentalizing) and when you are finding it more difficult. We all have times when we are mentalizing well (only about 30% of the time), and many more times when we are doing it less well. Reflective Parenting is all about helping you to start reflecting back to your child what you imagine is going on in their mind a bit more of the time. And with this increased mentalizing, you will start to see an impact on how they behave and how you connect.

REFLECTIVE PARENTING SUMMARY

The origins of Reflective Parenting

What it is ...

Reflective Parenting is a way of parenting your child where you think more about what the thoughts, feelings and intentions are behind your child's behaviour than about the behaviour itself. When you are a reflective parent, you are curious and attentive in your approach to your child. You understand that minds are separate and different and your thoughts and feelings are not the same as your child's, and vice versa. You listen attentively and empathically to your child, validating their thoughts and feelings, but at the same time, you hold authority and set a boundary for your child's behaviour, which helps them to feel safe and secure.

It helps you by ...

Being a reflective parent helps you regulate your own emotions. When you practice Reflective Parenting, you develop the ability to reflect on your own thoughts and feelings and are curious about where they come from and what influences them. When you tune into your own state of mind, this helps you regulate your emotions, and the more regulated you are, the better prepared you are for understanding your child. This in turn helps them to be more emotionally regulated, leading to fewer difficulties in their behaviour.

It helps your child by ...

When you practice being a reflective parent, your child feels more secure with you. This secure attachment comes from them feeling you are interested in trying to understand what they think and feel (even if you don't always get this right). Your child's experience of feeling your curiosity and interest in them helps them to feel more closely connected to you, and this, in turn, helps them to regulate their emotions and leads to less explosive behaviour from them.

It helps your relationship by ...

When you become a more reflective parent, you are seeking connection with *not* correction of your child. When you try to understand your own thoughts and feelings and then your child's, you strengthen the security of your attachment to each other. This promotes greater trust, leading to a better understanding of each other's emotions as well as other people's. More mentalizing in a relationship also promotes stronger relationships between your child and other people in their life, such as friends and other relations.

Keep in mind . . .

1. The first principle of being a reflective parent is to be curious about and attentive to your own thoughts and feelings as well as your child's.
2. People have different states of mind and your own is not the same as your child's. Try to see things from different perspectives and introduce your child to the idea that there are different ways of seeing the same situation. This helps with problem-solving as well as supporting strong connections.
3. When you listen empathically to your child and validate their thoughts and feelings and different perspective, your child feels understood by you. This leads to a closer connection and more secure attachment. It is also more likely to help your child see your, sometimes different, point of view.

What to expect in the book . . .

Over the next chapters, I will introduce you first to a set of tools that you will be able to use when you adopt a Reflective Parenting stance. First, I'll look at the concept of 'the Parent Map' to help you regulate your own emotions and manage your feelings, before I guide you on mentalizing your child and helping them with their own feelings, using a tool called 'the Parent APP.' I will also explore the role of discipline and how to approach this tricky area, and I'll take a closer look at sensitive children, in particular, and how you may want to adapt your approach if your child has particular developmental needs and sensitivities. After walking you through the tools, I will think about the broader role of family, siblings and friends and about mentalizing in good times as well as bad ones. Finally, I will help you think about your older child's transition into the tricky teenage years and how to prepare for this momentous milestone.

2

THE PARENT MAP

In this chapter, my aim is to show you the importance of thinking about yourself – having self-reflection – in relation to your child. I will ask you to consider a number of things, including what might be influencing you to feel in particular ways, how you react and any patterns you can discern from your reactions, and what you think during situations. This may lead you to consider your strengths and weaknesses as a parent – we all have them. You may find that specific areas and roles associated with parenting might come quite naturally, whereas other aspects might be more challenging.

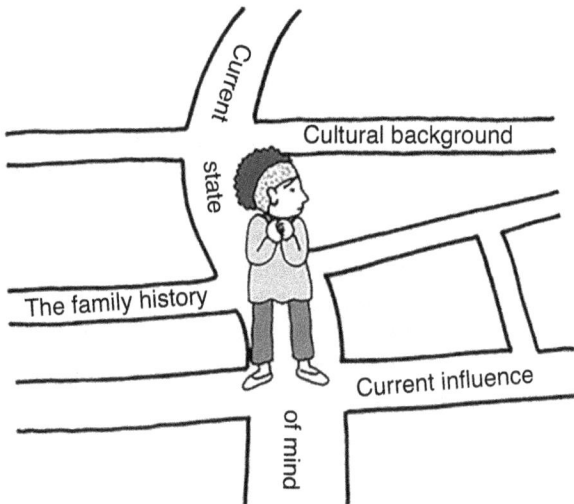

DOI: 10.4324/9781003483762-3

> *If I could get into your child's mind, and be able to see how they sees you as a parent, what would you want them to see? What would they say about you, what are your strengths? What qualities would you really want them to highlight?*

Being a parent takes a great many skills, and you often need to adopt very different roles in relation to your child depending on the situation. A parent is someone who at times teaches and supports, provides love and comfort, acts playfully, maintains firm boundaries and discipline in spite of upset or anger, instils routines and also strives to understand their child's perspective. How comfortable are you with these varied roles? Does one come more naturally to you than the others? One way of thinking about these questions is to think about your emotional reactions during situations, as they can help you to identify those areas of parenting that you might be finding more problematic. To help with this process of self-reflection and thinking about what makes you the kind of parent you are, I developed the idea of the Parent Map.

I think that becoming a parent is like going on an expedition into uncharted territories; you do not know what the destination is, how to get there or how the journey will affect you. A pre-prepared map would be very helpful, to show you a way to think, feel and act as a parent and help you through. However, there are none available as everyone's experiences and expeditions are unique and are influenced by different things. Instead, you can draft your own personal Parent Map. This means building up a picture of how you are as a parent and is a process that will probably continue to be pieced together throughout your child's childhood and often far beyond this point. You will undoubtedly start to draw up a new Parent Map when your child reaches adolescence. The process of thinking about, and working at, your Parent Map is more important than actually completing a finished picture. A Parent's Map constantly changes, mainly because your child changes what they think and feel as they develop and interact with their world. Also, aspects of your own life are probably always changing, so Maps need to change, too. The aim of this chapter is to start the process of constructing your Map, your own inside story put together through self-reflection, and thereby help you get to know yourself in a different way. Then, in Chapter 3, I provide you with strategies for both noticing and managing strong feelings.

Constructing a Parent Map: being aware of your own mind

Constructing your Parent Map, by becoming more aware of the influences on how you come across and interact with your child, is important to Reflective Parenting. Creating coherence in your Map is a lifelong adventure. Once you start to reflect more on your Map, you will be in a better position to think about your child, and how you approach your everday relationship with them. This can lead to some positive and long-lasting changes in behaviours that you might have previously struggled with. Note that this Map doesn't have to be a written or visual one, more a working mental document you keep on yourself. However, it might help at the start to get something down on paper or on a device that gets this process of self-reflection started.

Let me guide you a little with constructing your Map and suggest three important features that will help you increase your self-awareness. These reference points, when you become more attentive to them, will help you establish and define yourself as a parent.

> *Have you ever snapped at your child, and then later realised that you were really angry because of something that had happened to you, and not because of anything that they had done?*

Reference point one: current state of mind

The first important step of creating your own Parent Map is to be aware of *yourself* and be curious about your own state of mind. Try asking yourself the questions: 'How do I feel right now? What has made me feel this way?' and 'What am I thinking?' Start to observe your thoughts and feelings from the outside. Of course, this is work in progress for all of us because we are never constantly aware of ourselves. We often act without fully knowing why, and react without thinking. While this is fine a lot of the time, by increasing your awareness of how you are feeling, and focusing on what's going on inside *you*, you will discover how you can enjoy a better quality of interaction with your child. The reason this is important is that your own feelings have a powerful impact on how your child both feels and behaves and how you handle your relationship.

Why do we have to feel?

A big part of being aware of what is going on in your mind is being able to understand your emotions and feelings. But why do we have to have feelings? What function or use are they in our lives? We often don't have any choice over whether or not to have an emotional life – our feelings are just there. Over the centuries, our brains have evolved and changed, but the parts of our brain that have remained constant are those areas responsible for our emotions. This means our ability to experience emotions came first, and other functions such as reasoning and rational thought developed much later, suggesting emotions are essential to our survival in some way.

Because of the architecture of our brains, the emotional centres have greater power over the rest of the brain, including power over our thoughts. This means the emotional brain can take over the rational brain quite easily. We can be hijacked by intense feelings and have explosive outbursts, not always knowing why this happens or understanding what came over us. In terms of how we act then, our feelings are often more in charge than our thoughts.

Consider the following scenario. Imagine you are travelling home by train during a busy rush-hour commute and a man standing nearby becomes increasingly agitated as he is jostled around by the other passengers. He suddenly gets extremely angry about the fact that, as he perceives it, someone is intentionally trying to prevent him from sitting down in a vacant seat. A sudden rush of fury, driven by adrenaline, overwhelms the man being pushed around and he starts shouting at the man who pushed him (even though this was probably unintentional) and an actual fight ensues. In this example, an intense feeling takes precedence over any rational thoughts about what to do in the situation, or about what might have been the other person's actual intentions or thoughts.

Emotions are perhaps best thought of as impulses to act, providing instant plans for handling life that we may or may not be aware of. The tendency to act is there without us knowing it or consciously controlling it. So why do we have feelings if they have the capacity to affect our behaviour and relationships so negatively, as in the previous example?

Compared with other animals, we humans have a far more complex and varied range of emotional responses to situations. Our social lives are equally complex and our emotions can help us to manage socially. From the moment we are born, we are hardwired not only to seek out the warmth, food and comfort of our mothers (our physical instincts) but we are also driven to connect with and relate to other people (our emotional instincts). Through these emotional connections we learn not only about others but also ourselves. To underline just how important emotions are, when the emotional centres within the brain are removed during brain surgery, patients lose all interest in people; they report having no feelings and fail to recognise feelings in others. They are able to converse with those around them, but they seem to prefer to spend time on their own. So emotions can act as *signals* within relationships and help us connect to others. Although we are not conscious of the process happening, when we feel an emotion it tells us something about the external world and how we have reacted to it.

The reason I want to draw out the importance of becoming more aware of how you feel is because when we know how we feel, and even understand *why* we feel a certain way, we can use our feelings to make good decisions in life and learn to control our impulses. If we find ourselves snapping at our child, we might be able to make more sense of whether this was really about something that we felt about ourselves or our own lives. By making sense of the feelings we are experiencing, instead of just reacting, we can start to moderate our emotions and become better able to express them appropriately.

Think back to the busy train commute. If the man near to you had been more aware of how he was feeling and thinking and how these thoughts and feelings were causing him to become increasingly agitated, he might not have reacted so impulsively or aggressively. Alternatively, if he had been more aware immediately afterwards, he might have been able to reflect on his over-reaction, explain and apologise for his actions. Being aware of how you are feeling offers the opportunity to analyse whether or not to react, and how. Following on from this increased awareness, if you then start to share emotional experiences with other people, it is possible to feel more connected and understood.

How this part of the Map applies to Reflective Parenting

So we know feelings are essential for relationships and our communication with others in the social world around us, and it follows that an awareness of our feelings can help us to be more reflective about what's happening with our child. How does noticing this reference point on your Map apply to Reflective Parenting and help you become more self-aware, and how does this help your developing relationship with your child? Let's think through an example of how thinking about your feelings can be helpful.

> *It is a cold and wet Saturday afternoon. Finn is indoors looking after the children. He was meant to be seeing friends in the evening, but his friends had cancelled. His wife Lisa has gone out with her friends instead. Meanwhile, the children are either being clingy or misbehaving and being oppositional and this is really getting on Finn's nerves. His 4-year-old daughter Ella looks up at him with tears in her eyes and says, 'You don't want to play with me today daddy.' Finn feels ashamed that he has made his daughter feel so upset and begins to wonder why he hasn't been playing with his kids. Finn notices that he has been feeling bored and irritated. He begins to understand that he is annoyed that he is not going out with his friends and feels resentful about being in with the children when he was looking forward to going out. By becoming more aware of his feelings, especially his frustration towards the children's behaviour, he has a greater awareness of how he might be behaving towards his children. In other words, Finn's awareness of his state of mind and how this might be impacting on him increases his awareness of how he might be impacting on his children. A sense of guilt enters his mind. He is asking them to entertain themselves and getting frustrated at them when they won't. By becoming curious as to why this might be, and by thinking about himself, he can start to think about altering his behaviour.*

In the example above, the last sentence is really the most important one to consider first. Finn starts to become curious about why the children might be misbehaving and starts to make the connection with his own feelings about being frustrated and let down. This important first step, of being curious, is interestingly one that often gets missed, or lost, in our everyday interactions as we often just react. However, being curious about how you feel is crucial to Reflective Parenting as it allows you to understand how your own emotional state is impacting on your children, and it also allows you to reflect further and to link together your emotional states to what might be going on in your world. What matters most is the message that our children receive, and not the one that we think we're giving

(1). So, understanding the difference between how we *intend* to come across and how we actually come across is really very important to understanding how our children perceive us. Being able to develop a curiosity and understanding of what makes you feel negative feelings will help you in future exchanges with your child.

Curiosity involves first being interested in your own emotions and then observing the emotional 'tone' of your child's communication. And once you become curious about your child's world, you start to develop the ability to think differently about the reasons your child is behaving in a particular way – you start not just to notice, but also to interpret, your child's behaviour. If you can become more aware of your emotional states, you are less likely to react impulsively to your child's behaviour, which can only be a good thing. Let us return to the example:

> *Finn realised he was initially interpreting his children's behaviour as being whiny, clingy and oppositional. After Ella's tearful reaction he realised they were misbehaving because they were feeling ignored. He then started to think that perhaps they were feeling unwanted when they saw his lack of interest in them, and that maybe the acting up and misbehaving was a way to get noticed and get him to play with them. By making sense of his state of mind, Finn was better equipped to see that his mood was affecting his children and that his children wanted to spend time with him. This allowed him to connect with his children, tuning into them and finding a way to spend a more positive time together.*

This guide then, to trying to understand what might be going on inside your child's mind, begins with trying to understand what's going on inside your *own*. It will be harder sometimes to get his inside story when you lose the thread of yours. Reflective Parenting, then, encourages you to create an awareness, or space, in your mind for thinking about how you feel, and what's going on in your mind. In other words, being reflective helps you to see the importance of shifting your attention to yourself and how you are currently thinking and feeling so that you can then create space in your mind for thinking about what might be going on in your child's mind. You start to disentangle your own thoughts and feelings from your child's. The real benefit to doing this is that you then start to interact with your child in a different, more understanding way. When you start to interact differently, you begin to see real and significant changes not only in how your child behaves but also in how you and your child actually feel about each other. Adapting your thinking in this way isn't easy and takes some practice, so don't feel too worried if it doesn't come naturally at first. However, doing this often enough builds continuity and helps build a story of how you react to your child.

Reference point two: past experiences, relationships and development

It's in our common language to refer back to what our parents did, sometimes blaming them for things that we feel and do now, and sometimes paying tribute. Phrases like, 'He's just like his father,' however innocuous they may sound, are evidence of our tendency to think of the influence of the generations that went before us. Clearly these early relationships have a major impact on our sense of security, and on our personality and development. In the world of academic psychology, whole books have been devoted to the subject of the influence of early childhood experiences on our current emotions and our ability to deal with our emotions and enjoy healthy relationships, and I can't possibly do this topic justice here. All I am asking you to do, in terms of being aware of yourself and your own emotions, is to reflect on the influence of your past experiences on how you might be feeling right now, or on your everyday interactions with your child. Hearing voices from our past relationships might make us stop in our tracks and do something completely opposed to how our parents would act, or conversely, may make us smile at the recollection of something helpful and familiar. Whatever your own reaction as a parent, the imprint of your own parents, or those who looked after you when you were growing up, will remain inside your head and be more or less accessible depending on the nature of the experience. What I mean by this is that some of us can feel very preoccupied by early experiences, while others may be more detached from their past; what's certain is that how you deal with your past influences could be much more important to how you handle your relationship with your own child than you might realise. Being aware of this influence, and not ignoring the importance of it on your current emotional state, will be a big help in your relationship with your child.

There are times when we might catch ourselves doing or saying something where we can hear the echo of our mother's or father's voice. We may have inherited small mannerisms: for one mum,

Constructing your Map means reflecting on how you were parented.

rummaging through her handbag full of papers, lipstick, phone and so on, for a set of keys, immediately took her back to a memory of her own mum rummaging for her purse in a shop while she stood by somewhat awkwardly, feeling embarrassed by her mother's forgetfulness. A totally benign memory as it happens, but the mother experienced a very strong sense of herself doing something that she had somehow unconsciously 'inherited.' However, it was only when her own child nudged her out of this memory by saying 'Mum, hurry up! You are so embarrassing' that she became aware of how she might be impacting on her child in the present.

Fortunately, most of us have had a sufficiently good experience in early life, which means we are able to transfer a sense of security to our relationship with our own child. Crucially, what all babies need is a parent who is emotionally available to them and present – that is aware of their baby's needs (2). I can't emphasise enough how babies need their parents to notice what is going on inside their minds and to be able to respond to this in a way that is in tune with how they are feeling, and to a certain extent with what they are thinking. This is not so easy for all parents and some of you will find yourselves actively trying to tune out of your own early experiences, learn from them and act in an intentionally different way with your own child. This is great, and there are no parents who can't benefit from adopting a Reflective Parenting approach, whatever your early experiences.

Developmental history

When you think back to your early experiences, think also about anything important in your own development. For example, were you a child who struggled to pay attention, or was particularly clumsy? Or perhaps you were a child who struggled with friend-ships? Conversely, you may have had a large group of friends and been academically extremely bright. Your own developmental his-tory will influence how you parent your child now. I have worked with many parents who are either neurodivergent or had difficul-ties at school, and these factors play a significant role in how they parent their children. Again, just being aware of this aspect of your history and reflecting on whether or not it is relevant, or even inter-fering, with how you think about your children, is an important part of learning to mentalize yourself.

How this part of the Map applies to Reflective Parenting

Our experiences with our own parents can sometimes lead us into patterns of behaviour that may feel way beyond our control. So when you become a parent, you may find that you are carrying around the belongings from your own childhood experiences – a bit like setting off on a journey, carrying a backpack that's got a lot of someone else's gear in it and not much of anything that looks or feels like your own. At the very bottom of the backpack, you may find something that's useful, or it may feel as though you are carry-ing a really heavy bag on your back that seems to be dragging you down each time you embark on a new day and the responsibilities of looking after your child. One of the steps towards learning to become a more reflective parent with your own child is about tun-ing in to the part that your own history plays in this relationship, and this may not always be a totally comfortable experience. Let's look at an example.

Karen's parents argued for as long as she could remember. Meal times with family friends could be fraught affairs as they frequently became battlegrounds between her mother and father. Karen used to wish that any contentious topics were avoided as she learnt that disagreements could easily escalate into conflict. When Karen and her husband Tom became parents, they found themselves frequently disagreeing about how much they should intervene in the siblings' disagreements, and Karen often felt a strong wish to pacify and defuse tensions quickly whereas her husband thought that their children should learn how to do this for themselves.

In the above example, Karen might start to reflect on what her need to intervene in disagreements is about, and what it is linked to. Understanding the link between her unbearable childhood experiences and how she manages situations in the present would be very helpful for her and Tom to understand and be aware of, not because she is necessarily wrong to intervene, but because her urge to act in the present is driven by strong emotions that belong more in the past. Karen might then be more able to separate her own feelings of anxiety and worry from what she brings into her relationship with her children.

However, while past experiences can clearly influence current emotions, it's also incredibly important to be aware that your history is not necessarily your destiny. When you became a parent, you may have resolved that you were 'not going to do things the way my parents did them.' You may even be actively working hard to forge a different kind of bond and relationship with your own baby. But for some people, this is not so easy. So how do you turn your mind to your own baby, with all his demands for food, comfort, attention, love and interaction, when your own early experience was less than ideal? Or what if your young baby's demands feel just too much for you and you can't quite bring yourself to give them everything they need because there are many things you feel in need of too? By increasing your self-reflection and constructing your Parent Map this will help you to work on preventing these negative experiences from your past impacting strongly on your current relationship with your child. It may sound strange or somehow unbelievable, but it is the active process of thinking about yourself and finding this meaningful that makes a difference. Over time, linking together your reactions and feelings, the influence of memories and past relationships, and considering how these influence patterns of behaving and interacting, starts to prevent past negative experiences impacting strongly on how you interact with your child. Being aware is the most crucial step. We will all find ourselves at times slipping into patterns of behaviour that we aren't happy with, and which are part of our past experiences – be assured that this is normal.

Reference point three: current influences

Just as past relationships can affect your state of mind, current relationships, beliefs and circumstances can also have a significant impact. In Chapter 8, I talk about the impact of parental conflict on parents' states of mind as well as the impact on your child. We all have our own individual needs, independent to our children. We have a need to feel validated, empathised with and listened to, and if we can get this from our current relationships (e.g. a partner and friends), it can really help you in how you relate with your child. This does not necessarily have to come from the other parent of your child; it may come from a close friend who is also a parent. For example, a supportive relationship with a partner, friend or relative in which your needs are taken into account, and in which you have a strong sense that how you feel is both thought about by others, empathised with, and validated, is likely to have a calming, containing and generally positive impact on your current state of mind. You need to look after yourself first in order to help others. It is like being on a plane during an emergency and the oxygen masks come down – the advice is to put your mask on first, because then you are more able to help your child put his one on. I wonder how many parents would do this in a real-life scenario, but the message is clear. Get your current relationships right and you will be more able to help your child.

On the other hand, a relationship characterised by criticism will leave you feeling more intense feelings of worthlessness, anger and helplessness. It may not be that this criticism comes from your partner, or the other parent to your child; it may come from your friend, work colleague or your extended family. The reference point on the Map is really the emotions brought up by the current relationships you find yourself in, and their influence on you. These strong, negative emotions can be intense and make it hard to think clearly, both about yourself and about others, and when you do find you are able to think, they can have a major impact on the type of thoughts and feelings you have.

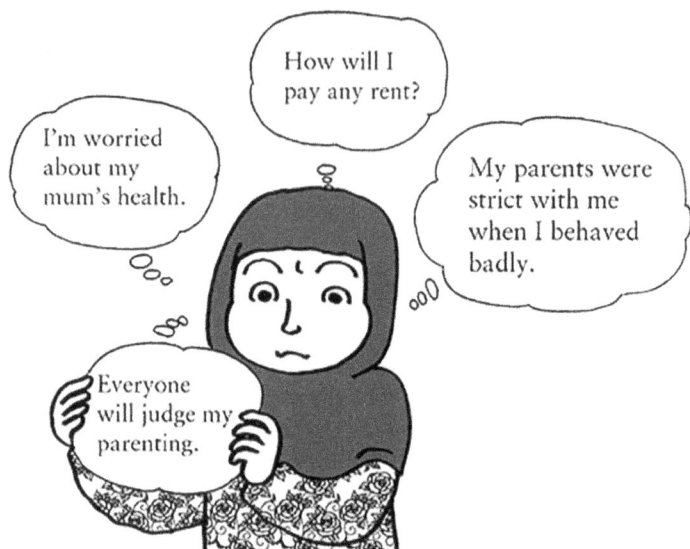

Your current relationships may not be the most important reference point for you to consider when putting together your Parent Map. For many of you, your religious and cultural beliefs may be the predominant guiding influence on how you want to parent your child. The important point is to understand yourself well enough to bring into your awareness the influences that are around you right now that go into making up your identity as a parent. For many parents, society's expectations and cultural norms have a huge influence. For example, in Western cultures, there has been a shift away from mothers as the sole carers of children, to fathers taking a more active role in day-to-day child-rearing, including childcare and feeding regimes. This type of societal expectation may or may not fit with how you want to parent your own children, and so it's important to reflect on these expectations, along with your other current influences.

How this part of the Map applies to Reflective Parenting

When you are with someone who seems to be in tune with how you are feeling, this is likely to bring your own feelings into greater awareness. Being in a relationship with someone who allows you time and space to reflect, or having time and space to yourself to reflect, helps raise awareness of what you are feeling and thinking.

On the other hand, being in the presence of one or more people who are bringing their own intense feelings to a situation, or simply making demands, makes it hard even to bring into your vague awareness your current thoughts and feelings. Equally, being aware of the influences on your current life, including any religious or cultural beliefs you might have and what you think that society expects from parents today, and being aware of the social and cultural environment you and your children live in, will help you to decide if these are a strong enough influence to consider in putting together your own Parent Map, based on the coherent story you have built up inside yourself. Becoming more attentive to this reference point can help you increase your awareness of your parenting.

The process

I have shown you the reference points, the features of your emotional life, to notice and pay attention to, but how do you fit them together? You will see that the process of thinking about yourself involves both emotions and thoughts, and perhaps a slowing down of situations in your mind, in order to get more of a sense of yourself.

First, try to work out your triggers for experiencing certain strong emotions. Triggers can come in many forms and may include the following:

1. A particular situation or interaction
2. A tone of voice your child uses sometimes
3. A comment someone makes
4. A thought you have
5. A strong belief system

These triggers can often elicit a strong emotional reaction in everyday situations with your child. When parents think about what might have triggered their emotions, they are often able to link a number of other similar experiences and discover repeating patterns. A helpful strategy for identifying triggers is to think back to situations where strong feelings caused you to overreact to a situation and work out what happened to create the emotion. For example, if I go back to the example of Finn earlier in the chapter, he noticed that when he felt he hadn't had any time to go out with friends for a long time and have time away from the family, he was snappier with his children and less likely to feel willing to meet their demands. He could feel frustrated, and only see his children as being deliberately demanding and irritating. In this situation, Finn's trigger was having his plans cancelled by his friends, which resulted in him having no time away from his family.

It was helpful when Finn noticed this so that he could step out of the cycle and get new understanding and meaning. He was able to begin a new inner dialogue – 'when I feel isolated from my friends I can feel frustrated easily at home, so when my children ask for things I often feel they are being unreasonable.' The next time this happened Finn could see that it wasn't his children's behaviour that was so troubling, but rather his own feelings were having a strong influence on how he was dealing with their behaviour. Finn was able to keep in his mind in future situations and interpret that what his children's behaviour really means in these moments is 'Daddy we need you to pay attention to us.' It is highly unlikely that Finn would be able to change his reaction straight away, as he might continue to feel let down by his friends, but over time once he has identified these triggers, it will get easier to anticipate how he might feel in certain situations and at certain times. At some point, he might think during these emotional times, 'Oh no, here I go again, taking my disappointment out on my kids,' and this might be enough to shift him into a more helpful state of mind before it effects his children. This trigger becomes part of Finn's Parent Map, part of his profile and something that would be very helpful to keep in mind for future times with his children.

> When you have identified a strong feeling, ask yourself, 'What is this feeling about?'

Once you are able to reflect on your feelings during a situation the better able you will be to think ahead. So, asking yourself questions such as, 'what situations are likely to bring up these difficult feelings?' will be helpful to you. Reflecting on times where you feel less able to cope can be very informative. Let's look at one mum's account and think through how it might help.

> Lisa said that she had become really angry at her 6-year-old son Charlie last week when he was refusing to put his shoes on, and shouted at him harshly. She felt that this was out of character, and because she felt so guilty and bad about the incident, she decided to think about what had triggered

*her to act in this way. She focused both on the circum-
stances of the event and her feelings and thoughts leading
up to the event, as well as thinking about what Charlie's
motivations might have been for being uncooperative.*

*Lisa remembered that she was running uncharacter-
istically late while getting Charlie ready for school, and
had felt very rushed and flustered. When Charlie seemed
oblivious to her need to get ready and out of the door
on time, Lisa believed Charlie was deliberately stalling to
irritate her.*

When thinking about your triggers, it is important to try to think
about your own reactions and the meaning behind them. For example, what are your beliefs around particular situations and why are
these situations important to you? In this example, the trigger for
Lisa would be a strong belief system; Lisa always liked to be on
time for everything, and so really didn't want to be late for school,
so she could identify a general anxiety around lateness.

For Lisa, her feelings around lateness were a reference point that
was important to her Map. Holding this in mind helped her to
plan ahead to try to reduce the chance of similar situations happening. The most obvious thing she could think of was to start getting ready earlier, for example to turn off the television 25 minutes
before leaving the house and to structure the time in the morning
more effectively. She also thought about explaining the situation to
Charlie and then helping him make some choices around getting
ready, as well as providing incentives for him, such as explicit praise
for getting ready on time and spending five minutes in the school
playground playing together.

Some emotions are pretty straightforward, but in our relationships with others, however, emotions can become more complex,
and a whole host of factors can govern how we are feeling at any
particular moment in time, and in relation to another person, or even
to several others. Take the following scenario, where feelings are
influenced by both past and present experiences and linked to more
than one person, and it's easy to see how complex emotions can be:

*Karen is preparing a Sunday lunch for her family. Her mum
has come to stay for the weekend and while Karen cooks,
the children are in and out of the room asking for snacks,
and if they can play on Mum's tablet. At the same time,*

Karen's mum is asking what time they will be eating lunch, and is it beef that Karen's cooking as she doesn't like beef.

The next time her son, Sam, comes into the kitchen, he asks if he can have a biscuit as he's starving. Karen suddenly shouts at him, and everyone jumps, startled by the aggression in her tone. Her mother comments 'Calm down Karen, it's only a biscuit!'

What are the triggers for these feelings? Your first reaction might be that it's obvious that Karen is busy and trying to meet many needs at once, and she's being criticised by her mother. However, it's likely that a combination of past and present experiences is interacting here at a level that's outside of Karen's immediate awareness. The actual triggers for Karen experiencing these feelings are the comments made by her mum that she doesn't like the beef that Karen is cooking. If Karen reflects on her feelings about her relationship with her mum, she might recognise that she has felt in her past that she has to take care of her mum more than she would like, and that there has been some criticism in the relationship that often has left Karen feeling that she doesn't quite meet her mum's needs, and even that she can be a disappointment to her mum. Furthermore, Karen becomes aware of a feeling that she has never been allowed *not* to take into consideration her mum's feelings, so that they have somehow got in the way of her own thoughts and feelings. Combined with a current feeling of being the person with sole responsibility for meeting the needs of others, the question from her son about the biscuit becomes the final straw that leads her to snap. What kind of steps could Karen have taken to help her to deal with this situation differently? And how can she take the first step of becoming more aware of her own mind?

First, stepping back and realising that this interaction is important to the process of learning about herself and developing her Map. It will be helpful for Karen to recognise a pattern of behaviour as well as her state of mind. Is it the case for example that whenever her mum makes a criticism of her, she 'lashes out' at others? Noticing this tendency in herself could start to help her to be able to think more about what's going on for her son at this particular moment, or just to respond to him in a calm way. Karen might also become more aware that the comments from her mum that imply criticism or demands easily trigger her to feel an emotion that is extremely strong, and that she needs to take control of. She is likely in this type of situation to sometimes overreact to any small demand from her children, and so being aware of this can help Karen to separate her feelings and thoughts about her mum from her thoughts and feelings about her children. When Sam asks for the biscuit then, the answer might still be 'no, you can't have another biscuit before dinner' but the more measured delivery will ensure that the situation doesn't escalate unnecessarily.

Here is another scenario involving Rachel and her children.

Rachel has been feeling isolated from her friends and struggling to find any space in her mind for anything other than the children, worries about her finances and her difficult separation from Matt. She has been looking forward to her friend Stella coming over to see her. Rachel feels this is a good time to leave the children to their own devices, and as they are usually good at entertaining themselves and playing happily and harmoniously together, she feels happy to spend some much needed time talking to her friend. Stella, a relatively new friend, was telling Rachel how she wished she could be as relaxed as Rachel with her kids and Rachel was saying how getting stressed about the small stuff really wasn't worth it. Just then, Lilly, age 7, came into the room blowing her recorder in a way that Rachel found really annoying as she was trying to talk to Stella. Lilly had been doing this for a while, and Rachel found she couldn't listen to Stella properly, and she suddenly lost it with Lilly, telling her she was making her feel she was losing her mind. She yanked the recorder off Lilly and tossed it up above the oven where she couldn't reach it. Rachel left the room for a minute and quick as lightening, Lilly climbed up on to the worktops to retrieve it, knocking all of Rachel's glass jars full of pasta and chutneys all over the floor, as well as her brand new, very expensive food processor (including the glass jug part). Everything was smashed to smithereens and baby Jack and Stella's baby Joe were left sitting in a sea of broken glass. There was silence and then Rachel started shouting at Lilly, who was not at all remorseful. After Rachel and Stella spent nearly an hour sweeping up the glass and cleaning the floor, Rachel finally calmed down enough to speak to Lilly and explain why she was so cross. She explained she was angry because these were her special things and it was like Lilly having broken all her favourite toys. Lilly was very sorry and wrote her mum a sorry note. Afterwards, Rachel reflected that she had reacted so strongly because she felt that her much needed and longed for time with her friend had been taken away from her, and she found herself reacting more strongly than she normally would have done to something that was essentially an accident.

For Rachel, her triggers were her strong feelings about her current circumstances – including her stress about her feelings of being stuck at home with three young children to care for on her own, her stressful separation from Matt and her worry about money. She felt a strong need to talk to a friend, and her reaction to the accident with the glass jars, which was probably a result of her children feeling that they were not getting the attention they wanted for themselves, resulted in an outburst that took time to repair and left both Rachel and the children feeling bad. In constructing her Parent Map, Rachel could try to identify that these current stressors are making her more impatient than she would normally be with her children, and hypersensitive to their demands. She might want to ask a friend if they could have the twins for an hour, or meet her friend during school hours with baby Jack, so that she could have some uninterrupted time talking to her friend and feel free to concentrate on her own needs.

Matt was reflecting on an extremely challenging Sunday looking after Grace and Lilly, who had just left to go back to their mother's. Matt had repeatedly become irritated and rejecting of Lilly, who he perceived had been clingy and cloy and overly needy and demanding. Rachel had called Matt and expressed upset and anger that Lilly had a temperature and seemed ill.

Upon hearing that Lilly had in fact been ill, Matt became tearful and had a strong feeling of shame and guilt for not realizing this and being more understanding of her need for his comfort and nurture. His mind turned to his own childhood memories with his parents, and specifically to a time when he was 10 years of age and had returned home from school. He had tearfully told his father that he had been bullied at school and his father had responded with anger and criticism and told him to 'stop being a baby'. This was the first time that Matt had looked at that memory from a different perspective – he realised that he needed comfort and love from his father, as did Lilly earlier in the day, that just like Lilly he deserved comfort but that his own father struggled to give this to him. He was able to begin to see that this role of parenting was difficult for him, because of the impact of how he was parented himself, but resolved himself to try and keep this in mind in an effort to give his own children a different, more caring experience of a father than he had.

What makes constructing and applying your Parent Map difficult?

If you have reached this far in the book and started to think about some of the reference points you would like to put on your Parent Map then you are already starting to become more reflective in your parenting. Taking time to think about all the things that influence you in your approach to parenting your child is an enormously helpful step towards creating a better connection with your child. This will probably take you some time and effort though, and there are obstacles that can get in the way, both to constructing your Parent Map in the first place, and then in applying it in your relationship with your child.

Tiredness

We all have times of the day when we feel at our sharpest. For some this might be 6.30 a.m., while others might be at their best at 10.30 p.m. But for all of us, tiredness usually has an impact on our level of self-awareness. Waking up in the middle of the night with a newborn baby, two, three, or maybe more, times, is not only physically exhausting but mentally too – the 'baby brain' that mothers often refer to is quite an accurate description of a brain that at times is literally unable to think. Being aware that how tired you are has a major impact on how aware you are of your state of mind is important as this self-awareness is an essential part of becoming reflective, helping you to recognise your limits and have empathy with yourself at these difficult times. You are not likely to be your most acutely self-aware, and therefore able to be reflective, when you are sleep deprived. Wait until you are more rested, and then it will be a great deal easier to think about your own feelings clearly.

If you are a new parent who has been sleep deprived for months, try and find a pocket of time in the day when you can have some time to yourself to reflect on your feelings. And before you do this, if you can, try to get in a time to have a nap whilst your baby is sleeping, so that you are more rested and able to reflect. Equally, you may have an older child who has an erratic sleep pattern, and it may feel harder to get the empathy of other parents who have passed through this stage with their babies, but it is still important to reflect on the influence of tiredness in your relationship with your child, and in other close relationships. You may need to voice aloud to your child sometimes that your mood, or tone of voice, are due to the fact that you are tired, and not a reflection of the degree of warmth you feel towards your child.

Drugs and alcohol

Excessive use of drugs and alcohol dims levels of self-awareness, but even mild use of alcohol and drugs can impair your ability to be aware of your state of mind and also impact your mood. Understanding that if you drink or abuse drugs this will impact significantly on both your level of self-awareness, and capacity to think about how you are feeling, is an important part of thinking about how and when you can best be aware of your own mind. Times when people drink alcohol or take drugs are often coupled with tiredness, and the combination of the two is a recipe for an almost total absence of a reflective self.

Physical health

Your state of mind might feel quite separate from what's going on in your body. But take a moment to think about how you feel emotionally when you have a really bad dose of flu. It's hard to think positive, happy thoughts when your body is wracked with aches and pains. In fact, it can be hard to think of anything much more than that you feel unwell – and it is especially hard to think about other people and their needs. Where someone experiences more extreme pain or has a chronic illness, it can be hard to think about emotional states at all. Again, bring this awareness of your body into your mind and understand that it is an important part of your own inside story and strongly influences your sense of vitality and the degree of energy you bring into your relationship with your child.

Mental health

It is clear that an acute mental health disorder such as psychosis or schizophrenia will have a major impact on a person's state of mind, causing confusion about themselves and the world around them. But even 'low-level' mental health problems, such as anxiety and depression, will shape your state of mind, causing you to see the world and the people in it through a very particular lens. If you are feeling anxious or depressed, recognising that these feelings will affect your viewpoint will help you to validate how you feel and allow you to reflect on your current state of mind as normal and understandable. Even everyday low moods, rather than an ongoing feeling of depression, will have an impact on your ability to reflect on your own feelings and state of mind. Of course, when you are feeling robust, it will be much easier to reflect on your state of mind in a clear and open way. If the problems you are experiencing feel more severe, it is important to seek professional help for these if possible. Going back to the oxygen mask analogy, it is only when you feel robust enough in yourself that you are able to really focus in on what's going on inside your child. So addressing any mental health issues you might have will be in the interests of both you and your child.

Life events

Significant life events such as bereavement, a birth, divorce and separation, moving house, or losing a job, living with financial hardship, or being below the poverty line and having inadequate housing, all interfere significantly with our emotional well-being and have a major influence on our state of mind. Parenting undoubtedly becomes more of a challenge when you are experiencing these life events, and it's important to acknowledge this and accept that you are under additional strain. Major life events can lead to depressive feelings that can endure and therefore need to be acknowledged (3). It is important to reflect on the impact they have had, or are still having, on you, as it is to accept that they have changed how you feel and think. It is equally important to reflect on these within your relationship with your child. For example, if you have experienced the loss of a parent, you will undoubtedly show feelings of sadness and loss around your children. This is perfectly normal, and it will help your children to understand that the relationship was an important one to you if they know that you are sad because you have experienced a loss. This will be far less confusing for them, and actually helpful to their own emotional development, to know that you can show these feelings and come to terms with them, rather than showing an emotion which doesn't seem to fit with the experience of loss.

Societal and global events

I spoke about the changing landscape of parenting in the Introduction, including the impact of a global pandemic on children's development and on many people's mental health. It's clear that major events in society have the potential to significantly impact our state of mind and can affect how we parent our children from day to day. I was acutely aware of the negative impact the daily news updates on TV about the number of Covid deaths had on my own state of mind, eventually deciding to boycott the news. I'm sure if I rewound back to some of these moments, the news impacted my mood in a way that could easily have come into some of the conversations I was having with my children. Give yourself space to reflect on how world events, or your own particular circumstances, are impacting your state of mind, noting these on your Parent Map where they feel important. Again, it will help you to make that important distinction between your own state of mind and what's going on in your child's mind.

REFLFECTIVE PARENTING SUMMARY

THE PARENT MAP

What it is . . .

The Parent Map is a way of reflecting about yourself and how you parent your child. It encourages you to map out and think about what influences your parenting, such as current feelings, your past experiences and wider influences, such as beliefs and relationships.

It helps you by . . .

The Parent Map helps you become more aware of yourself and how you relate to your child. It also helps you to be more aware of the difference and separateness of your emotions from your child's. It helps you identify times when you are more likely to have strong feelings, which can be unhelpful in some situations.

It helps your child by . . .

The Parent Map helps your child because the more reflective and aware of yourself you are, the more stable your relationship can be. Your child will experience you in a more regulated and considered way.

It helps your relationship by . . .

The Parent Map makes links between past and present, which helps prevent past negative experiences impacting strongly on how you interact with your child. Your relationship benefits by being more stable and less reactive.

Keep in mind . . .

1. Think about the need to be aware of yourself.
2. Think about what influences your parenting, include your thoughts and feelings, the influence of past experiences.
3. Use strong feelings to trigger self-reflection and make a connection with how this influences your parenting.
4. Identify times when you think there might be a link between current and past experiences.
5. Build a story of how you got to feel and think the way you do now:
   a. Did your level of emotional reaction fit the situation?
   b. What do you think may have contributed to you reacting in this way?

    c. How might a friend have experienced you in this situation, what would they have seen?

    d. Can you link your reaction in this situation to previous situations?

6. Use your awareness of your 'triggers' to help guide you during future interactions; imagine, predict and reflect on where and how similar feelings and thoughts may arise.

3

MANAGING YOUR FEELINGS

Rachel was sitting on her sofa, lost in her own thoughts and texting a friend. She was vaguely aware of her 7-year-old twin girls, squabbling together, and half-heartedly called over to her daughter Grace, 'Stop annoying your sister!' Grace cried out in distress and ran up the stairs in tears, feeling blamed and picked on when really it was her sister who had hit her on the head with a toy, which Rachel had missed.

Grace came back downstairs and continued to niggle her sister as Rachel watched with increased irritation. Her irritation grew until she suddenly got up, snatched the toy they were arguing over out of Grace's hand and said 'I'm going to throw this toy away. If you can't play nicely you won't play at all!'

You are now hopefully more aware of the reference points on your Parent Map and the types of emotions that arise for you in the midst of your parenting. Noticing what triggers you to feel certain feelings and act a particular way is hugely important. Next, I would like to help you to think more about how being more aware of what you're feeling can help you to *manage* your emotions when you are interacting with and responding to your child. In the example above, Rachel could start to think about all the things that are making her irritable and unable to think about what is going on really with her children, but she also needs to start to think about how she can manage this irritation if she is going to make any changes in these tiresome exchanges.

The emotional thermometer

There's an expression, 'strike when the iron is hot' – to act decisively and take your opportunities as they arise, however, when it

DOI: 10.4324/9781003483762-4

comes to our emotions, this isn't always the best advice. Often it is better to wait until our feelings have cooled down a little, especially when it comes to responding to our children – and to strike when the iron is *warm* rather than hot.

Imagine that you have a thermometer with a line in the middle that moves up and down as it responds to the temperature. However, instead of measuring temperature, this thermometer measures your emotional arousal: how intensely you are experiencing a feeling. On the thermometer, there is an 'ideal' range, where you are able to use your emotions in a constructive and informative way when interacting with your children. If the thermometer is too cold, indicating that there is little or no emotional intensity, this makes it difficult for you to identify how you feel, to connect with your mind and be aware of what you are experiencing. One of the first ways to manage how you are feeling, then, is to use this thermometer as a gauge of when it's best to act, and when it might be better to wait. Most of us are inclined to leap in when our emotional thermometer is near to boiling. This is because we aren't mentalizing, or reflecting on any thoughts at all, so instead we leap to action. It's at these moments when we are more likely to shout or snatch a toy away, maybe even send our child away to their room. Let's think about how you could use this thermometer more helpfully so that situations between you and your children don't escalate beyond your control.

With little awareness of your own emotions, it then becomes hard to connect with your child in a meaningful way. When the emotional thermometer gets too hot, indicating high emotional arousal, it means you are vulnerable to becoming overwhelmed by your feelings and more likely to act impulsively, as we can see in the example of Rachel.

Being in a 'warm' emotional range is ideal as it means you are likely to be more aware of what is going on in your mind, which then makes you more receptive to your child. But how can you keep in this range? In this chapter, I look at strategies that can alter the level on your emotional thermometer, bringing it into a range that makes your relationship with your child go more smoothly and leads to better understanding between you and your child. I am going to help you to bring your temperature into a range where you are able to be more reflective. Try out the following strategies as you interact with your child:

Emotional Thermometer

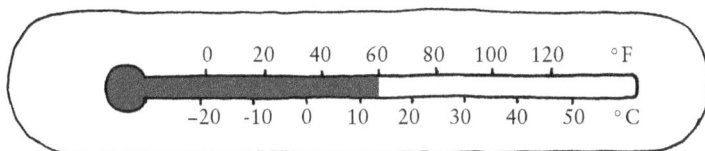

Too cold to mentalize	Warm enough to mentalize	Too hot to mentalize

Recognising and labelling feelings – where are you on the thermometer?

Let me start with the obvious, what are you feeling? Most of us remain unaware of the emotions we are experiencing much of the time. In fact, when everything is going well, we can get by without really having that much awareness of exactly what we are thinking and feeling. However, if you want to make some changes in your parenting style, then it is important to take a step back and start to consciously think about how you are feeling so that you can bring this awareness into your new style of Reflective Parenting. You won't need to be doing this all of the time – that would feel odd and a little stilted – but it is a helpful first step and also helps you to separate what is going on in your own mind from the things that are going on in the mind of your child. In the example at the beginning of the chapter, Rachel would start to become aware of her general level of irritation, which may be related to a text message she was getting from her friend, or a leftover mood from a previous event in the day. Recognising the feeling and owning it as hers is an important first step.

> Ask yourself the following question: 'What am I feeling right now?' Imagine you are asking yourself this question whilst you look at yourself from the outside.

So, although we may be largely unaware of how we are feeling from moment to moment, there are other times when we can be jolted into thinking about our thoughts and feelings, when something happens that shifts our attention on to ourselves. Let's look at the following example:

Karen was driving to work one day and listening to some music on the car radio, not really thinking about anything much at all, when suddenly a dog without a lead ran across the road, right in front of her car. Without looking in the rear-view mirror she braked suddenly, and then noticed that the people who were queuing at the bus stop were all looking in her direction, probably alerted by both

It's so important to reflect on what goes on in your mind.

the sound of the car tyres and the dog on the loose (which she had managed to avoid). Her heart was pounding, and Karen felt pretty furious, not only at the dog and the missing owner who had let him run off, but at the thought that she might have caused a crash, injured someone else and possibly injured herself. The feelings were strong, but also relatively short-lived, but notably, she couldn't fail to notice them. In the heat of the moment, though, Karen certainly wasn't able to do much thinking (not reflectively at least) about the consequences of what she was doing, or of what else might have been going on around her. We could say that in this moment, due to being highly emotionally aroused, Karen had a lapse in being able to think about others.

Sometimes then, when we are forced into feeling a strong emotion, such as the example of Karen, we become compromised in our ability to think about what might be going on in the mind of our child. If you imagine in the above scenario that Karen had had her three children with her in the car, with Sam telling her that he had too much homework again and was feeling fed up, and Maddy complaining that Molly gets away with behaving badly in the car, understandably Karen would have found it difficult to turn her mind to what they were thinking and feeling. Using an emotional thermometer at this time, to become more aware of the impact that being in this boiling range has on her ability to think about other people's minds, would be helpful in preventing a possible conflict between Karen and her children as she struggles to take notice of their thoughts and feelings. It might start with Karen simply recognising 'I'm too hot on my thermometer to say anything helpful right now.'

Once you start to think about noticing your thoughts and emotions, you can then develop your ability to be a more reflective parent by noticing those times when it is more or less difficult to identify these thoughts and emotions, as this will inevitably vary from day to day and circumstance to circumstance. In the previous example, we can see that there are times when you can't help but notice how you feel because you are jolted into this awareness by something so arousing that it's impossible *not* to acknowledge your feelings. The rest of the time, though, when we aren't in a state of high emotion, our awareness of how we are feeling varies.

This means you might not know where a growing feeling comes from or how a feeling might be influencing you in a situation. The more you are able to name what you feel, the more you can bring the feeling into your awareness and moderate it, if necessary. Sometimes just this action can lower the intensity of a feeling. Take this example of Lisa picking up her daughter from nursery after work:

> *Lisa rushed out of work to her car, increasingly preoccupied with whether she would miss the terrible rush-hour traffic on the main road out of town and be in time to collect her daughter Ella. As she swerved out of her parking space, she narrowly avoided hitting a colleague in the car park. A beep from a car behind jolted Lisa into thinking about what was going on. She managed to think to herself 'I am stressed, I am not calm.' She then was able to start saying other things to herself that helped her feel less stressed. 'There is nothing I can do to get to the nursery any quicker. I don't want to have an accident.'*

Becoming more aware of how she felt in the moment meant that Lisa was more able to rationalise her feelings and then lower her emotional temperature. Once Lisa understood what she was feeling, she was better placed to understand what she needed to do, which was to calm down and realise that she could not do anything about the traffic. The other advantage of being aware of how she was feeling is that Lisa was able to separate her own feelings from other people and things going on around her. On another day though, Lisa might have really struggled to do this, as, like the rest of us, it is not always easy to reflect on our emotions in the moment. Awareness of your own feelings then will help you to separate your mind from other people's, and this is a great step towards becoming more reflective and being able to mentalize about other people.

Being aware of our emotions helps us to notice what else is going on around us, so it's good to accept and embrace our feelings. And just as being aware can help us to moderate our emotions, being unaware can have the opposite effect. In the previous example, Lisa said that when she was unaware of what she was feeling, she acted like a robot fuelled by strong emotion. Very strong feelings still make us act and interact, but in autopilot, and often in ways that are unhelpful. For Lisa, the jolt of a car horn helped her to switch off from autopilot and made her think about her feelings, bringing them back into her awareness. You might think back to the last time you had an argument with someone and recall that your strong emotions made you say or do things that you later regretted, and perhaps later on when you were able to think back you could start to think about the reasons you felt annoyed in the first place and perhaps think that the strength of your reaction and feelings might have been out of proportion with what you said in the heat of the argument.

It can be difficult to acknowledge some of the feelings that are related to parenting – perhaps you feel guilty about negative emotions and think that you shouldn't have them. But it is normal for parents sometimes to feel bored, angry, hopeless and depressed in relation to parenting, and this is not surprising when you consider what a life-changing experience having children is. However hard it might seem to be aware of your thoughts and feelings, it is important to try not to deny them, or to increase negative emotions by feeling guilty for having these feelings. It is also important to acknowledge that for some people it can take a long time to adjust to becoming a parent.

> When Matt and Rachel lived together, and Grace and Lilly were little, the twins cried a lot. Matt used to detach himself from their crying and imagine himself in another place. He would start to think about his past travelling experiences and feel far away in his mind. He said that it took him a couple of years before he could really start to understand what the crying was about, and how he could do something to respond to it and make it better. By connecting with his feelings of wanting to remove himself when his twin daughters wouldn't seem to stop crying, Matt was able to reflect on the difficulties of parenting, and also on his need to manage this feeling and try to help his daughters to settle with his help.

For others, this response comes much more naturally and quickly, but everyone will learn these things at a different pace and the first step is to just acknowledge these feelings and think about what they mean.

Watch, listen and step back

Another way to start managing the emotions that are brought into your awareness when you are interacting with your child is to take a step back from the feelings. Recognising and labelling how you are feeling makes that feeling 'visible': a feeling that is seen, felt and thought about. Once you learn to name feelings in this way, you can try the following technique.

Once a feeling comes into your awareness, wait before you do anything else. Step slightly away from the feeling, which can sometimes stop you reacting immediately. Once you've stepped back from the situation, watch and listen, maybe only for ten seconds, and then see what happens and what you notice.

> When Tom walked through the door on his return from work, he was immediately bombarded by his children's demands. He had been aware in the car that he was feeling stressed from his day at work; there were some difficult meetings and conversations that had really irritated him. The fact that he had identified how he was feeling meant he was able to check himself before responding to his children. He stopped and closed his eyes for five seconds and consciously told himself he was stressed by the difficult day. When Tom opened his eyes, he paused and just watched the scene unfolding in front of him – like an observer removed from a scene. This helped Tom to name what was happening around him without judgement. What he saw was that he was home, away from work. He saw Maddy, Sam and Molly eager to interact with him after missing him all day. He also recognized that the fact that he was not at work meant that he was away from his main stress. His stress was about something that had happened earlier, not about anything that was happening now. He saw his children's excitement at seeing him home. He immediately felt pleased about this and put down his coat and gave them all a hug, and started to enter into their world, leaving his own day behind.

In this example, Tom was able to access his feelings and in doing so he learnt that his feelings were really to do with events that had happened before he arrived home. He also had an increased awareness of his children's excitement at seeing him, which he might otherwise have missed if he had remained preoccupied by the day's events at work.

What could you learn from a situation if you listened to your feelings? The next time you experience a negative feeling, try to let it into your awareness more fully, pause and watch. What do you see? By watching and stepping back, and waiting for the thermometer to be warm, it is more likely that the interaction between you and your children will be a positive one.

On a note of caution, this technique can be extremely difficult if the scale on your emotional thermometer is too high. Watching, waiting and wondering are almost impossible when you are experiencing very strong feelings in the heat of the moment. If you think back again to the last time you were involved in an argument with someone close to you, it was probably impossible to wonder about what you were feeling – you were too caught up in it. In arguments, we are classically unable to mentalize well – to think about the thoughts and feelings of other people – so later on when the emotional temperature has come down is a good time to go back to thinking about what might have been going on in the mind of the person you were arguing with.

In this case, I would recommend that you walk away from the situation if you cannot think clearly about how you think and feel. You can then reflect on what happened when your ability to observe your feelings returns, and your emotional temperature has gone down. If you imagine that you are driving your car with your children in the back, and suddenly a cyclist, who has been in your blind spot, shouts loudly that you were about to run right into him, you are unlikely in that moment to be able to observe your own feelings and step back from them. You would probably just feel shocked, maybe even angry. However, you might be able to do this later, when your emotional thermometer has cooled down.

You can even share this image of a thermometer with your child and tell them that you are a bit too overheated to think clearly right in that moment. You can also check in with your child about where they are on the emotional thermometer as young children can become so consumed with feelings to the point that thinking and even talking rationally becomes impossible. Asking your child whether they are hot, warm or cold may be easier for them to connect with than asking them what they are feeling and why. For example, think back to the last time your child had a full blown tantrum, or when your older child was much younger. Were they able to articulate how they felt, or were they writhing on the floor, or stamping their feet, red-faced with fury or screaming? Letting your child know that we all have moments where our thermometer becomes too hot to be able to explain to each other clearly what is going on in our minds can be really helpful, and allowing them to cool down and explain later, is often a better way to resolve a tantrum than trying to get to the bottom of it in the heat of the moment.

It might be quite difficult to think that a feeling is temporary and may pass if it is a particularly strong one, but it is important to realise that feelings pass, no matter how strong or difficult they are. This technique of watching, listening and stepping back helps you to deal with negative emotions, unless they are extremely intense. It encourages you to accept a feeling in the moment that you are feeling it, to put up with it for a short while. That's it, nothing more. It will pass. Whatever the strength of the emotion, all feelings are transitory. I find that parents and young people alike can become quite anxious when they experience an intense, particularly negative, emotion as the accompanying thought is often 'I'm always going to feel like this,' so knowing that all feelings are temporary is really helpful.

How am I coming across? Looking at yourself from the outside

Another strategy that will help you to manage the emotions that arise during the course of parenting is one that can help both in the heat of the moment with your child, or after an event, when you are thinking about what happened.

We are often unaware of how we're coming across to others, unless we are acutely self-conscious. However, we can learn to be aware of our body language and tone of voice, which are responsible for a significant proportion of our communication. Being conscious of how you're coming across to others when you are experiencing negative emotions is really important. Children are very receptive to subtle communication cues and are sensitive to the whole range of emotions. So, without you being aware of it, a negative feeling in you will be communicated rapidly and automatically to your child and will impact on them. The main point is not that your negative feelings will necessarily damage or traumatise your child, but that they can affect their emotional state and lead to an increase in disruptive behaviour. Their behaviour will then impact on how you feel, creating a cycle of escalating emotions.

> Lisa came downstairs early in the morning, following Charlie who had got up again at 5.45 a.m. Charlie was sitting happily on the sofa, but Lisa was irritated and frustrated at being woken so early and her face was communicating this in a scowl. Charlie saw this and immediately felt upset and sulky. 'Is it my fault you feel so grumpy mum?' The

*impact of Lisa's face on Charlie was to make him experi-
ence a strong emotion, and he may have felt blamed or
experienced shame – these are hard feelings for children to
manage and can be easily avoided with a simple change in
the parent's expression.*

In the above example, I am not criticising Lisa or judging her to
be wrong, and indeed situations like this probably happen in most
households each day. However, what I am highlighting is the importance for Lisa to be *aware* of how she looks to her child. If Lisa
could have imagined what she looked like to Charlie – if she could
have seen herself through his eyes – she might have been able to
change her expression and so influence the communication with
her son. These are small details that can have a large impact on
your relationship. Importantly, Lisa might have managed to create
an interaction where she could talk to Charlie about why she was
feeling frustrated. Or she might simply have checked his expression,
realising that the situation wasn't important enough to make him
feel bad about it. The main point is that in failing to take note of
how her emotions were coming across to Charlie, she actually made
an already tricky interaction between them even more difficult and
upsetting for both of them.

Imagine being able to make a movie of your life. You could
record yourself, perhaps playing with your child, or sitting around
the dining table together at mealtimes. You could press a pause button and notice the moments when things were going really well,
the moments when you felt very in tune with your child, and you
could see what you did to help that happen. In my work, I use a
technique with parents called Video Interaction Guidance (1) which
gives me the advantage of being able actually to do this. By film-
ing a parent and child in an everyday interaction, I can then show
back clips to the parents, highlighting times when they were managing to interact and relate in ways that were positive and helpful
for their child's development. Of course, none of us has the luxury
of this in our everyday lives, where it can often feel more like a
fast-forward button has been pressed rather than the pause button, especially at hectic times, such as getting everyone ready in the
mornings. However, when you start to notice your own feelings,
you can then reflect on how you are coming across – try imagining you are on video and thinking about how your actions might
look from the outside – which is a very important step towards
being able to notice, and ultimately change, the impact that you

are having on your child. Video Interaction Guidance is really great for showing parents what happens when they change their body language towards their child. For example, parents can actually see how looking interested, maintaining eye contact and having a friendly voice and posture encourage children to interact. Video work is particularly helpful for parents who have a negative perception about their relationship because it helps to highlight how when they are positive in their interactions, and aware of how they feel, this has a magical effect on their children and how they interact. And although as parents we generally don't get to see ourselves in action with our children, we can use the principle of imagining an audience to check our responses and think about how our children experience us.

We've all got footage of our children, family and friends on our smart phones or tablets, but more often than not, we don't feature in these clips. We're the cameraman and camerawoman, the observer of others. But imagine if you were in the film yourself, alongside these other important people in your life. How do you look? As well as thinking about yourself in a snapshot of time like this, you can take a look at your life over a longer period of time and see how your decisions and patterns of behaviour are affecting your relationships. Take the following example:

> *When Ella was born, Lisa gave up a full-time job to look after both her and Charlie, and she found herself setting a series of goals to achieve, in order to feel that she was being a good parent. She developed a whole checklist, including making sure they had a healthy meal each day, an outdoor activity, spent only an allotted amount of time on any screens, visited friends, had playdates... the list got bigger as Lisa set out what she felt was her job of being a part-time stay-at-home mum with two young children.*
>
> *When Lisa reflected on what she might have looked like relentlessly working her way through this list each day, mentally checking that she had achieved all her goals, she saw that often she didn't enjoy spending time with her children and that frequently they seemed unhappy. She saw that trips to the park were sometimes greeted with screams and complaints about being too tired, and reflected that this might be the result of her setting such a full schedule in a bid to meet her daily targets. She saw that she was stressed around the children, preoccupied with this list of*

things to achieve, and ultimately felt unrewarded by her children, who seemed not to appreciate this huge effort she felt she was making. Looking at herself from the outside at this 'ideal' mother she had created, Lisa saw a stressed-out, slightly anxious woman rushing around trying to pack everything in, out of synch with her children. The pace of the day looked exhausting, even to her, when she examined it from the outside looking in.

Lisa made a decision to change the focus from her own goals to her children's needs and interests. Following the children's lead, she first noticed that the pace of the day was a lot, lot slower. A morning that had previously been filled with a baking session, a trip to the park, preparing a healthy meal, and a visit from a friend with similar-aged children, shifted to something altogether different. As she watched this new 'film' of herself, it was as if someone had hit the slow-play button. Following the children's lead, everything seemed to take much longer, and yet the relationship between Lisa, Charlie and Ella looked much more enjoyable, for everyone involved.

Remembering your child is just a child

Rachel was getting increasingly annoyed with Grace, who was whining that she didn't want her mum to keep stopping on the journey back from school, chatting to other mums on the way. She started to play up and looked sulky and Rachel snapped at her to 'grow up and act your age.' Grace hung her head in shame, feeling upset at being embarrassed by her mum in front of others and feeling unable to manage how she was feeling in that moment.

Being a reflective parent means you are able to accept that there may be different perspectives to take on why your child has behaved in a particular way. It follows therefore that having fixed assumptions about the motivations behind your child's behaviour can be a large barrier to being able to adopt a fresh perspective. In the example above, Rachel was expecting Grace to act like an adult and to be patient and interested even in the conversations she was having with her friends on the way home. She had perhaps forgotten that a seven-year-old child at the end of the school day is tired, wants some time with her mum and is susceptible to being easily embarrassed if attention is drawn to her (particularly negative attention) in front of other people. Her instruction to her daughter to 'grow up' means that Grace isn't allowed to act her age and express the kind of emotions that go along with being a seven-year-old child. This causes a great deal of confusion for children as they are experiencing a set of emotions that are real and intense, whilst simultaneously being told they shouldn't feel this way, but should instead be behaving a certain way and experiencing a different set of feelings that are perhaps more appropriate for an adult.

Often, though, we are unaware that we are carrying around underlying assumptions, which makes it tricky to identify and challenge them. Moreover, I have found that many parents have assumptions about their children's abilities that, developmentally, are just not possible. A helpful statement to hold in your mind is 'My child is just that – a child,' they have a child's view of the world and childlike abilities that will develop only as they grow older. Remembering this can really help you to reduce negative emotions either during a difficult interaction or when reflecting on one afterwards. For example, if you, like many parents, assume your child is knowingly manipulating you into getting something they want, or crying because they want to upset you, then this can be infuriating. However, are young children really capable of deliberate manipulation in the way that it can feel to parents? Do children understand other people in such a sophisticated way? By assuming that a child is doing something so knowingly and deliberately, the parent is attributing grown-up, adult characteristics to the child. I once heard a parent saying to her eight-week-old baby, 'are you trying to beat me up?' when the baby was writhing and wriggling in her arms. A clear example of a parent attributing adult-like thoughts and feelings to a newborn. Often parents feel manipulated, or feel upset, and think therefore this must be the case – that their child has set out to do something to upset them. Remember, our strong feelings can affect our understanding of other people, so we think 'because I feel manipulated that means I am being manipulated.' However, it is important to have more realistic assumptions about what your child is capable of. Children are constantly learning to understand other people, and this process continues. Although children are extremely sensitive to how their parents feel, and react to how they act, in terms of truly and accurately understanding their parents, they are a long way off. Remembering that your child is just being a child – with limited emotional capabilities – can help you not to react strongly to them.

Recruiting supports

Another important way to help you manage your emotions is to think more deeply about how you can get help from other people. Underpinning the model of Reflective Parenting is the principle that we influence and are influenced by other people, and that something good can come out of relating to others in a thoughtful way. It follows then that when you are struggling with parenting issues, support and understanding from friends and family is really beneficial and actually helps you to become a more reflective parent. Drawing on other people's experience or just talking things through and feeling understood all support a more reflective stance.

You can start to seek support early on, even in pregnancy, by talking to others, especially other parents or prospective parents, about your thoughts and experiences, which will also help you to think about the baby growing inside you. And once in the world, seeing the adults around him enjoy supportive and understanding relationships will show your child the benefits of relating to other people.

It's worth mentally compiling a network of supportive adults who are interested in you and how you see things. It's also worth looking into parenting groups such as antenatal groups, parenting groups or local parent support groups, and finding drop-in cafes where parents can meet and talk. It can be helpful to begin with thinking about how you feel about asking for help. Some parents feel awkward or embarrassed, and fear being shamed for their parenting if they show weakness or vulnerability. As much as parenting can be a time in your life when you feel connected to other people, it can also be a time when you might experience great loneliness, or a sense of inadequacy as you compare yourself to what you see as the ideal parent. If you find this hard, or are feeling especially isolated, online chat groups and forums can be good places to start to feel more connected to other parents. Finding a place where you can talk honestly and openly about yourself and your struggles as a parent is really important, and I would advocate that finding relationships where you can talk about your own feelings and not just what your baby or child is doing is vital. In my clinical practice, I run Reflective Parenting groups which are both psychoeducational and therapeutic, as they provide a supportive environment where parents can hear about other people's experiences and benefit from sharing their struggles and learning new perspectives on common parent–child difficulties.

Forgiving your child's behaviour and self-acceptance

As parents we can all easily feel filled with self-criticism and self-doubt about the way we acted and felt in a particular moment with our children. At the same time, in the midst of difficult exchanges, we can feel critical towards our children and find it difficult to let feelings go. There's no doubt that parenting is a really difficult job for almost everyone at least some of the time. So it can be very helpful to remember that we all act on strong feelings at times; sometimes, it is really hard not to act, and not to do and say things we regret. This applies to you and your actions as a parent, and also to how your child acts. So this strategy is about being able to accept that you have strong feelings and sometimes act in ways you are not happy with, and having the same acceptance of your child, too. Children find strong emotions extremely difficult to cope with, and intense feelings often manifest in their actions, influencing what they do.

Parents who have a history of trauma, or even just difficult experiences, can be overwhelmed by thoughts and feelings, making it even harder to think about what is happening in another person's mind. I have shown how understanding your own history, including your own experience of being parented, is important to your ability to think about other people's feelings and states of mind. These early experiences also govern how comfortable you feel with closeness. If you had an early experience of feeling insecure with your parents, you will probably find it harder to see your child's actions, and those of others, for what they really are. None of us can change our early history, but I can't emphasise enough that history does not need to be destiny, that is that patterns from the past do not need to be repeated in the present or future, and an awareness of our feelings, however complicated and troubling they might seem, is part of the path towards developing a different, hopefully secure, relationship with your own child. Equally, developing a more rounded, or flexible, view of your own early history is important, as even childhoods that had traumatic or insecure aspects to them could also have featured love, pleasure and intimacy. Accepting then that you had these experiences in your childhood, and that they have shaped who you are and how you feel, is an important strategy when trying to bring your temperature into the right range in your interactions with your child. An understanding of your own inside story, and the history of relationships that helped to form this story, will help you to bring the temperature on your emotional thermometer into a range where you can think more clearly about your child and what's going on in their mind.

Being able to forgive yourself and accept your feelings is an important step in managing your emotions and moving towards Reflective Parenting. Acceptance and forgiveness of yourself for experiencing a certain emotion or state of mind is all part of thinking in a more flexible and reflective way. In other words, it is a good thing generally to be aware of your feelings, even when these are difficult or unpleasant. Conversely, if you are frequently judgemental about your own and others thoughts and feelings, this will have a major impact on your general emotional state, which in turn will impact on how you handle important relationships.

In Chapter 4, I will introduce you to ones of the core tools of the Reflective Parenting approach – a concept known as the Parent APP. This tool will help you become even more mentalizing in your stance as you seek to understand the meaning of your child's behaviour. Armed with some ideas of the things you want to plot on your Parent Map which you know have influenced your feelings and parenting, and with some tools for managing your emotions better, the Parent APP is the next step. I will show you how to use this in your everyday relationship with your child. I hope that it will really help both you and your child to feel better connected.

REFLECTIVE PARENTING SUMMARY

THE EMOTIONAL THERMOMETER

What it is . . .

The emotional thermometer is a way of keeping in mind how strong your feelings are at any given moment. Use this thermometer as a gauge of when it's best to act, and when it might be better to wait.

It helps you by . . .

The emotional thermometer helps you become more aware of what you are feeling and how intensely you are experiencing the feeling. This awareness will allow you to find ways to reduce the impact of your feeling and bring you into a calmer state of mind.

It helps your child by . . .

The emotional thermometer helps your child because the more regulated you are feeling when you interact with him, the less likely you are of overreacting. Your child will see that you take responsibility for your feelings.

It helps your relationship by . . .

Keeping in mind your emotional thermometer makes it less likely situations will escalate beyond control and will help you to understand your child's feelings and bring you closer together.

Keep in mind . . .

1. Use the concept of the emotional thermometer as a gauge of when it's best to act, and when it might be better to wait.
2. Notice your thoughts and emotions to develop your ability to be a more reflective parent.
3. When you start to notice your own feelings, you can then reflect on how you are coming across.
4. Use friends and networks to help you.
5. Be accepting of how you feel and how your child feels.

Remember, your child is just a child, with a separate and totally different set of thoughts and feelings from you, which represent both his age and the things going on in his life.

4

THE PARENT APP

Have you ever wondered what goes on inside your child's head?

Maddy (aged 12) came to the dinner table after the third time of her mum calling her to come to eat. She brought her mobile phone with her and carried on texting her friends as her mum Karen tried to engage her in a conversation about her day.

Karen:	'How did the end-of-year tests go today, Maddy?'
	Maddy shifted uncomfortably in her chair, and picking her food hung her head down whilst she carried on texting her friend.
Karen:	'Maddy! Can you get off your phone, please, I'm asking you a question.'
Maddy:	'Er, what? What did you say?'
Karen:	'I was asking how your tests went?'
Maddy:	'Er, can't remember.' *She carried on texting.*
	Maddy's dad, Tom, who has been watching this interaction, suddenly explodes, 'Maddy, come OFF your phone, eat your dinner and show some respect to your mum.'
	Maddy pushes her plate away, gets up from the table and yells, 'I'm going to my room, nobody around here has a clue what's going on in my life.'
Karen:	'What was all that about? How am I supposed to know what goes on inside her head?'

By now you will be familiar with a few of the fundamental principles to becoming more reflective in your parenting, the central aim of which is to raise a happy, secure and resilient child. The focus in the previous chapters has been on how to start to notice your own

DOI: 10.4324/9781003483762-5

emotions, where these have come from, and how, through developing a greater self-awareness, you can begin to bring your emotions a little more under control during interactions with your child. Now you are following these principles, it will be easier to turn your mind to the mind of your child.

I have developed a tool called the Parent APP, which helps you see what is inside your child's mind and to connect you with what you *think* is in there. It's not an APP for your phone, but rather a handy acronym to help you remember the core principles of being a Reflective Parent with your child. It will help you to attune to your child's experience by appreciating what is going on *inside* your child's mind, rather than simply responding to the behaviour they display on the *outside*. This will give a whole new insight and meaning to your child's behaviour and can produce noticeable and tangible changes to your relationship. It will help you to avoid difficult moments that I illustrated with Maddy and her mum (earlier) and show you that through starting to be curious about your child on the inside, you will both feel a greater connection. I have called this the Parent APP as it stands for three main elements. The elements of the Parent APP are:

Attention
Perspective Taking
Providing Empathy

Attention

The first element in your reflective attitude towards your child is attention. To understand your child, and the cues and messages underlying their behaviour, it is important to pay attention to them. This might seem obvious, but I mean paying attention in a special way, which includes being interested in them, watching them, turning towards them and having a friendly posture while you watch and interact with them. This type of interaction will both appear and feel very different to your child from you simply looking at them. This is because when you pay attention in this meaningful way, you are more likely to let your child know that you are interested in them. Through my video work with parents (using Video Interaction Guidance), where the work is about becoming more attuned to your child, the first step is to help parents notice the positive impact of paying attention. Parents often are surprised and delighted to see how paying attention in this way encourages more fun and positive moments together.

Paying attention by definition involves being curious. When observing what your child is doing, there is always more going on than just what you can see. Being curious is the quality that helps us to be interested in seeing our child more from the inside – *why* they are behaving in a certain way, rather than paying attention only to what's happening on the outside – *what* they are actually doing. You can see from the example at the start of this chapter that this doesn't necessarily mean firing questions at your child about what they have been doing when they are not in the right frame of mind to talk, but it is more about showing a general curiosity for their state of mind. For example, it might be more helpful to ask yourself 'What are they feeling right now that is making this difficult to talk about?' In many ways, being attentive and curious are the most important qualities of Reflective Parenting as you are being actively interested about your child's thoughts and feelings. In the moments when you are able to be a reflective parent, you are being willing to be open to discovery about your child's actions and behaviours:

You are interested in how your child experiences their world. This interest can start at day one of a child's life and continue throughout childhood.

An ambulance whizzes past a window and 9-month-old baby Jack turns his head in that direction. His mum Rachel looks at her son then towards the window and back again, 'Oooh what was that sound? You seem to like that noise.'

Rachel is thinking about her baby: 'You are an interesting person who sees things in his own way and I'm interested in what you think about things.' She notices what her little boy notices, is curious in how Jack is experiencing her world and tries to understand his view on events that happen around him.

When you think about how to pay attention to your child, it's helpful to imagine how you will appear to them. Imagine if you are standing in a queue at the supermarket checkout and a baby in a buggy in front of you smiles. Your automatic response is likely to be to smile, raise your eyebrows, perhaps open your mouth in an exaggerated way and soften, or even use a sing-songy voice to say 'hello' back. This is the kind of attention I mean, having an animated facial expression, making sustained eye contact, taking an interested friendly posture, actively listening and encouraging and softening the tone of your voice – all these things will increase the impact of your paying attention from your child's point of view.

Luckily, these factors will also make each interaction with your child a more interesting and enjoyable experience for you. You may become self-conscious about your behaviour and feel a little inhibited. Yet it's worth trying to overcome this feeling as I know how important a parent's responses are when I see the dramatic effect it has on a child when parents make positive changes to the way they communicate.

Imagine a parent notices their two-year-old about to pull themself up onto the table with sticky hands and says, 'What are you doing?' This is said with an accompanying smile and outstretched arms, about to lift the child down from the table, and with a soft voice. In this way, by being aware of the impact of her own state of mind on her toddler's, and by adopting an open and friendly face, the parent can pay attention to what her child is doing, but manage her child's behaviour without the situation escalating into conflict and tantrums. For example, imagine if this scenario was dealt with in a different way. The parent comes into the room with an angry expression, shouts 'What ARE you doing?' and grabs her child down from the table. This may well get the child down quicker, but the resulting tantrum and upset in the child becomes the next problem for the parent to deal with. Often the resulting behaviour when taking this kind of authoritarian approach can be even worse than the original behaviour itself.

The same can be said for the type of questions that we parents often ask of our older children. How was your day at school? Who did you spend time with? What did you have for lunch? Whilst these types of questions are perfectly normal, they don't necessarily help you to connect in an emotional way with your child, in a way that makes them feel understood emotionally, or you feel close to them. Instead, your interest in what is going on inside your children might lead to you to notice that they need to relax for a while before they are asked about their day. You might say instead something like, 'Are you in a chatty mood or do you want to catch up later over dinner?'

The impact of paying attention

Stepping back and observing allows you to begin to wonder about what your child is doing, and what you notice can be the first step in looking at an inside story that will enable you to understand their behaviour. Often parents feel they need to engage their children actively all the time, either feeling they have to take the lead in interacting with them or making sure they are always occupied with something. It might feel like a novel idea at first: just to stop and watch what your child is doing. However, a lot can be said for just enjoying watching your child, following their lead and wondering about what they are doing and thinking and their motivations might be. One parent, observing her own behaviour, said:

> I used to overwhelm him a lot of the time. I thought I had to entertain and do something with my son all of the time and felt under pressure to show I was doing something. I had to learn that just watching and showing him I was interested in what he was doing was actually doing something. I guess I was following him.

The impact of being attentive to what your baby or child is doing, thinking and feeling cannot be overestimated. Attention is one of the most powerful parenting tools you have and both giving your attention to and withdrawing attention from your child has a very significant impact on how they think, feel and behave. I often hear the phrase 'attention-seeking behaviour' used as a criticism of children, and sometimes adults. However, maybe the times when your child seems to act up to gain your attention are the cues to step back and be more attentive to them. Once you start to think about what seeking attention is for, then you can increase your understanding of what's going on inside your child's mind, and this in turn can lead to a fairly immediate shift in the interaction between the two of you. For your child, the experience of being paid attention to, experiencing your interest and curiosity, can feel great. This will be easier to do if you are both aware of and in control of your own emotional state first.

> Rachel was trying to feed 9-month-old Jack, who was fussing around and refusing to be fed. Rachel wanted Jack to hurry up as they were late in meeting some friends for a play date. She had already noticed herself becoming more frustrated with her baby son, which she knew was probably disproportionate and unhelpful. She was getting nowhere with the feeding, so she decided to try and stop worrying about being late and just watch Jack instead. Rachel put the spoon down and said to Jack, 'It doesn't matter if we are late does it! What are you doing sweetie?' She then found herself beginning to actually feel more interested in

what Jack was doing, and turned her attention away from her thoughts of getting ready to go out. As well as feeling interested, Rachel actually looked interested and had a friendly face, and noticed that Jack in turn looked up at her. Jack had noticed that his mum was watching him interestedly and he appeared to relax, caught his mum's eye again and smiled. Rachel and Jack carried on noticing each other, smiling. Rachel noticed that Jack was reaching out to the spoon and so she said 'Do you want the spoon? Did you want to hold it all this time sweetie? Ok, here you go, here is the spoon.' The result was that, in his own time, and under Rachel's watchful gaze, Jack began to eat his food, albeit more slowly and in a messy way.

When Rachel paid more attention to her son, adopting a friendly posture and expression, she was able to notice that Jack was interested in holding the spoon himself. Importantly, positive effects were experienced by both Rachel (who felt less frustrated) and Jack (who felt more at ease and able to eat in a relaxed way). The end result was for both of them to feel more connected to one another. This kind of mindful approach of just staying present and calm helped to make this feeling of connection a pleasant one for both mum and baby.

Being interested and curious about the reasons underlying your child's behaviour has further benefits to your relationship with your child. Let's look at an example of how curiosity can help.

Finn is playing with his two children in the park. He picks up his 6-year-old son Charlie and playfully pretends to throw him in a stream. His 4-year-old daughter Ella becomes immediately distressed and shouts 'Don't Daddy!' She then runs over to her mother and cuddles furiously into her, looking scared. Finn starts to think about what might be going on for his daughter and why she feels so strongly. A little later, Finn comes up to his daughter, deciding to follow his curiosity about why she might have got upset and worried, and said 'Did you think Daddy was really going to throw Charlie in the stream?' Ella looks away and buries her head in her mother's arm. About ten minutes later though she walked up to her dad and said 'I got scared Daddy didn't I?' Finn said back 'Yes, I think you did, did you think I was going to do it?' She replied, 'Yes, I thought Daddy was going to throw Charlie.'

In being curious like Finn, you can actively show your child that you are interested in them and what's going on inside their mind, and that they are someone to be interested in. This example shows that Finn's curiosity in Ella's reaction, and his ability to share his curiosity with her, enabled his daughter to be curious herself about why she acted in that way. This teaches your child to think about their emotions more and what they mean. Over time, this is a really good way of helping your child to learn to regulate, or manage, their feelings. As a parent, you can sow the seed of curiosity in your child in this way, and over time your child will begin to show curiosity in others and wonder why others behave in the way they do.

You might also find that by adopting a genuinely curious stance about your child's actions, you will naturally be less critical towards their behaviour.

> Tom was at the park when his 2-year-old daughter Molly indicated that she wanted to get out of the pushchair. Tom unbuttoned her straps and Molly immediately ran off. Tom felt a surge of anger within him (which he luckily recognized in himself) as he called out to shout to her to stop. Tom then remembered another dad talking to him about his son who also used to run off whenever he had an opportunity. This got Tom wondering why young children would want to run off and what doing this might feel like from Molly's perspective. His curiosity about the situation reduced his anger immediately as he thought about how much fun running off might be for his child (taking her perspective), and so he decided to playfully make up some running exercises for Molly, backwards and forwards, setting markers around the park for her to run to and turn around and run back. Molly had great fun, and Tom started to enjoy their time together at the park more.

Children love it when you really notice them and pay attention in a friendly and curious way to what they are doing. To get a sense of how this attention feels to your child, it may help you to imagine how different it feels when you have someone's full attention when you are expressing yourself, compared with when you feel that you are being ignored, particularly when you are in a state of heightened emotion. It doesn't feel great to say the least. Attention and curiosity are the building blocks to your reflective attitude towards your child. Get this first quality right and become genuinely interested in your child's mind, and the next two qualities of perspective taking and empathy will follow quite naturally.

Perspective taking

The second quality to have in your relationship with your child is perspective taking. We tend to take for granted that, as adults, it can be hard to know what's going on inside someone else's head. Why don't we apply the same rule to our children? It can be easy to assume that a child sees the world through the same lens as their parents, or as parents that we know exactly what is going on in our child's mind but this is not the case. There is even a pressure that comes with the role of parenting, that somehow we *ought* to know what our children are thinking and feeling all the time.

Most of the time we interact reasonably well with those around us, accepting that we cannot know exactly how other people think. Although at times a struggle, we take a good guess about what another person is thinking or feeling. If we saw someone walking around a city with a map, checking backwards and forwards between a street name and the map, we might conclude that they are lost. While this is a more obvious scenario than trying to figure out why your child is upset or misbehaving, remembering that your child has a different set of thoughts and feelings to you, but that you can still take a guess at what these might be, can be helpful. Being accurate in our 'perspective taking,' or getting another person's point of view, is of course desirable but in a way it is the *effort* to understand another person's perspective that is in itself valuable. This effort is all part of being curious and paying attention. When we think about parenting, and the sometimes bizarre and confusing behaviour of children, it is both normal and highly likely that you could be wrong about what you think your child is thinking and feeling, just as you can be wrong about the thoughts and feelings of your partner, friends and family.

The same experience can look very different from different perspectives, and sometimes in the heat of the moment, when a child is mid-tantrum, it can be easy to forget this. How often have you found yourself thinking that surely your child knows they are annoying or upsetting you? This kind of assumption is predicated on the (false) belief that your child can read your mind and knows what you're thinking and is probably driven by you feeling either annoyed or upset.

It is important to note that children are not able to see things from another person's perspective fully until they are at least three to four years old. It is worth bearing this in mind because as parents we can often believe that our children are doing something intentionally to make us feel or act in a certain way. One parent said that she felt her child was repeating the same question over and over again 'just to wind me up.' Her friend wondered whether there might be other reasons why her child felt the need to ask the same question over and over again, on reflection the parent said that she thought her daughter might be 'anxious that she's not going to get what she really wants.' In this instance, taking the child's perspective, and tuning in to the emotion behind the questions, was a helpful move away from perceiving her daughter as trying to intentionally annoy her and move towards a more attuned relationship. Being aware of this developmental framework can help us to see that our 18-month-old toddler is not lying on the floor screaming because they want to punish us, as this would involve a cognitive skill that he hasn't yet developed. It's more helpful to try to be curious about what it is that's making them feel quite so angry. So perspective taking involves not only trying to see what your child might be thinking but also how they might be feeling. All the time, keeping in mind that this is quite likely to be something different from how you think and feel.

> When they first had their twins, Grace and Lilly, Matt and Rachel were going on holiday and were arguing in the front of their car about who was supposed to have brought the keys to the holiday cottage they've been driving to for nearly five hours, and Grace and Lilly were crying in the back seat. If the babies could verbalise their feelings in this moment, they would probably say a whole range of things including, 'We've been sitting here being really still and quiet for nearly five hours now, and now we're tired and want to get out, and you are making us feel a bit frightened because you're shouting at each other, and we don't know if you like each other, or if you are cross with us as well?'

Imagine if Rachel and Matt stopped their arguing and said some of what they thought might be going on in their babies' heads right at that moment. What would this feel like for Grace and Lilly? How might thinking about each baby's experience both help the parents to look at the impact their own emotions are having on the babies, and calm everybody down? If the main aim in that car were for everyone to reach their destination harmoniously, then trying to imagine how it feels for the two young babies would certainly be a very positive move forwards. For example, if Rachel and Matt stopped halfway to their cottage and said to Grace and Lilly, *'lets have a break now and get something nice to eat, you must both be getting really bored and fed up in the back all this time?'* and had organised their journey around the young twin's needs as well as their own, things may have gone a lot smoother. What is so noticeable when we start to do this with our children is how differently we then behave, and even our tone of voice changes. For just becoming aware of how our children might be feeling, rather than making an assumption about what is going on in their minds, has an immediate impact on how we feel and then behave. It is likely in the above scenario that once Rachel and Matt thought about the experience from their babies' point of view, they felt differently about arguing with each other during a long and tiring journey for their babies.

If you think about the times when you feel particularly strongly about your child's behaviour, it is quite likely that you experience negative emotions when your child is misbehaving and when you are feeling more stressed and harried than usual. Your feelings guide your perspective-taking ability, so if you find yourself feeling particularly stressed, angry or upset, it will be harder to step back and think about your child's perspective. It's easy then to misinterpret your child's behaviour. If you remember, one of the landmarks on your Parent Map is your current strong feelings, so by becoming aware of these influences on your parenting, you can then learn how to manage your own emotions. All of which will help you to step back and think about your child's mind and their own particular experience of the world.

All too often we can let our emotions get the better of us and lead us into interactions and altercations with our children that we later regret. Understanding and accepting your child's state of mind, and noting the difference between their mind and yours, is not the same as accepting their behaviour, which you might feel quite rightly was extremely challenging and unacceptable. What is really interesting to observe is how when you do make an effort to see things from your child's point of view this can lead to a change in the very behaviour that you found challenging. This comes back to the concept of the power of being paid attention, and in addition to this, feeling understood. It's actually quite amazing to see how, following a little bit of understanding and perspective taking, children and adults alike can change both how they are feeling and how they are acting. Imagine if, in the first scenario of this chapter Karen, the mum, had said, 'I don't know if you feel like talking about the tests over dinner, or if you'd rather just forget about them for now and eat with us? I'm just happy to sit and have a meal with you.' It would be interesting to see if Maddy had then been able to open up about the school tests, feeling that her mum understood a little of her experience of being tired and fed up from the day. In the case of a younger child, watch how differently your child reacts if instead of shouting at them for not hurrying up with their tooth-brushing, you observe out loud how much of a rush it is in the morning sometimes for them, and if only there was a lot more time for brushing teeth.

Try taking this approach: next time your child is shouting, see if you can step away from your own emotional response and try to take the perspective that your child is shouting because they are having a problem managing how they are feeling. Your child may be behaving in a way that is unreasonable, but for a reason that is entirely reasonable.

Let's look at an example of this from a family with an eight-year-old child.

Karen and Tom and their three children were having a family barbecue where their son Sam, who was eight at the time, had been bouncing on the trampoline with his cousins, who had become too boisterous. Karen asked Sam to come off the trampoline and go inside, but Sam refused. Karen tried to coax him in, but then her parents joined in and started telling her that she was 'too soft' and didn't know how to discipline her son. Feeling embarrassed and under pressure from her parents, Karen shouted at Sam to get off the trampoline and let his cousins stay on. Sam swore at his mum, and Tom laughed at this.

What might they have done differently if they had been more able to take other people's perspectives? Karen might have reflected that Sam was feeling upset about being pushed around by his cousins and then more upset that he was asked to come off the trampoline whilst they got to stay on. Karen might also reflect on her shouting and per-haps conclude that she had been feeling pressured by her family to act in a way that she didn't feel was her normal parenting style. If she had seen that this was her parent's perspective and not her own, then she would probably

not have resorted to shouting. She also felt that Tom had
undermined her authority by laughing at Sam's swearing,
and Tom accepted that he had done this out of embar-
rassment. Karen and Tom could then start to think about
Sam's mind, and how this differed from their own state of
mind and perspective, which could help them handle the
situation differently next time.

Some parents report being upset or worried that they do not understand why their children behave in specific ways. It can be reassuring as a parent to understand that it is normal to be puzzled by why
a child is reacting or acting in a certain way and this does not make
you a less competent parent. In fact, there are times when puzzling
about your child's mind is helpful. We are not mind readers so there
will be plenty of times when we simply don't know what our children are thinking, and it is often helpful to say this out loud to
your child and show them that you really don't know what they
are thinking – but by showing curiosity and interest, we may gain
insight that will help us to influence our child's behaviour.

The impact on your child of perspective taking

There are important consequences of being good at taking another
person's perspective. Not only does this help your child to understand
their own mind, because you are showing that it is separate from
yours, and is interesting and with valuable thoughts and feelings,
but also because exercising the ability to step into another's shoes
is one of the most important elements of being socially skilled. This
means that, not only are you working on your own relationship with
your child when you think about what's going on inside their mind,
but you are also helping them to become socially skilled – popular
and well-liked. Research shows that there is a well-established link
between perspective taking, secure attachment and popularity with
friends (1). The impact of perspective taking on relationships, including siblings and friends, is explored in more detail in Chapter 7.

Recent studies have found that having very poor perspective-taking
skills is linked to social anxiety. Where children find it difficult to
understand and manage social situations, this is largely due to being
overwhelmed by the multiple states of mind that are present in a
group of people. The anxiety this leads to in the child may also cause
them to become hypervigilant to perceived 'threats' in their environment, and this combination of factors causes the anxiety to escalate.

Providing empathy

The final quality on the Parent APP is providing empathy, which is the part that helps you connect to what you imagine is inside your child's mind after you have used the stance of being curious and taking their perspective. When I talk about providing empathy I mean being able to understand and be sensitive to your child's feelings and points of view. The difference between perspective taking and empathy is subtle but important. While perspective taking just involves you appreciating that your child's view on events is different than your own, empathy involves an emotional response to how you think they are experiencing the event: it is being touched by how they are feeling and then letting them know that they have touched you. This is what helps make the connection between them and you. The ability to experience empathy within our relationships helps us to be more deeply attached to our family, friends, communities and even strangers. We could see someone begging for money on the street and either choose not to think about how the person might feel or connect with what it must feel like to be homeless and hungry. Similarly, it's the experience of empathising with other people's distress that leads people to donate to charity. People feel for the victims or beneficiaries and this is further enhanced when they or loved ones have also been affected by the charity's cause, or they feel connected to a community or group. Feeling empathy makes us behave in a very different way.

Empathy is a human capacity that children themselves learn as they develop. As a parent, there are plenty of opportunities to provide empathy, for example when talking to your child about situations that happen at school, around exciting times, proud times or particular events such as when your child brings a picture home from school. You might feel particularly empathic when your child is upset and you want to help them to get over this feeling, as empathy has incredible powers of changing emotions. It is easier to empathise with your child when they are upset but it can be much harder to empathise when they are angry. However, empathy can really help children when they feel angry. It can even help when you need to discipline your child; while you may need to tell them that an action was wrong, by also showing empathy, whether through a simple statement, a well-timed hug or a concerned look, you demonstrate in your communication with them that you understand how they feel. Providing empathy has two important functions: connecting with your child's feelings and letting them know you get how they feel. When you feel empathy for your child you experience their experience, you imagine how they feel and walk in their shoes.

> Lilly comes home from school and tells her mum Rachel
> about something that happened in the playground:
>   'Susan and Jade were playing a game in the playground
> mum and when I came out and asked to play they said I
> couldn't play. They walked away and played at the other
> end of the playground.'
>   'Oh Lilly, I'm sorry to hear that! That sounds really
> hard,
>   I bet you felt really hurt and left out!? You poor thing.'
>   'Yes I did. I felt really sad, they didn't want to play with me.'

In this example, Lilly's mum was imagining how Lilly must have felt in that situation by using her own feelings to guide her. By being open to her own feelings about Lilly in the situation, she was able to picture accurately how Lilly would have felt. It can be hard to really feel what your child is experiencing and so we need to work hard to try to tune in to their experience. We can't actually *feel* the same emotion that our child is experiencing, so it's important to try to imagine what that feels like and verbalise this.

For empathy to be effective, your child needs to know you get how they feel. It is not enough simply for you to get how they feel inside; you need to communicate your understanding to them in a way that is helpful. For empathy to be truly communicated to your child, spoken words need to be authentic, non-verbal communication needs to be matched with your words and the energy and vitality of your communication needs to be pitched at a level that fits with how your child is feeling.

It is a great feeling for your child when you stand alongside them, experiencing their feelings and connecting with their experience of an event. The impact of empathy on your child cannot be overestimated: it can be used positively in almost any aspect of raising children and in any situation. Combine a consequence for bad behaviour with a big dose of empathy, rather than annoyance or anger, and see how much more effective this is. When I have suggested this to some parents I work with, they sometimes ask:

> *But wouldn't it weaken the effect of limits and consequences if I back off and be comforting by being empathic to my child?*

Parents can seem reluctant to recognise their children's feelings and perspective for fear that this will increase the negative behaviour they are facing. There is often an anxiety that it is somehow letting a child off the hook. However, providing empathy is not the same as comforting your child and saying 'Sorry, everything is going to be okay, let's forget about your behaviour.' Instead, for your child, it can feel comforting knowing you understand them. After all, empathy is communicating a sense that you get how your child feels, and that you are alongside them. Being understood feels good and children thrive when they feel understood and acknowledged. So rather than reinforcing bad behaviour, when you provide empathy the opposite is true. Children are more likely to be cooperative when they feel their parents are trying to understand them. This is because the best and easiest way to get your child to understand your perspective is to connect with their experience first. In fact, one of the most powerful tools in therapy is to communicate empathy and validation. Often only when a client feels understood and has a sense that their therapist genuinely gets and cares about their view can they hear what the therapist has to say. Having someone show them that they get how they feel helps people to hear about other points of view. The same applies to your child. Let's look at an example of this in the following conversation between a mother and her son. The mother asks:

> 'How come you got so angry at daddy just now?'
> 'Because he is so unkind and a horrible daddy.'
> 'Oh, what makes you say that?'
> 'Because he always bosses me around and tells me what to do!'
> 'Really, is that what you think? Wow that is really hard, that must feel so unfair to you.'
> 'It does, he doesn't like me!'
> 'Oh OK, well that's even harder having a dad you think doesn't like you! I'd really hate that if I thought my dad hated me.'
> 'I do hate it. It feels horrible.'
> 'Yes I bet it does. Yes, horrible. Well I'm sorry you feel so bad about it. You know it's probably hard for your dad as well!'
> 'Really, why?'
> 'He loves spending time with you but gets very frustrated when he asks you to do something more than three times.'

By being curious and communicating empathy, the parent here was able to help her son explore how he feels about his father. If she judged her son's perspective as being wrong and tried to correct him, he might have felt judged. Instead, she focused on his experience rather than fact. By listening and being empathic, the child was able eventually to see the situation in a different way, because he first felt understood and accepted. When children feel this they are much more receptive to hearing other points of views.

The impact on your child of providing empathy

When children feel understood, they are more able to discover other people's perspectives. It is the same for adults. If you think about how you feel if a partner or friend really shows that they understands how you feel, you are much more likely to be interested in what *they* think or feel than if they show you no empathy. Providing empathy to your child, in how I have begun to suggest, will encourage their empathy for others. It is long recognised through research into the effects of ongoing traumatic events on children that the normal development of empathy in children can be significantly disrupted. When children have not been thought about and their thoughts and feelings not been cared about it makes it harder for them to think about others and care about how others feel. Lacking empathy for others can then get in the way of forming supportive relationships and being able to feel cared for.

One of the most important ways of trying to help your child manage, or regulate, how they are feeling is to validate their feelings. This is vitally important because it helps your child to be more comfortable with how they feel and to be reassured that they have a right to feel this way. In Chapter 5, I look much more closely at this because conveying to your child that they are right to have the feeling they have is an important part of Reflective Parenting. Whatever the nature of the feeling, it is very real as far as your child is concerned, and to have this feeling either minimised or completely invalidated creates a great deal of confusion.

It is really important to apply the Parent APP during everyday moments with your child, and to comment on and discuss emotional events and experiences. However, while this approach is helpful a lot of the time, it is important to keep in mind that it may not always be a good time to talk about things. Focusing on the inside all the time does not always feel comfortable for your child. Ask yourself whether it is a good time to interact with your child and see things from their perspective because as we have explored in previous chapters, your own stresses and strains at a particular moment can really get in the way of being reflective towards your child. Choosing the moment when you are emotionally calm and timing talks with your child when your child will be more receptive is important to the Parent APP's success. Don't force a discussion with your child when they can't cope with it.

REFLECTIVE PARENTING SUMMARY

THE PARENT APP

What it is . . .

The Parent APP is a stance which helps you to think about what might be going on inside your child's mind and to connect you with what you think is in there.

It helps you by . . .

The Parent APP will help you to appreciate what is going on *inside* your child's mind, rather than simply responding to the behaviour they display on the *outside*. This changes your focus during inter-actions with your child and will help you have new insights and meaning to their behaviour.

It helps your child by . . .

Each time your communications with your child follow the princi-ples of the Parent APP, you will be laying the foundations for their skills of perspective taking and empathy. It will also help develop their awareness of what they are thinking and feeling, too. This will make it more likely that they grow up relating well to others.

It helps your relationship by . . .

As the Parent APP helps you see your child from the inside, it will help you respond emotionally with how they are feeling and think-ing. The result will be that you will both feel a greater emotional connection and understanding.

Keep in mind . . .

1. Start to notice and be curious about what might be going on in your child's mind.
2. Be more aware of your tone, expression and the words you use.
3. Be curious about what's going on inside your child's mind, show them you are interested in their inside story, rather than just what they do on the outside.
4. You cannot be expected to always know what their inside story is because you have separate minds. It is normal to be puzzled by why a child is reacting or acting in a certain way and this does not make you a less competent parent.

5. Taking your child's perspective will help them enormously. They don't see the world in the same way as you, and letting them know this will help you become more reflective, and then feel better understood by you. This leads to a better connection.
6. Show empathy to your child's feelings as when they feel understood and accepted, they will be much more receptive to hearing your point of view.
7. Your child may be being unreasonable for a reasonable reason (forgive them). Understanding and accepting your child's state of mind doesn't mean you have to accept their behaviour.
8. Choose a moment when you are calm. You will find this makes the Parent APP more effective.

5

HELPING CHILDREN WITH THEIR FEELINGS

In our efforts to help our children navigate their way through life, it can be easy to make their behaviour the focus, rather than their feelings. But in many ways, helping your child to manage their feelings is the most important thing you can do as it not only impacts on their behaviour but also on their relationship with you, and with others. All children struggle to manage their feelings, especially when they are tired and hungry, or if they really want something.

> *Lisa is in the local shop with her 6-year-old son Charlie, buying some bread and milk, when Charlie spots a magazine with a toy on it at the counter. He asks his mum if he can have the toy and Lisa says,*
>
> *'No, we've just come to get bread and milk, I'm not buying you a toy.'*
>
> *Charlie starts to whine and pulls at his mum's coat, 'I want it, why can't I have it?'*
>
> *Lisa replied, 'Because you can't have a toy every time we come into a shop. OK?'*
>
> *Charlie says, 'It's not fair. I want it.' He starts kicking his mum's ankle and cries, 'I want a toy, I want a toy.'*
>
> *He starts crying loudly and refuses to leave the shop so, with her son still crying, Lisa has to pull him by the arm out of the shop and walk home with him crying all the way. By the time they get home, both are exhausted, upset and angry.*

Have you ever been in this kind of situation? Have you wondered 'why can't my child just stop crying, accept what I'm saying and learn to move on?' How would the situation be different if Charlie's mum could help him manage his feelings? And why is this so important in the first place?

 DOI: 10.4324/9781003483762-6

There are three main reasons why it is important to know how to support your child to help them understand and cope with their emotions:

1. **To help your child in their development**
   When your child first came into the world, they were not born with the ability to understand how they were feeling and why they had feelings. For babies, feelings are diffuse, all encompassing, overwhelming experiences, because they have under-developed brains. They need your help and support whilst their brain matures to deal effectively with strong feelings and this continues well into childhood and even adolescence.
2. **Your child's emotions greatly influence their behaviour**
   If your child becomes more practised at understanding their feelings and managing them more successfully, they will be less likely to react strongly or behave impulsively. Keeping in mind the link between emotions and behaviour will make it easier for both you and your child to understand the inside story behind how they act and help bring some stability to their relationships.
3. **It will help you stay connected with your child during conflict**
   If you do not see your role in helping your child with their emotional experience, and instead focus solely on their behaviour, it will be harder to resolve situations. In some circumstances, you might actually inflame the situation and create disconnection, and then conflict can often last much longer. This is because their brain will be overheating with emotion, which means they will be unable to think about what they are doing, let alone manage their behaviour.
   With these three reasons in mind, I will now turn to some strategies to help your child manage their emotions.

Strategies to bring down your child's 'emotional temperature'

As the example at the start of this chapter illustrated, when your child's emotions get the better of them, it's easy for both them and you to feel overwhelmed, and this quickly leads to a breakdown of the connection between the two of you. There are several strategies you can try to help your child to manage their feelings, and to help you stay connected to your child at the same time. In the next chapter, I look in more detail at how the misunderstandings you have with your child can actually be used to build a better understanding between the two of you and to help strengthen your relationship. However, this is most effectively achieved when your child has calmed down and their emotional temperature has cooled slightly, as only then will you be able to think together about what happened.

> *Before beginning with these strategies, and to make sure that you have the full story of how your child is thinking and feeling, it can be helpful to ask your child the question: 'Tell me a bit more about…,' leaving a space for them to tell you.*

The following is a list of strategies that you can try and keep in mind, which can work on their own or in combination, depending on the situation and the intensity and type of feelings your child is experiencing.

Empathy and validation

The main aim of being empathic and validating to your child's experience is that it will help them feel understood by you, and the impact of being understood is that it will lessen their emotional experience. Thus, expressing empathy and validation is a helpful way of trying to help your child manage how they are feeling and is important because it helps you connect with your child at the same time. It also conveys to your child that they are right to have the feeling they have, which is an important part of Reflective Parenting. The impact on a child of not feeling understood can have the opposite effect:

> *Ella was feeling very unhappy about her Grandma coming to look after her while her Mum and Dad went off to a wedding for the whole day. At first she grumbled at the talk of Grandma coming to stay for the day, and then became quite rude and angry about her. Eventually, by the time her Grandmother arrived she was crying that she didn't want to see her, and she 'didn't like' Grandma anyway. Ella's parents told her off for being rude to Grandma, and told her 'You should be happy to spend the day with your lovely Grandma. She wants to play with you.'*

In this example, Ella wasn't allowed to feel angry or upset, or even express anything negative about her Grandma. For her, the feeling was connected with not wanting her Mum and Dad to go away for the day, and her upset about this was related to feeling that she hadn't spent much time with them all week. Usually on Saturdays they all did something nice together, and now she was being left out. Ella's feelings weren't validated and she felt that she was not understood, and as a result, became increasingly angry and upset. Moreover, she was told that she should be experiencing a different feeling to the one she had, and so she started to get really confused about why she didn't feel the way her Mum and Dad said she should.

As you are aware, providing empathy is part of the Parent APP, and is a quality I have encouraged you to bring to your relationship with your child in order to connect with what you imagine is going on inside their mind. Being able to make an accurate statement about what you think is going on inside your child's mind is an excellent way of helping your child to be able to manage their emotions and also helps them to feel better connected to you. An important part then of showing empathy and validation is to have a mind-minded approach to your child.

When your child is having an emotional outburst, you may not feel like being empathic, however, empathic statements can show your child that you understand how it feels to be them, and this can really help to calm the situation and stop it from escalating further. Empathy has a strong emotional component to it, where you show your child that you get and feel what they feel. Empathy mirrors back a feeling that matches (is contingent with) what your child is feeling. Naming and mirroring back the feeling in your face in a marked way is important. When your expression matches how your child feels this is known as marked-mirroring. We all do this quite naturally much of the time, but when we are preoccupied with something, or overwhelmed with a strong emotion ourselves, it can be much harder to mirror in our face what is going on inside our child.

For example, using an expression that matches her upset, Ella's parents could have tried saying:

I know you're really disappointed you can't spend time with us. I know you love Saturdays where we all spend time together and it doesn't feel fair right now.

The other advantage of making an empathic statement is that it tends to also bring your own emotional temperature down because when you start to imagine what it feels like from your child's point of view this can resonate within you when you start to feel empathic. This then naturally impacts on your communication, for example lowering your voice, appearing calmer, relaxing your facial muscles, which then makes conflict less likely. So this, combined with the impact on your child of the statement itself, can really take the heat out of the situation.

Sometimes, especially if your child is angry at you, being empathic can make them angrier. Another way of being empathic, if you have a partner present, is to express to him in front of your child how you imagine your child is feeling and why, rather than speaking directly to your child. This can be a less intense way of helping your child feel understood and can work particularly well for a younger child. Let's go back to the example of Charlie and his mother Lisa from the start of the chapter.

> By the time Charlie had got home he was very angry at his mum, both about the way she said 'No' but moreover about his subsequent experience of not being understood or validated. In the car Lisa had tried empathizing with her son, but Charlie just seemed to get more and more angry. When they arrived home Lisa turned to her partner Finn and said in a sympathetic voice:
> 'Poor Charlie, he is so upset and angry with Mummy. He really really wanted a magazine in the shop just now. It was very hard for him when I said "No" and Charlie got really angry at me and I think I got mad too.'
> Charlie's dad cuddles him and says:
> 'Oh poor Charlie, that sounds hard for him. He must have really wanted that magazine!'

Getting your partner, if you have one, to intervene can be really helpful sometimes, either in the way shown here, where Charlie is spoken about, rather than spoken to directly; or, if your child is angry at you, encouraging your partner to step in to help resolve the situation can be more helpful than trying to battle through yourself.

Additionally, you might find that when your child is extremely upset, empathic comments during the situation might encourage them to carry on expressing more negative emotion. So, if Charlie's mum became really empathic in the shop, this could have magnified his feelings and not help resolve the situation. It could have encouraged Charlie to express his feelings more strongly in the hope of changing his mum's mind and might plant an idea that expressing strong feelings gets him what he wants. Instead, choosing a validating statement can be more effective.

Validation is similar to empathy as the aim is to help your child see that you get his point of view, but differs in that it does not take the child too deeply back into the experience of what they are feeling. It does this because the tone that you communicate your understanding can be quite different from empathy. When you make validating statements you are more likely to express your concern and interest, rather than reflecting back a marked emotion congruent to theirs. Sounding genuine but not being overemotional, combined with a brief statement, can be enough to validate what your child is feeling. Furthermore, these statements have a mind-minded quality – in other words, they 'fit' with how your child is thinking and feeling. Take a look at a mind-minded statement from Karen towards her two-year-old daughter, Molly:

> *Karen is watching Molly pretend to understand a game that her 10-year-old brother is playing, and getting bit frustrated that she can't play it, and comments, 'Molly wants to be just like Sam.'*

In this statement, Karen is accurately guessing, and most importantly, verbalising, what she thinks is going on inside Molly's mind. The accuracy of these statements is important, but if you really don't know what your child is thinking or feeling, then being explicit about the fact that you are taking a good guess is also helpful to him. In the earlier example, Charlie's mum in the shop could have said:

> *I know you would really like it if we got a toy every time we came to the shop, and it is hard for you, but that's not going to happen. It feels really disappointing and annoying.*

A simple validating statement like this acknowledges Charlie's disappointment with not getting a toy and communicates that from his point of view his mum gets that it is hard, but it also holds a line. When you convey your understanding for your child's experience, this does not necessarily mean that you like or agree with what they are doing or feeling. However, it does mean that you understand where they are coming from.

Tips for making validating statements using the Parent APP:

a. Pay attention and actively listen – make eye contact and stay focused.

b. Be aware of how you are coming across, especially non-verbal communication such as tutting, rolling your eyes.

c. Can you hear what your child is saying and communicating? Allow space in your mind to think about what is going on in the inside and try taking their perspective – what is their experience in this situation right now, what are they feeling?

d. Reflect back their feeling without judgement. The aim is to let them know that you understand their point of view: 'I understand that you are angry because..., I can see that this really frustrates you.'

e. Show tolerance. Look for their inside story and how it all makes sense from their point of view; even if you do not approve of how they are acting, you can still try and empathise with how it might feel for them.

f. Respond in a way that demonstrates that you take them seriously. For example, Charlie's mum might think with him about how he might be able to save up for a magazine with his pocket money.

Using humour

Lilly is angry at her father Matt for asking her to tidy her toys away. She turns to him and shouts 'you are a bogeyman', he dramatically hunches over and puts his finger to his lips and says, 'Shhh! You can't tell anyone that's my real name!'

Injecting some humour into difficult exchanges can be a great harmoniser, bringing you and your child closer together. Humour can be especially effective when you are trying to help your child lower their emotional temperature as it breaks the tension quickly in heightened situations. In this situation, Lilly was so amused she laughed back, 'No, you're a poopy head.'

Disciplining and making sure your child is well behaved unfortunately can feel like such a serious issue but why should it? The ability to be able to laugh at either yourself or a situation you find yourself in with your child can be extremely refreshing and a lot less stressful. It follows that once you have got to the point where you can both step back enough from a situation to be able to laugh and joke about it, then you have already managed to deescalate the situation. Having a playful relationship with your child can really make you both feel more connected. You could try using funny voices, tripping over dramatically, rephrasing angry requests like 'For the last time, put your pyjamas on now!' with a friendly voice, 'I've been standing here so long I think a spider has managed to spin a web between my shoulder and the wall! Can you check for me?'

However, using humour isn't without its risks and it can be a bit of a balancing act as you don't want your child to think you are laughing at them as this results in a feeling like shame. If you described to a friend something that was important to you and she made a joke, you would probably feel teased or even shamed, which can be irritating at best. In your relationship with your child, making a joke at your own expense may be a safer bet, and more helpful. This might be telling a funny story about you when you were a child, or admitting that sometimes you must be the worst mummy or daddy in the whole world, probably the whole universe. The ability to be able to laugh at either yourself or a situation you find yourself in also has the advantage of showing your child different perspectives, and mirroring for them that you can look at yourself from the outside too. When you look at yourself from the outside in a humorous way, it takes the heat out of the emotion you are feeling, so you may go from feeling intensely angry about something to mocking yourself and laughing heartedly.

Distraction

Diverting attention from one thing to another is a strategy that all of us employ, often very successfully. How often when you feel worried about an upcoming event, such as an important meeting at work, or a social event with people you don't really feel comfortable with, do you try to focus on something else to take your mind off the thing that is bothering you? Similarly, distraction can be an excellent way to deal with a child's feelings.

Distraction can take a few different forms. For younger children, it can be as simple as noticing something of interest outside the window and excitedly saying something like 'Oh wow, look at Felix the cat outside on our fence, how did he get up there?!' For older children, you might have to be more elaborate. You can use an earlier conversation about something your child has been talking about and is interested in and try to steer his thinking back to this. For example:

> Grace was feeling angry at her mum Rachel lay on her bed yelling and crying. Rachel had told her she couldn't have any more biscuits before dinner and they had argued over

*this, with Grace getting more and more angry. Her mum,
with a puzzled and curious expression on her face, says:*

'Look Grace, I know you are furious at me at the moment.'
'Go away, you are so mean.'
'I know you think that. But look, I've been thinking all day
about something you said earlier.'
'I don't care.'
'Listen, I know you're angry with me Grace, I understand
that, but what you said earlier was really important. You
wanted to know how to get more bonus fruits in that
game on your tablet!'
'AND?'
'Well I think I worked it out, you need to get more bananas
by getting into the bonus area.'
'Really, how do I do that?'

Grace and her mother spent a few minutes talking about this further until Rachel decided to revisit talking about the situation that
had happened earlier.

Another way to use distraction is by talking about your own
experiences to draw your child's attention away from their current
concern. Instead of trying to think of something you talked about
earlier in the day to reconnect with them, try to think of a time
when you felt similar to how they are feeling, and talk about this.
For example:

'I know Grace you are furious at me at the moment.'
'Go away, you are so mean.'
'I know you think I'm mean. You probably hate me at the
moment as well. Do you know how much I hated
granddad and grandma when I was younger?'
'I don't care.'
'No, I bet. I used to get so mad at them. Do you know, once
when I was really mad, I poured away grandma's special
perfume, I got in so much trouble for that! Oh no, that
was bad, she got so angry!'
'Really! What did she do?'
'She didn't let me go outside for 2 years!'
'Really?'
'No, probably not 2 years, probably only for a week, but she
did shout very loudly at me!'

Rachel decided that it was probably a good time to leave Grace to have a bit of space as things had settled down between them and she felt somewhat more connected. However, she resolved to come back a short while after this to think through with her what had happened and to try to understand any misunderstanding.

In both of these examples, Rachel managed to distract Grace by generating her interest in something else. However, she did not dismiss her daughter's point of view or her thoughts, she clearly connected with them, but at the same time, she also confidently persisted in drawing Grace's attention to something else. When you use distraction techniques like this with your children, you can take them away from the tricky feeling they are having right in this moment by shifting their attention to a more positive, manageable experience. This also shifts their attention to a different emotion. Bear in mind, though, that while using distraction helps your child to *shift out* of a difficult feeling and think about something else, it is sometimes important to revisit the initial feeling after a short period of time, perhaps by having some sort of discussion about what happened or just commenting on it – often it's easier to think about a situation after some time has passed. In shifting Grace's attention away from her own feelings, towards the story of how her mum Rachel felt when she upset her parents, also helped to lessen the intensity of how Grace was feeling. When your child is feeling sucked into a feeling, helping them orientate to future events – to think about how they will move on from this unpleasant moment – can be really beneficial. This gives them a perspective that their current emotional state will pass, and that life changes day by day and hour by hour. They can also begin to be curious about feelings and talk about them, all the while understanding that they won't last forever.

Time alone

Parents in some parts of the Western world are familiar with the concept and practice of 'Time Out,' traditionally used as a form of punishment that involves temporarily separating a child from an environment where undesirable behaviour has occurred, with the aim of reinforcing desirable behaviour. Sometimes, Time Out is used as a way to communicate to children that they need to get anger and frustration 'out of their system' or for children to think about their behaviour. However, the strategy has its limitations, especially when it's used in a punitive way. 'Time Alone' is different. When children get slightly older, around five years and upwards, they may actively choose to spend some time alone if they are upset and angry at their parents, and to use this time as a way of self-regulating. And, of course, at times, trying to speak directly to your child only serves to inflame the situation, so having time apart can be really beneficial for your child. To make this a supportive strategy, it shouldn't be perceived as a punishment by your child, for example 'Go to your room for five minutes,' but rather as a suggestion to help them calm down:

> *Okay, you seem really upset and angry at me at the moment and I'm sorry I can't help. I think me being here is making you feel worse. I can go downstairs for a bit, maybe that will help.*

As with learning all new skills, the ability to use Time Alone to calm down and move into a 'warmer' range of emotional control will not just come naturally to your child. It is important first and foremost that they do not feel you are sending them off to be alone as a punishment, but that you are teaching him a new skill. This skill involves not just calming a mood but is an exercise in learning to self-regulate. However, children do not learn new skills when they are angry and upset so it is a good idea then, with you as your child's trainer, to ask them to practice when they are calm. Remember, this is a practice of how to be alone in a space where they can learn to bring their emotions under their control (to self-regulate). You might even want to model this by using the time to sit quietly yourself in a different part of the house. When your child has managed to practice this skill, and you can help them devise their own name for it (one child I knew called it his 'chill time'), you should then praise them for learning this new skill. After they have learned to do this under your guidance, they will soon be able to use Time Alone independently to help them calm down and think about their behaviour.

Older children who have learned how to regulate their feelings a bit better can often decide that they want to take themselves off to spend time alone and calm down, and you can both encourage and facilitate this. For example:

> *12-year-old Maddy came home from school after a long day and the minute she walked in the door her mum Karen started firing off questions at her about her day. Maddy started to get agitated and argumentative with Karen, to*

the point of shutting her out and telling her to 'back off'. Maddy's mum got upset about this and said 'I'm only taking an interest in what you did today.' Maddy shouted back, 'I'm really tired, it's been a long day, I'm going to my room.' Later that day, Karen thought that maybe she should ask her if it would be a good idea if every day after school Maddy had 20 minutes alone time in her room, which she could take or not, to relax after the school day, and that they could have a catch up after that. Maddy agreed to this and a pattern was set whereby most days she would come in from school, chill in her room, and then come down to talk about her and Karen's day together. This time alone created a better connection between Maddy and her mum, and also taught Maddy a bit more about how to regulate her feelings.

Use of touch with sad and difficult feelings

Touch has calming effects on children and can act as a helpful cue, along with verbal statements, to help them start to feel better. A warm, loving touch with close body contact can release oxytocin (the bonding hormone) and so this has the almost immediate effect of making both you and your children feel calmer. This can be accompanied by words, for example putting both your arms around your child and saying, 'You seem really frustrated with that; let me help you calm down.' Alternatively, saying nothing at all, and simply holding your child in a secure and comforting embrace when they are experiencing a strong emotion will help you both to feel better.

You know that soothing, warm, loving feeling you get inside when you hug someone close? That's oxytocin. It's a hormone released in the body and brain in response to affectionate touch, hugs, and also in young infants, breastfeeding. Oxytocin has many positive effects including promoting feelings of calm and nurturance; promoting feelings of trust, security and closeness; promoting infant bonding; lowering blood pressure and regulating sleep patterns. The type of touch you give is important too as a casual pat on the shoulder will not have any of these positive benefits, whereas a really heartfelt hug where your whole chest and tummy touches your child's, and where your breathing is slow, full and relaxed will have the desired effect of bringing your child's emotional temperature down and bringing the two of you closer to one another. Some children who are more sensitive to touch may prefer a side-hug without full body contact.

Apologising when you get it wrong

It is highly aversive for your child to feel that they have been mis-understood and that you have 'got it wrong' when it comes to understanding the thoughts and feelings behind their behaviour. However, this experience and their associated feelings about having been misunderstood will be felt even more keenly if you are not able to tell them that you got it wrong. An important element of Reflec-tive Parenting is being open about the fact that you don't know what is going on in other people's minds, and to make it clear to your child that you are taking your best guess at why they behaved the way they did. This curiosity should be equally matched by an attitude of self-reflection, and being able to admit that you thought you knew what your child was thinking, or why they behaved in a certain way, but that you may have got this wrong, is very helpful to your child. They will feel closer to you and your connection with them following an emotional outburst can be re-established both when you accurately guess what might have been in their mind *and* when you make an inaccurate guess, but acknowledge that you got it wrong. As parents, we all make mistakes, but acknowledging this with your child is another important aspect of being reflective.

REFLECTIVE PARENTING SUMMARY

What do we mean ...

Reflective Parenting reminds us how important it is to help your child to learn to understand, and eventually manage, how they feel. Reflective Parenting encourages you to take an active stance in helping your child build up ability to do this independently.

It helps you by ...

Stepping back and seeing how you can directly help your child build up their ability to cope with their feelings is a stance that is more likely to help you remain calm and empathic. Also, focusing on your child's emotions will help resolve situations quicker, reducing your levels of stress and increasing your confidence. When your child becomes more skilled at managing their feelings, they will be better behaved, bringing further benefits to you.

It helps your child by ...

Being a reflective parent by focusing on feelings and finding ways to help your child manage these independently has a direct impact on their capacity to manage their feelings in other relationships. The consequence of this will be more stable and positive relationships with peers and other family members.

It helps your relationship by ...

A focus on feelings, in some circumstances, can be of enormous benefit to resolving situations and encourages connection, which is so important to security in relationships, as well as shortening conflict. When you can match your feelings and expression to your child's, it will help them to both manage their own feelings and develop resilience through feeling understood by you.

Keep in mind ...

1. Helping your child to manage their feelings is important as it impacts on their behaviour, but also on their relationship with you, and with others.
2. Keeping in mind the link between emotions and behaviour will make it easier for both you and your child to understand the inside story behind how they act.

3. Empathy and validation are both important to helping your child manage how they are feeling and connecting with them, which reduces conflict and difficult behaviours. Validation expresses interest and concern, and empathy expresses feeling for how your child feels.

4. Make statements about what you imagine is going on in your child's mind and body. Making these mind-minded comments can help them understand what they are thinking and feeling.

5. Humour can break the tension between you and your child, make you feel better connected and show them that you can look at yourself from a different perspective.

6. Distraction comes in a few different forms and helps children with their feelings; it can take your child out of a difficult emotion.

7. Make Time Alone a supportive strategy, by turning it into a suggestion to help both you and your child calm down.

8. Be aware of your facial expression when verbalising what you think your child is feeling. Try to match your expression to your child's feelings (marked-mirroring).

6

DISCIPLINE

Understanding misunderstandings

Let me start with the obvious: all children misbehave many many times during their childhood. In fact, misbehaving is so much a part of their development that it would seem incredible and completely out of the ordinary if a child didn't misbehave. Yet naughty behaviour concerns the majority of parents, and generally parents want their children to be well behaved.

Why is bad behaviour such a concern to parents? Why does this issue motivate so many parents to ask the advice of friends, look online or to buy a parenting book to look for solutions? The answer is complex and multifaceted and slightly different for each one of us. It might be linked to any or all of the following: the powerful

feelings children being naughty and pushing limits bring up in parents; pressure from other parents, or grandparents, for children to behave in a certain way; messages implicit within society regarding authority and respect; concern about where bad behaviour now might lead a child in the future; or simply that it makes life easier when children comply. Of course I understand all of these concerns and why they often motivate parents to seek advice from others. A central aim with this book is to provide ideas that will indirectly, and sometimes directly, reduce problematic behaviour. One of the core principles of Reflective Parenting being that emotion regulation leads to more manageable and regulated behaviour. I hope this chapter can address your concerns while challenging some commonly held ideas around discipline, its purpose, and how useful it can be to your child.

In this chapter, I want to explore and challenge the idea that bad behaviour simply needs to be discouraged or managed. Instead, I offer you a broader view: that actually the occasions when you respond to your child misbehaving also provide excellent opportunities to support their emotional development and to help them to understand their own thoughts and feelings and other people's. In fact, young children in particular are not meant to behave and be obedient all the time, and the reason for this is that their needs are frequently completely at odds with those of their parents. Think

Parents can feel judged by others for their child's behaviour

about your view for example of your need to keep your child wrapped up and warm for the walk to school versus your child's feelings about wearing a jumper under a coat while trying to ride fast on his scooter to school. Your young child isn't actually feeling at all cold and wants to have as much movement and freedom as they can possibly experience while riding on their scooter. Understanding these different perspectives is one of the key elements to understanding why it's inevitable that there will be everyday conflicts. What if I told you that falling out with your child is actually helpful sometimes, but only if you spend time afterwards actively trying to repair the relationship and explore what happened? The key is to help your child to mentalize their experience, which will help to reduce the incidence of difficult-to-manage behaviour in the future. If you recall from the introduction, when people are mentalizing, they are trying to understand the mental state (or thoughts and feelings if you like) of both themselves and others that underlines overt behaviour. So in the experience of the child refusing to wear a jumper, the parent would start to try to understand what it was the child was thinking and feeling and ideally would be explicit about what they were thinking too (e.g. 'I'm just worried that you might get cold without noticing and then feel ill at school all day').

The first important step in this approach is to take a stance of curiosity about your child's behaviour, rather than blame. If this seems odd or counter-intuitive, I would like to reassure you that the ideas in this chapter do reduce problematic behaviour, not only when these ideas are being applied in situations where your child is behaving badly, but also, importantly, in the longer term as your child develops. I am going to help you see that within conflicts there can be important developmental lessons for your child that bring benefits to them and to you and most importantly to your relationship.

Bad behaviour, conflict and connection

It is extremely common and normal for a child to act inappropriately and for there to be some conflict that follows with the parents. The feelings that come with conflict can be difficult for most parents to manage and can lead to feelings of personal inadequacy or disappointment in their children. But it's important to remind yourself that your child's motivations are often completely at odds with yours; after all, you are two very different people, and so it is very normal for them to behave in a way you consider inappropriate.

It's reassuring to know that bad behaviour and conflict is not a sign of poor family relationships. Conflict arises normally between parents and their children. How these conflicts are resolved and understood is key to Reflective Parenting. Despite having different needs, parents still have to maintain boundaries and correct behaviour that is inappropriate. It is a parent's role to set boundaries and limits on behaviour in order to help children learn what is expected of them, what is safe, appropriate etc. Children on the other hand are grappling with issues of autonomy and their own emerging identity, one that is quite separate from their parents. This is one of the day-to-day aspects of parenting: balancing your children's needs with the need to help them behave within acceptable limits. The potential for conflict is great as you constantly try to judge an acceptable level of independence for your child while providing support and direction to conform to your expectations.

The potential for conflict in adolescence is even greater (as I go on to describe in Chapter 10), and it is therefore even more important to think about creating communication patterns early on in the family that will carry on through into the teenage years, and so setting the environment for understanding misunderstandings early on is helpful. There is a growing body of evidence that suggests that the ability of parents and their older children to continue to feel connected to each other while disagreeing on critical issues is the hallmark of secure relationships (1–3). If parents and teenagers are able to state their opinions while accepting the other person's point of view, they are more likely to feel secure in their relationship with each other. What is important here is not that parents and teenagers never fall out, but that they continue to feel connected during a conflict or are able to re-establish a feeling of connection quickly after times of conflict. This is synonymous with the key concepts in this book that aim to help parents connect to the minds of their children, irrespective of the child's age. If you want to know more about the parent-teenager relationship, you can find more out in my book *How Do You Hug A Cactus: Reflective Parenting with Teenagers in Mind.*

The importance of connectedness with children around times of conflict cannot be overstated. There is growing awareness of the role and, impact of, shame during parenting practices (4,5). Shame, the sense of feeling bad and awful for doing something wrong, seems to play a very important role in shaping young children's behaviour to fit within moral and social norms. This is because the main feeling that young children feel when told off by their parents is shame. And when young children feel shame they become quiet, hide their eyes, and become inhibited in their speech and movement. You can probably recall a time that you told your children off and they might have hung their heads in this way or curled up into themselves. Within this unpleasant state, children feel a sense of threat to the bond with their parents, in other words they feel they are not accepted or loved. Children then learn to anticipate what might result in the same feeling of shame and learn to behave in ways that might be more in line with their parents' preferences, especially if their parents reward positive behaviour, and as children grow, they learn to inhibit their behaviour somewhat and select other more socially acceptable behaviours. Children do not like to feel disconnected from their parents, in fact it feels threatening to them, which is why they adapt their behaviour. Parents who can acknowledge the shame in their children can easily help reconnect to their children quickly, strengthening their bond with them and helping their children learn that they are okay and the state of their relationship with their parents isn't damaged.

> 9-month-old Jack was crawling around his front room and became interested in a plug socket. As he fiddled around with the plug, he suddenly heard his mum Rachel shout 'Jack, STOP! Get away from there now!'
> Jack froze and became very quiet. He looked at the floor, stiffened and refused to respond to his mum. He felt shame. His mum picked him up, held and rocked him for a few minutes, and affirmed how much she cared about him and loved her. Jack started to relax and together they went over to the plug socket and Rachel told him a bit about plugs and that he should not be around them. He felt better even if he didn't really understand why plugs are dangerous.

If there is a lack of acknowledgement of shame and children experience this emotion too much, it can create alienation and weaken the parent-child bond. Children learn to cope and defend against feelings of shame, bringing in other negative states of emotion, such as resentment and anger. Children can also learn that negative interaction cycles still bring desired attention and some sense of connection to their parents, albeit with more shame and resentment. So short experiences of mild shame, followed by repair and reconnection, are positive and strengthen your child's relationship with you, whereas prolonged experiences of moderate-to-severe shame, followed by little repair and further disconnection, are negative, weakening your relationship and actually increasing bad behaviour.

If you're worried about your child experiencing feelings of shame, remember that disagreements happen regularly in families, and if you were totally attuned to your child's experiences, without bringing in an understanding of how they impact on others, your child would never learn about different perspectives and understand that people have needs that are different from their own. Furthermore, it is from these conflicts that you can learn a lot more about each other than you might from times when you are getting on really well.

The important message is to find ways to interact positively with your child, during or after conflict. This brings security to your relationship and reduces negative behaviour cycles. So while conflict between parents and their children is to be expected, it is how the parent and child negotiate conflicts and sustain their relationship that is most important. Children who feel understood by their parents trust their parents' commitment to the relationship, even in the face of conflict and strong differences of opinion. They are more able to move forward confidently from one developmental stage to the next, learning to tolerate and resolve conflict, and feeling confident that they can trust their parents while also feeling valued in their views. When you are able to work your way through disagreements with your child, they will see and learn how to manage conflict and negotiate situations without resorting to aggressive behaviour or heightened emotion. Then, by noticing and praising them when they are able to resolve conflict and alter their behaviour, they learn that you like this and will want to do more of it.

I will help you to see that within these conflicts, there can be an important developmental lesson for children, namely to help them explore the underlying reasons for their behaviour. Also, you can start to understand your child's world a little more and discover what is important to them. I would also like you to consider to what extent it's important *all the time* to get your children to do what you ask of them or to bring their behaviour under control? I know from working with parents of very young children that there can be a fear that if behaviour isn't controlled very early on, 'nipped in the bud', that their children will become out-of-control monsters. There isn't any evidence for this, and the approach I would like to advocate here might actually lead both to an understanding of the behaviour but also to a better mutual understanding in the relationship between the two of you – even if your child doesn't behave perfectly all of the time.

The other important point to note is that through conflict and managing negative emotions, your child sees that you, their parent, can tolerate and manage these feelings. This is an important lesson for your child in both seeing things from another person's perspective and learning that differences in opinion don't have to lead to rejection or a loss of warmth or empathy. However, your children do have to see that there are expected boundaries and limits to behaviour, and that even if they push these limits and boundaries, they will reach a point where they have to adapt what they want to do to fit your expectations for their behaviour.

Karen had made a Sunday lunch for her husband Tom and the three children and gone to some effort to make it a bit special, as it was a miserable day outside and so everyone was stuck in the house. The eldest two children, Maddy (12) and Sam (10) sat down at the table and started to eat, but Karen's youngest, Molly (aged 2) came to the table, took one look at her dinner and said, 'Yuck, me don't like cheesy sauce. Yuck! No! Me not eating.' She didn't bother to come to the table with her brothers and parents and instead sat on the sofa, sulking and saying she wanted peanut butter on toast instead. Karen said, 'I'm not doing you separate food, I've gone to quite a bit of trouble here Molly, don't be fussy.' At this, Molly threw her toy doll at the Christmas tree, knocking some of the decorations off and throwing a cushion after it. Karen suddenly exploded and shouted at the top of her voice, 'I've spent ages cleaning up today, don't you DARE start wrecking everything.' Older sister Sam muttered to Molly, 'Silly little baby, can't eat your dinner at the table.' At this, Molly burst into tears of upset and anger and saw that she had broken her doll's arm off in the fracas. She stormed out of the room, slamming the door. Karen shouted after her, 'Come back, and tidy up your mess.' Molly ignored her and went into the other room. The rest of the family left Molly and continued to eat, then, after a few minutes, Molly came back into the room and went to her daddy saying, 'Me don't like it when mummy shouts at me. Not tidying up. Not talking to mummy. She says sorry.' Molly's dad said, 'No, it's not nice when people shout. But maybe you need to say sorry too for wrecking the room, and the tree. And look, you've broken the toy you really loved, what a shame.' Molly hung her head, looking shamed and feeling upset, about being shouted at, the broken toy, and the feeling that she had been rejected by her mum, and furthermore made to feel like the baby by her 10-year-old brother. Her dad asked Karen to come and tell Molly that she was sorry for shouting and that she loved her. Karen, having cooled off, told Molly that she didn't like shouting either, and was sorry she had made her feel bad, but she had been looking forward to a nice family meal. 'I still love you, and I'm sorry you broke your toy. You must be very upset about that?' Molly took some time, but after around ten minutes she had calmed down, and her posture changed to sitting up straight. She looked at her dinner and started to pick at her roast potatoes as her mum gave her a cuddle. And after she had finished some food, Karen suggested that she tidy up the room, but offered to help her. Molly played happily for the rest of the afternoon.

I would like to encourage you to see that when your child either empathises or conversely fails to appreciate the impact of their behaviour on others, both these instances can be training opportunities where they can learn to understand other minds. Within a safe and secure relationship, conflicts can be resolved in a positive way, without leading to distancing in the relationship, as you can see from the example of Molly. In fact, quite the opposite: conflicts surprisingly can even lead to an increase in closeness and understanding. Naturally, it is incredibly difficult for both you the parent and your child when feeling misunderstood, and as I've highlighted from the beginning, this feeling of being misunderstood by others is one of the most aversive feelings we can experience, both as adults and children. This is where conflict provides the chance to turn a perceived misunderstanding into a deeper understanding of how the other person feels.

In healthy relationships, there is conflict and children misbehave. A parent's job is both to respond to disruptive behaviour and care about the child's feelings and points of view. I don't believe that responding to their feelings and taking their point of view undermines the boundaries you have set. You can see from the example of Molly that children need limits, but these should be set in such a way that preserves the relationship and actually supports the child in learning from the circumstance as well as supporting his wider development. Karen was clear that she still needed Molly to eat her dinner and tidy up her mess but also acknowledged how bad it feels to be shouted at, and how she had lost control in that moment because of her own feelings. She was able to name and own her feelings of upset about having been looking forward to a family meal and having spent time tidying the house. You can see that connection through bad behaviour and conflict helps their development; so falling out with your child can actually be extremely helpful to your relationship, and discipline can actually help strengthen your bond. While parents may ask themselves, 'Is it more important to correct him or to connect with him?', my Reflective Parenting approach allows you to connect with your child *while* you are correcting him. If you spend time actively trying to repair your relationship after conflict, using the principles of the Parent APP in Chapter 4, and rewinding and exploring what happened, you can help your child understand other people's points of view and their underlying intentions. I have given some examples of the types of ways you might do this, but I would like to make it even more explicit and give you a tool that you can use to help you combine these two things, correction and connection, as it can feel quite tricky to imagine how you might do both things at the same time.

The 'Two Hands' approach

Children behave and misbehave for many different reasons. While the reasons are not always clear, it is helpful to respond to your child's difficult behaviour and to try to understand what led to the behaviour. Think about your hands; in one hand you are juggling with your child's behaviour and in the other hand trying to get to grips with why your child misbehaved in the first place. This is often overwhelming and too much to handle. There is a great concept used by clinical psychologist Daniel Hughes and kindly given to me for my Reflective Parenting model; the Two Hands approach (6). Two Hands invites you to have two important components to your parenting around discipline: one hand is for focusing on understanding what led to the behaviour and the other hand is for dealing with the behaviour. I have developed this idea by adding my idea of the Parent APP to Hughes's useful concept.

Explaining the Two Hands approach

On the first hand is 'dealing with behaviour' – this represents what you do when you respond to your child's bad behaviour, for example

the consequence you give to your child. It might be a behavioural consequence or it might be about your child taking some responsibility for what they have done. You could think of this as the 'action' hand.

On the second hand is understanding the behaviour – that helps you to understand the underlying reasons and motives that led up to your child's behaviour. Using the Parent APP in this hand helps you see the reasons why your child behaved in a particular way, not just the behaviour outside. This is the more mentalizing, or reflective, hand, if you like.

Two Hands reminds you that it is just as important to deal with behaviour as it is to understand a child's experience that has led to the behaviour. As with most of the ideas in this book, this approach is useful both in the heat of a situation and afterwards.

> *Charlie was playing outside with his friend William while Lisa, his mum, was inside speaking to William's father. Suddenly William came running inside crying, and told his mum that Charlie had kicked him on the shin. After making sure William was okay and waiting until her own embarrassment subsided, Lisa decided to wait a further few minutes before going outside to see Charlie.*
>
> *Using the ideas of the Parent APP, Lisa guessed that Charlie might be feeling ashamed about kicking his friend, but also probably in Charlie's mind there must have been a reason for him to lash out. If she were to use the Two Hands approach, Lisa knew she would have to give Charlie*

a consequence for kicking (dealing with behaviour hand), but she also wanted to understand what had happened as it was very unusual (understanding the behaviour hand). Lisa sat down next to Charlie and, trying to set the tone for the conversation and to help his probable feeling of shame, gave him a quick cuddle. She then said in a friendly voice: 'What happened there Charlie? I thought you liked William?

What happened just now that you didn't like?'

'I hate William Mum!'

'Really? You usually like him. He's your good mate isn't he? Something bad must have happened?'

'He said his trampoline is much bigger than mine. He said his garden is bigger and that my games are all rubbish!'

'Oh, that doesn't feel nice.'

'I don't like him. Why was he saying that?'

'I'm not sure, love. People can say things like that for a lot of different reasons. I can understand why you got so mad.'

Charlie looked up at his mum, a bit uncertain. Lisa went on.

'I can see how you feel. I don't like it either when someone says something that upsets me. But it's not okay to hit people when you feel mad. I know you know that.'

Charlie was silent and hung his head down. 'You do know that's wrong don't you Charlie?' Charlie was silent and nodded.

'You need to say sorry to William when you go in. I'm also going to speak to your dad, too, and talk about it with him. We need to help you to find something else you can do when you feel upset; being kicked on the shins really, really hurts. You wouldn't like it if he'd kicked you.'

Children are helped enormously when they experience the Two Hands approach to discipline. Charlie felt understood by his mum but still understood that his own response to what had happened was not acceptable. All children need limits and consequences, and as your child grows older and aspects of their brain development make it easier to understand feelings and inhibit urges, they will become more able to make choices around how to respond to a feeling or perception of an event. In turn, their behaviour will improve and more desirable behaviours will become more frequent. Helping them to become more interested in their feelings and why they act the way they do will increase these more desirable behaviours.

At bedtime, Lisa decided to speak some more to Charlie about what happened earlier. Charlie had expressed some interest in why his friend might decide to say things to him that felt hurtful. Lisa thought exploring the reasons would be a good way in and an opportunity to look at different perspectives. After talking through different ideas as to why William might have said the things he did, Charlie decided the perspective he liked best was that William might actually be jealous of what he had. Charlie also decided that he had felt angry because he felt William was criticising his family. As a consequence for kicking someone Lisa decided that Charlie was not allowed to have his friend Ollie round to play.

How does this approach help reduce behavioural problems? First, it encourages you to approach bad behaviour and interactions during conflict with interest and curiosity, which in turn means you will be more able to approach your child with a positive mindset. Just being less irritated and angry can help the outcome of situations. In the previous example, Lisa had consciously decided that she would have to approach Charlie carefully just after he had kicked his friend. She was actually really concerned and interested to know what had happened and was able to reflect on what Charlie might have been feeling, creating a space for a helpful conversation. If she had confronted Charlie straight after the incident, while she was feeling angry and embarrassed, and demanded an apology for William there and then, this would have most likely inflamed the situation.

Secondly, adopting the Two Hands approach helps you ensure that not only is there a consequence for your child's behaviour but also that you also consider the internal experience that led up to the behaviour. This helps foster positive self-esteem and helps your child to deal with feelings of shame by allowing them to explore with you why something happened and understand that this was wrong but also ensuring that they feel understood by you. Again, in the previous example, Lisa managed to empathise greatly with Charlie. She thought about some friends she knew who tended to brag about things and how she could never really understand why they did this. By stating this to Charlie, it helped him to experience his mum as someone who understood him, and this felt good, even though he felt ashamed that he had kicked his friend. This also links in with a concept I touched upon in Chapter 1, namely that it is easier to influence others when they have had a feeling of being understood and connected with. Nowhere is this more important than when disciplining your child. The Two Hands concept helps your child see that you are trying to understand their thoughts and feelings and point of view. In the previous example, feeling understood by his mother made it easier for Charlie to accept the later consequences.

Authoritative vs authoritarian parenting

One of the many questions that friends raised when I discussed this book with them was 'Am I supposed to always see things from my child's point of view then, and never tell them that they are wrong, or have been naughty?' It was interesting that often people equate being empathic and 'mind-minded' with letting children get their own way and take control. Empathy can be seen as somehow letting children get away with things. This is not the case, and I hope that this chapter will assuage this myth and instead look at the powerful role that the skills I suggest in the Parent APP can play in achieving a better relationship with your child and resolving difficult behaviour and exchanges. I want to address this issue by showing you the difference between two styles of parenting: authoritative and authoritarian.

A line I often hear from parents saying is 'He doesn't respect my authority'. In a conflict situation, whether it's a major or minor fallout, the issue of who is in control and whose voice and opinion carries the greater weight can be one that generates extremely strong feelings, in both parent and child. I would like to show you how you can use the Two Hands approach and keep an *authoritative* stance with your child so that you understand how they are feeling, while simultaneously managing their difficult behaviour. This is quite a complex thing to do, and most of us won't be doing this a lot of the time. However, when we do manage to take this approach, it's notable how quickly and significantly things change, both in the way your child is behaving and how you both relate to and feel about one another.

It is generally thought that being authoritative is a good thing and something that children both need and respond to. It's important, however, to be clear about the difference between being authoritative and *authoritarian*, and the benefits of one over the other.

In contrast with authoritarian parenting, which involves high levels of parental control, exerting power, and strict all-or-nothing boundaries without any explanation, authoritative parenting is about achieving a balance between granting too much freedom (as is the case with permissive parenting) and being too strict.

The benefits of authoritative parenting

Contrary to how the word may sound, authoritative parenting is an approach to parental control that emphasises empathy, parent-child communication, and a rational explanation of rules. The authoritative parenting style is about setting limits, reasoning with children, and being responsive to their emotional needs. This approach is linked with very successful outcomes in children when it comes to managing behaviour and achieving harmony in the relationship. It is also linked to secure attachment between children and their parents. Managing conflicts and misunderstandings in your relationship with your child using an authoritative approach would involve being able to balance the two hands well; this would make children less likely to engage in antisocial behaviour and be more well-behaved. This is borne out by research that suggests that having at least one authoritative parent can make a big difference to how a child behaves (7).

So what are the criteria for authoritative parenting? What will this look like if you practice it with your child?

The qualities of authoritative parenting

With an authoritative parental approach, you will be nurturing and responsive to your child and show them respect as a rational individual, with thoughts and feelings that are separate from yours. You will start with the expectation that your child will cooperate with you and you will expect a level of maturity from them, while at the same time offering them the level of emotional support appropriate to their age. It is important to emphasise that authoritative parents don't let their children get away with bad behaviour, unlike permissive parents, who don't enforce rules and boundaries, often expressing a wish to be their child's friend rather than a parent figure. As I emphasised with the Parent APP, it is important to show empathy, to see things from your child's perspective, and to be *mind-minded* in your approach to your child's behaviour. In addition to these elements, you will need to emphasise and enforce the rules for appropriate behaviour with your child and give not only the rules but also the reasons for these rules. Taking this 'complete' approach allows your child to see that you are being explicit about what's going on in your mind and that your role as the parent entails responsibility for both caring for your child and managing their behaviour. The message you will be giving your child when you parent in this way is that you expect them to behave responsibly.

When you treat your child with this level of respect, during a misunderstanding or incident of bad behaviour, you will attempt to reason with them and to explain the consequences of good and bad behaviour. And, importantly, when you treat your child in this way, it is much more likely that you will get a good outcome, both in terms of their behaviour and in your relationship with one another. I must emphasise that this is not about letting your child off the hook and condoning what is unacceptable behaviour, but it is about setting a boundary around the behaviour and trying to show your child that you are interested in learning what lies beneath the behaviour, that is what's going on inside their head – showing them how their behaviour affects others, and how they can change it in the future.

When you adopt this type of respectful and thoughtful approach, you also avoid the negative consequences of a more authoritarian approach, such as harsh punishments that shame your child, or having to withdraw affection from your child, which is completely unnecessary, even if your child has behaved very badly in your eyes. With a more authoritative approach, you give children the space to consider the consequences of their actions and work out themselves better ways to behave.

Let's look at the following example and how the two different parenting styles would influence the management of the child's behaviour:

> Rachel walks into the sitting room at home and finds her 7-year-old daughter Lilly smashing up her dolls tea set and kitchen, throwing all the pieces around the room in a fury, and hurting her baby brother Jack with one of the tea cups. Jack starts screaming, and Lilly carries on pulling her kitchen set to pieces and chucking it around the room, so that pieces are flying into walls, the TV screen, everywhere.

Authoritative approach

The authoritative approach to dealing with this situation might look something like the following:

> Rachel walks into the sitting room, her expression is serious, but also curious as to what all the noise was about.

Seeing the scene, she gives all her attention in the first instance to Jack, and begins by immediately checking if Jack is hurt or injured. Having established that Jack is okay and comforted him, she then puts him into a safe place. Rachel then tells Lilly in a very firm voice to stop throwing her toys around the room immediately or she won't be allowed to have her friend Amy round to play later that day. She gets down to Lilly's level and asks her why she is so angry. Lilly is too angry and upset to be able to articulate how she feels, so Rachel hazards a guess and asks if anything happened to her kitchen and tea set to make her feel so furious. Lilly screams that Jack tried to take her best tea pot from her, and wrecked her kitchen hat she'd spent hours setting up in the process. Rachel says that that must have been extremely annoying when she'd spent so long putting it all together, but it's never okay to hurt someone, and so she is taking her new tea set and kitchen away for now and wants her to apologise to Jack for hurting him. When she sees that Lilly is still really furious and too upset to be able to apologise just yet, Rachel takes her onto her knee and wipes her face telling her that can see why she is so mad, but she underlines that it is never okay to hurt anyone. Lilly's cries start slowly to subside, and feeling that her mum knows how hurt she felt by having her brother spoil her game, she finds that she is more able to think about whether Jack is hurt or not, and goes into the other room to see if he's okay. Before she leaves the room, she checks whether Amy is still coming over to play later. Rachel says she can come as long as Lilly makes friends with Jack and says she is sorry for hurting him. She tells her, though, that she can't play with her tea and kitchen set now and must put it away. Lilly is cross about this, but Rachel insists that her playtime is over for now. Rachel adds, 'I will tell Jack that she mustn't take your toys when you're playing with them, because that's really annoying isn't it?'

We can see in this example how the Two Hands approach helps Rachel to balance showing an understanding of what might be lying beneath Lilly's behaviour with holding a line around managing her behaviour. In one hand, she is using the Parent APP, showing a curiosity in why Lilly got so angry and trying both to see Lilly's perspective and to get Lilly to see how her brother feels. She is also providing empathy to her. In the other hand, she is giving a consequence for Lilly's actions that lets her know that there is a firm boundary.

Authoritarian approach

An authoritarian approach to the above scenario might look something like this:

Rachel, hearing the noise from the sitting room, walks in with a scowl on her face and shouts at the top of her voice, 'What on earth are you doing Lilly? Did you hurt your baby brother? You naughty child.' She goes straight over to Lilly, snatches the tea set out of her hand and throws it aggressively to the floor, shouting that she is going to throw all her new toys into the bin for being so naughty. All her attention is on Lilly, and Jack is still crying. Lilly starts to cry more loudly as well now, and hangs her head down in shame. 'I'm going to tell your dad what a naughty girl you've been when he comes home Lilly, and you can forget Amy coming over to play. She's not coming, and it's too late to make friends with Jack. You've hurt him.'

If we look at what is communicated in the first, authoritative approach, we can see that Rachel gives a punishment for Lilly's behaviour (Lilly is not allowed her toys anymore, and Rachel gives all her attention and empathy initially to Jack). She sets down a clear boundary around her behaviour, telling her that she isn't allowed to throw toys or to hurt her brother. She also keeps hold of the boundary that unless she can empathise with her baby brother and communicate that she is sorry for hurting him, she won't be able to play with her friend later. At the same time, she shows Lilly that she can see things from her point of view, too. While it's not okay to hurt her brother, it is understandable that she is really cross with him for messing up her game when she spent so long setting it up. The empathy, perspective taking, and 'mind-minded' approach that Rachel takes means that the outburst is soon resolved and Lilly calms down. She takes some responsibility for her own actions but at the same time feels understood. The key elements to Rachel's authoritative approach here are that she shows a level of warmth, while emphasising the reasons for her rules, thus teaching Lilly something important about both her own behaviour and how it affects others. Plus she gets to understand the reasons behind her mother's actions, so although this may be difficult for her to accept, it is clear and understandable and can be taken further forward into the next time there is a misunderstanding between her and her mum or an argument with her brother. Rachel has helpfully given Lilly some important feedback about her behaviour and about the boundary she sets around this behaviour, while still maintaining a warm and loving relationship with her. Rachel keeps Lilly's sense of shame small and helps her to resolve these feelings and stay connected with her.

In the second authoritarian approach, Rachel gives all her immediate, negative attention to Lilly, therefore communicating straight-away that bad behaviour gets attention. She then goes on to criticise not the behaviour but Lilly herself, labelling her naughty. This leads to feelings of deep shame and upset in Lilly, who then can't resolve or understand how she's feeling but instead feels at the same time blamed and misunderstood. Struggling to make sense of her fury, because no one has been able to reflect this back to her, her feelings of distress escalate until she is crying uncontrollably. In this frame of mind, she is unable to empathise at all with her brother as her ability to think about other people's minds is totally lost in her own heightened emotional state. She loses the playdate with her friend and her toy at the same time.

Taking an authoritarian approach often involves exploding with anger towards your child or punishing them by withdrawing affection. You may find yourself resorting to bribing your child in order to get him to comply. While it may feel as if some of these things work in the moment, they are generally not found to be good strategies for either changing future behaviour, or for having a harmonious relationship, and so conflicts end up unresolved, and potentially escalate very quickly, and future conflicts are likely to be even more dramatic. This type of approach also leaves children feeling insecure, both about themselves and about the relationship with you, their parent.

REFLECTIVE PARENTING SUMMARY

AUTHORITATIVE PARENTING

What do we mean...

Taking a Reflective Parenting stance to managing your child's difficult behaviour means seeing the times when your child misbehaves as an opportunity to support their emotional development and to help them to understand themselves and others. Bringing Two Hands to discipline means both responding to your child's inside story to their behaviour as well as responding to the behaviour itself.

It helps you by...

Disciplining your child in this way will make it more likely that you understand your child and their behaviour. This different focus allows you to connect quickly with them, whilst being effective in your discipline. This combination prevents negative interaction cycles, which in turn means a reduction in problematic behaviour over time and an increase in positive behaviour. When you take a reflective, but authoritative stance, you offer your child consistency, predictability, and safe boundaries within which they can express their feelings and respond to your limits.

It helps your child by...

The times your child misbehaves are excellent opportunities to support their emotional development and to help them to understand their own thoughts and feelings and other people.

Taking time to understand and respect their point of view, and then to actively reconnect, aids their emotional development, reduces shame, and brings feeling of security within the relationship with you.

It helps your relationship by...

Maintaining a Reflective Parenting stance during discipline will help your relationship by allowing you to stay connected during disagreements or reconnected quickly afterwards to understand what happened. Repairing ruptures in your relationship will help bring you both closer together. You will be a more authoritative parent, bringing consistency, calmness, and mutual understanding and giving your child a clearer understanding of the motives behind your actions.

Keep in mind...

1. In healthy relationships, there is conflict and children misbehave. This is normal.
2. You and your child have different perspectives; after all, you are two very different people, and so conflict and bad behaviour is to be expected.
3. Find ways to stay connected with your child, during or after conflict.
4. Think about dealing with difficult behaviour with having two hands – one hand for responding to the behaviour and the other hand for understanding the reasons underlying behaviour (getting an inside story).
5. Encourage your child to talk about their feelings.
6. Respect your child's opinion and encourage them to express these opinions, even if they are different from your own.

Being authoritative is a good thing. You should expect your child to cooperate but also offer them emotional support. Set a boundary and rules that you expect them to comply with. Afterwards show warmth and empathy.

7

PARENTING AROUND NEURODIVERGENCE AND TRAUMA

In the 10 years since writing the first edition of *Reflective Parenting*, I've witnessed a significant change in the language and approaches used around people who are neurodivergent. In my own clinical practice, I've noticed a sharp increase in the number of families seeking a diagnosis for their child and in adolescents seeking their own diagnosis or understanding of themselves. How you feel about this increase depends on your perspective. Personally, I view it largely positively, as I see strong evidence of people managing their mental health and their relationships, far better when they have an understanding of their mental health and their relationships themselves; helping them reach this understanding is the main aim of any diagnosis I give. However, I also understand that many people feel that labels can be stigmatising, leading to a division of neurotypical and neurodivergent people, with the inherent implication of 'typical/normal' versus 'atypical/not normal.' Alongside this increase in people seeking a diagnosis, I've witnessed an increase in the training programmes for people working to support the mental and physical health of people with autism spectrum disorder (ASD) (see 'Note on Language,' below), co-delivered by people with a diagnosis of ASD. Programmes such as those led by educational consultant and neurodevelopmental specialist Dr. Georgia Pavlopoulou, Professor at University College London, have made a huge difference to the lives of people with ASD. These approaches take what is referred to as a trauma-informed approach, taking into consideration that the majority of people with ASD have experienced traumatic events as a result of their neurodivergence that have impacted their mental health. For example, a child with ASD who has found it hard to establish a strong friendship group will have experienced a degree of trauma within the school setting where they felt repeatedly rejected, misunderstood, or, at worst, shamed, for not fitting in to the group

DOI: 10.4324/9781003483762-8

norms. Autistic children with and without a learning disability are three times more likely than their non-ASD peers to experience trauma that may expose them to violence and bullying (1). Experiencing adverse events and trauma more frequently, combined with a genetic vulnerability when it comes to self-regulation and understanding others, makes people with autism more susceptible to the consequences of experiencing adverse events (2). Researchers have found that social confusion, misunderstanding and rejection by others might lead to raised anxiety levels, affecting resilience to cope with stressors. A possible consequence is a severe overload in (young) adults with autism and their family and friends. This can lead to a range of additional problems in the areas of attachment, identity, anxiety and mood symptoms and subsequently a maladaptive way of regulating themselves through, for example, compulsive behaviour, restrictive eating, socially isolating themselves and/or substance use (3).

Note on language

In this chapter, I will use the term ASD, for autism spectrum disorder, rather than autism or Asperger's or autism spectrum condition (ASC). I am acutely aware that there are diverging opinions on the language used around describing children and young people on the autistic spectrum, and I have chosen to use the acronym ASD because it is most familiar to the families and young people I work with. I also often use the term 'neurodivergent' with young clients where this is their preference. Many adolescents I work with prefer to refer to themselves as neurodivergent rather than autistic, and I understand and respect this. My only concern is that children and young people develop an understanding of their own identity and that this understanding helps them to feel comfortable in their own skin, and feel more able to be their authentic selves.

Why focus on ASD?

Many parents picking up this book will have children with neuro-developmental differences other than ASD, such as attention deficit hyperactivity disorder (ADHD), dyspraxia and other specific learning difficulties. I have chosen to focus on the autistic spectrum, partly because this is one of my areas of interest and specialism but also because this group of children have specific difficulties in mentalizing. ASD has a strong genetic component and because I work with many parents who may consider themselves on the spectrum (often undiagnosed), I notice that these families can experience great difficulties, with different perspectives leading to frequent misunderstandings and emotions running high. Adopting a Reflective Parenting approach can be extremely useful for this group of parents, helping to bring about greater connection and feelings of being understood. That is not to say that if you have a child with another developmental difference, you couldn't use the same approach advocated here, for *all* children will benefit from you trying to understand their particular perspective.

According to the National Autistic Society (NAS), more than one in 100 people are autistic, and there are at least 1.3 million autistic adults and children in the UK. These numbers are not the same as the number of people with an autism diagnosis, but based on research about the likely true figure. The NAS offers support and information for parents of children with ASD and for young people themselves. They state that people of all ages, genders and ethnicities can be autistic, but people from marginalised groups, such as from minoritised ethnic groups or from no income families, face more barriers to getting a diagnosis.

The autistic spectrum

In the past, people thought the spectrum was a straight line between 'more' and 'less' autistic, which is incorrect. Today we understand the spectrum to mean each autistic person has a unique combination of characteristics. Autistic people can be very different to each other, with different sets of strengths and challenges.

Some of the most frequent difficulties that parents of ASD kids experience include dealing with restricted eating, which may include things like sensitivity around textures and tastes, sensitivities around areas such as the texture of clothes and materials, smells and sounds; rigid thinking patterns; excessive talking and detailed monologues; a need for routine; difficulty with change and transition; sensory sensitivities that make new places hard to accept; difficulty in sharing and perspective-taking; and sometimes (although not as commonly as described) difficulty with empathy, lack of friends despite wanting friendships and unstable relationships. Although not required for diagnosis, children with ASD also often display physical clumsiness and an unusual or idiosyncratic use of language.

The presence or visibility of certain characteristics can vary a lot between autistic people. These characteristics can also change over time, in different situations or if the person is 'masking.' Masking is more commonly found in girls than boys and involves the child with ASD working extremely hard to observe the way people interact, to mimic this in social interactions and to hide their true selves to fit in with a group. Masking can be exhausting for children and young people, and although it often leads to greater acceptance among their peers, it can result in burn out and sometimes low mood and poor mental health as the young person with ASD is unable to be their authentic self for fear of rejection. ASD is not a learning disability or a mental health condition, but a third of people with ASD also have a learning disability and ASD people are more likely to experience mental health problems.

A word about attention deficit hyperactivity disorder

Currently, there is an increase in the number of people being diagnosed with ADHD, and sometimes people with ASD will also have attentional difficulties. There is a certain amount of disagreement surrounding a diagnosis of ADHD in children and young people. Clinical psychologist Tom Manly, from the Medical Research Council Cognition and Brain Sciences Unit at Cambridge University, is extremely well qualified to help our understanding of attentional problems in children, having studied attention in children and adults for around 30 years and authored two versions of the 'Test of Everyday Attention for Children,' a quite widely used neuropsychological tool in the diagnosis of ADHD. Manly's view on ADHD is that we all sit at various points on a scale of attention capabilities, including our ability to focus attention, resist distraction, sit still, wait our turn and so on. For people at either extreme of these continua, it could be a problem that interferes with their ability to achieve other goals (for example, educational, occupational, or social) and they might benefit from help. If we need to call it a 'disorder' to get this help, so be it. We could use height as a readily understood example. We all vary somewhat in height. For people in the shortest 5% of the population, in some situations this could be a problem that requires extra help. Similarly, those in the tallest 5% may also struggle in a world built for people closer to the average height. We could call each end of the height continuum a 'disorder' if it helped people get the relevant assistance.

In the UK education system, formal diagnoses are often a requirement or can be of assistance, to get extra help through a 'statement of special educational needs.' However, having a diagnosis certainly doesn't automatically bring additional support or services, as many parents of children with special needs can testify. There are other ways in which having a diagnosis can help, for example, to help ensure that parents, teachers, colleagues and partners are more understanding and not thinking that a child is simply not trying hard enough or is not listening purposefully to irritate others. A diagnosis may also help young people facing these challenges show more self-compassion and feel less of a failure. In terms of treatments, there can be benefits to a diagnosis. For example, there is evidence that the drug *Ritalin* (methylphenidate) can reduce some ADHD symptoms and, hence, diagnosis could lead to access. However (and this is surprising), there is very little work on whether the drug has long-term benefits and it does have some unpleasant side effects. However, Tom Manly and I agree that diagnoses can also have downsides, for example, they lower others' expectations and exclude people with a diagnosis from opportunities or if they become a self-fulfilling prophesy or lower self-esteem.

So, apart from being at one end of normal variation is there any evidence that ADHD is a disorder like, say, diabetes is a disorder, where a well-understood mechanism leads to a certain set of problems and requires particular treatments? Not at the moment. To meet the current criteria for a diagnosis of ADHD, a person needs to exhibit 6 out of 22 possible behaviours, such as being fidgety and often 'on the go,' exhibiting difficulty waiting their turn and/ or being easily distracted. There is no blood test, brain scan, genetical assessment, cognitive performance measure, or other formal test involved in the diagnosis. Because of the way ADHD diagnoses are made, two people could receive a diagnosis *with no overlap at all in symptoms* or a person with five of the 22 criteria would not meet the diagnosis, despite their symptoms overlapping closely with a person who exhibits six of the necessary criteria. Furthermore, a high proportion of people with ADHD have other conditions, such as dyslexia, that create a complex diagnostic picture. It can be difficult and confusing for parents to try to navigate this system and receive a diagnosis for a child if that's what is desired.

Because of the complicated nature of ADHD diagnosis, including the analysis of neurone connections in brain imaging and the fact that the criteria for ADHD often shift because of disagreement between psychiatrists, rates of diagnosis vary hugely. For example, in some US states, >20% of school age boys have the diagnosis whilst, in the ostensibly rather similar France, the rates are less than 1%.

As the ability to pay attention relates to our capacity to mentalize, there is a strong argument for focusing on helping children to increase their attentional skills. If we think of learning to mentalize as being at the top of a developmental pyramid, then at the bottom of that pyramid is attention regulation, followed by emotion regulation. When we are able to regulate our focus, or attention, this leads to greater emotional regulation and, finally, to the ability to mentalize. Take the example of a small child who is looking around them and spots a bird in a tree. They point and possibly vocalise and their parent, following their lead, looks to where the child points and says, 'Ah, you like the birdy?' and the child smiles, feeling recognised and understood. In this example, the young child has been able to sustain their attention on the bird because their parent has followed their lead, which extends the period the child can pay attention for. In meeting them at their level, the parent helps their child to regulate their emotions. Imagine then that the parent says, 'I wonder if he's singing because he's happy, or if he wants some food?' The child will be able to mentalize (reflect on what the bird might be 'thinking' or feeling) because they will then have well-regulated attention and emotions. Any support you, or other people in your child's network, can give to increasing your child's ability to regulate their attention will help them to develop greater skills in mentalizing.

Think of your child's classroom as an example of how attention leads to mentalizing. Imagine a child is distracted in the classroom and unable to focus on what the teacher is asking them; next, the child is asked by the teacher how they feel about performing in the end of term show. It's highly likely the child will be unable to understand or respond to the question because they are too distracted to access their thoughts and feelings. A child whose attention is better regulated is not only able to take in the teacher's instructions but can also reflect on their state of mind and think about how they would feel performing in the show. Better regulated attention leads to more regulated emotions and a greater capacity for reflecting on thoughts and feelings.

Understanding misunderstandings within the parent-child with ASD relationship

In the previous chapter, I talked about the usefulness of understanding misunderstandings within your relationship with your child. How does this work, though, if you have a child who, due to their autism, finds it more difficult to see different perspectives and has particular sensitivities and a different way of thinking and interacting that are sometimes hard for you to predict or understand? In this chapter, I will walk you through the model of Reflective Parenting for children with ASD and will also talk about a different group of children who have experienced traumatic relationships in their early childhoods and are now either in the care of other family members (known as Kinship or connected care), in the care of local authorities (foster care), or living with their adoptive parents. This group of children may have experienced developmental trauma that can result in them experiencing difficulties in their relationships, behaviour and emotional lives; this, in turn, can make parenting these children more challenging. When things are not going well between these groups of children and their parents, it's all the more important for parents to remember their particular sensitivities. Applying a Reflective Parenting stance for both these groups of children will help support their needs and nurture their relationship skills outside of the family. The key thing to remember is that both children with ASD and those who have experienced early childhood trauma find it harder than other children to understand and be 'good' at relationships – but it's important to understand that *all* children want and need relationships.

How understanding others is difficult for children with ASD

Many parents fall easily into ineffective mentalizing; that is, they say, 'Oh, he can't help it, he does that because he's autistic.' Although this might appear superficially to be an understanding of their meaning of the child's behaviour, it shows no actual curiosity about this behaviour. Let's step into the shoes of a child with ASD and consider how important it is to mentalize their experience once you are in a calm state of mind.

Children with ASD are thought to find social communication difficult because they struggle to be able to take another person's perspective. This can mean they interact differently to others, and their peers can find them difficult to relate to because they might appear to want to do things always in their own way. In fact, behaving in an inflexible way is more about their feelings of confusion about how exactly to do things anyone else's way. I want to discuss how, in my view, this group of children and young people do have the capacity to take another person's perspective and give and receive empathy. I appreciate that, in fact, this view is quite contentious with some professionals and it is important not to ignore the fact that people with ASD are not quite as good as neurotypical people at understanding the meaning and intentions behind people's actions. Research evidence shows (4), however, that people with ASD do have the networks in their brains for understanding meanings, but that these are just active to a lesser extent. Neuroscientists in the field of ASD are researching whether children and adults with ASD can in fact learn skills of perspective taking. Ranging from studies giving children oxytocin nasal sprays (sprays which release the naturally occurring hormone oxytocin that plays a critical role in sociability) to engaging in social skills training programs, to combinations of both, there is emerging evidence that the brains of people with ASD may not be quite so fixed as had been thought. Some studies show that when oxytocin is used together with intensive interaction (which involves use and understanding of eye contact and facial expressions, taking turns in exchanges of behaviour and developing and furthering vocalisations) with a responsive parent, children with ASD become significantly better at taking another person's perspective. The bad news is that this effect doesn't last for long after the intervention, so in fact the brain hasn't permanently changed at all, just learned a new skill, which can't be sustained.

While there is ongoing debate and research as to the extent that this group of children have minds that are flexible, I have made interesting observations in my own clinic on work that I have carried out with young people, and this, together with research on interventions with this group of children and young people (5), has led me to conclude that the idea of Reflective Parenting as a means to increasing the flexibility of these children's minds is an important and exciting one. It is important to note that most research and interventions focusing on children with ASD has emphasised ways in which they can learn the skills to fit in more with neurotypical children. I believe it is important to support ASD children to be their real selves and for others to make some adjustments.

Let's further the experience of children with ASD and try to enter into their world.

Sensory sensitivity

As well as finding it hard to appreciate things from another person's point of view, for children with ASD, sensory sensitivity can be a major issue. That is, the feel, smell, sound and sight of things in their environment are experienced differently and more acutely than others. Let's look at an example of a ten-year-old boy, Jacob, with ASD, and his mum Laura.

Jacob became highly agitated because he didn't want to wear the pair of trousers his mum suggested he put on for a family trip out. He got more and more distressed and angry, and eventually became tearful, running away from his family and hiding in his wardrobe upstairs. Laura eventually took the decision to go out as a family with him still wearing his pyjama bottoms as these were the only thing at the time he found acceptable and comfortable enough. She reasoned some people might stare, but most people probably wouldn't even notice that they were pyjama bottoms. At least her son would join the family on their trip out. After an hour or so wandering around, seeing her son happily chatting away to his brother over lunch, Laura approached him and asked tentatively, 'Everything alright now?' Jacob replied, 'Fine, sorry Mum. But you see, it might just feel a bit itchy to you, but to me, wearing those trousers is like being inside a termites' nest.'

Several important things strike me about this scenario. At first, Jacob was showing his distress through his behaviour and couldn't express what the real problem was, aside from that he hated the trousers his mum wanted him to wear. Notably, once he had calmed down (think back to the advice on striking when the iron is warm), he was able to say explicitly that what he felt was entirely his own experience – and one that might be very different to his mum's understanding – 'to me' being the important words. Once he was calm, he was also able to let his mum know that something she might perceive as maybe a bit itchy and uncomfortable, to him felt as uncomfortable as being inside a termites' nest. This description made it easier for Laura to relate to him, to get inside his experience, much more so than had he said, 'I just don't want to' or something similarly oppositional – which is what was usually shouted in the heat of the moment.

Sensory overstimulation can occur as a result of an ASD child's environment. If you have a child with ASD, you may be familiar with after-school scenarios where your child is exhausted or unable to control strong negative emotions after a long day spent trying to fit into school life. For some ASD children, the structure and predictability of school is welcome, whereas for others, the effort involved in fitting in to the social norms, understanding teacher's expectations and managing many different sounds, smells and general frenetic activities of school life can quickly lead to burn out. ASD girls can be particularly adept at masking their social anxiety by spending hours studying other girls in their social group and mimicking their interests, attitudes and even tone of voice, in order to be accepted in a group. You can imagine how exhausting it must be to have to hide your authentic self for six hours each day. Bearing all this in mind, it's unsurprising then that when ASD children come home from school, their emotional thermometer is in the red range and their capacity to mentalize is low.

Parenting children with ASD

It is easy to fall into gross generalisations when thinking about children with ASD. Clearly, like everyone else, children with ASD are individuals, and there is great variation between people on the spectrum, in the same way there is variation among neurotypical children. I have an adult son who has a diagnosis of Asperger's because that was still a diagnostic category at the time of his assessment, but now he would think of himself as having ASD, or describe his 'autism' in certain aspects of his processing and personality, but wouldn't necessarily refer to his differences much of the time. In thinking about parenting a child with ASD, and particularly thinking about the application of Reflective Parenting, it's helpful to consider that the majority of children with ASD find it challenging some of the time to think about what's going on in other people's minds. For parents, at times it can be especially hard to comprehend what this is like if you don't experience the same difficulties.

If you think about your ASD child, there are likely to be many ways in which you are genetically and physically similar to each other. It's likely that when you compare your child to their peer group, and even to their own sibling, there may be more obvious differences.

When two people are neurologically (and to a degree physically) different from each other, they have their own standards of what normal is because they each have a different life experience that is defined by their own neurology. A person's neurology sets the potential of what that person can do physically and cognitively. It is not possible to relate to the other person's experience unless you have a similar neurological system, so ASD and neurotypical people will never truly know what the other experiences. They can compare cirumstances, but those comparisons will always be based on their own experiences, which is not the same as going through the same set of events.

Let's take an example of a child called David with ASD who might think, 'If I know there is no more chocolate cake left in the refrigerator because I ate the last piece, I would assume everyone knows that the chocolate cake is gone.' We call this a lack of 'theory of mind' (6), because David shows a difficulty in understanding a situation from another person's perspective. Without a theory of mind, or with a poorly developed one, David couldn't understand why, say his brother, thinks there is still cake in the fridge. There are many other factors that affect 'theory of mind.' Tiredness, distractions, stress, familiarity of a topic, how well the other person is known, how socially stressed we feel, past events, future plans, communication processing issues and disorders (such as ADHD) can all affect our perspective-taking skills. Hopefully, it's therefore easy to see how, in this type of everyday situation, a child with ASD could struggle to appreciate different perspectives and come into conflict with their neurotypical sibling or family member.

One factor that often plays a part in these everyday scenarios is sensory sensitivity, mentioned previously. If we envisage a busy family mealtime, where multiple people are interacting and perhaps even speaking at the same time, David may be so socially overwhelmed and overstimulated he cannot function. He may have language processing issues, so when his brother asks why there isn't any chocolate cake left in the fridge, David might find it extremely hard to express his thoughts for a number of reasons such as a delay in processing words and their meanings, difficulty in timing verbal interactions and challenges getting his point clearly set up so he can speak clearly. Feeling overwhelmed, David's behaviour may explode, leaving him unable to explain his thinking that everyone else knew the chocolate cake was gone.

As a parent to a child like David, it's important to realise that, if you don't take these factors of their differences into account, you are asking a person who processes things differently to adopt and adapt to *your* way of communicating. Would you be the one with the difference, or 'disability,' if you were in a group of autistic people and trying to carry on a conversation? Would your ways of speaking and comments be seen as at odds with the group? Definitely yes. You would feel out of place if your flow of conversation would be inhibited because what you expect to happen is not happening. If you are a neurotypical parent parenting a child with ASD, then it's important to reflect on the adaptations you need to make to your style of communicating with your child and try not to focus on your frustration with your child's difference or difficulty in seeing your perspective. If you had a child who needed a stair lift to get up the stairs and a wheelchair to get around, would you try to make them walk? I'm confident you would make adaptations and adjustments to make sure they could access the world around them, taking their differences into account. By the same token, if you want to support your ASD child to access conversations, activities and relationships in the world, it's important to think about what adjustments need to be made *for* them and not to focus overly on what *they* need to do to adapt. In addition, though, you might also try to be more explicit about what you mean and be clearer when you explain things from your perspective.

It isn't possible to anticipate every situation your child will find distressing or difficult any more than you can mind-read other people in your family, but of course, it is enormously helpful if you can take time to talk through situations that you know are likely to be triggers for your ASD child. For example, many families I work with say that 'special' events such as Christmas and holidays can be particularly troublesome for their child (and consequently the rest of the family) as they are occasions where the routine is not adhered to and where, even objectively pleasant, events can take their child by surprise and then lead to great upset. It is also extremely hard trying to anticipate all the possible eventualities that you might need to prepare your child for.

Challenges to the ASD child's parent

Before I get on to the very practical steps of how to use a Reflective Parenting approach to help your child with ASD, it is important to look at the experience of the parents of this group of children. Whether you are reading this chapter as one of those parents, or know other parents who have a child with ASD, I hope it will help to reflect on the experiences of parenting a neurodivergent child and help you to become more open generally to experiencing and empathising with other people's perspectives. While I, too, have struggled at times in understanding my son's perspective on certain matters, I am hugely grateful to him for opening up my mind to his way of seeing things. Reflective Parenting, and specifically mentalizing, is all about appreciating that all minds are opaque, we cannot read other people's minds, and by staying curious and attentive to the perspectives of others, we can learn that everyone sees things in either slightly or vastly different ways to ourselves. If we can truly validate these different perspectives, while not necessarily adopting them or agreeing with them ourselves, then we step into someone else's shoes and give them the feeling of being understood. For a child with ASD, sadly, this feeling of being met at their level and understood in their perspective is often frustrated by other people's insistence that their way of seeing and doing things is the *right* way, and when the different perspective, thoughts and feelings of the child with ASD aren't tolerated, this leads to them being further isolated and can negatively impact their mental health. Simple kindness towards people with ASD is hugely important.

So one of the first things I'd like you to think about if you are a parent of a child with ASD is that your child is not neurotypical. This might sound like an obvious place to start, but I want to begin by recognising that for many parents, controlling your reaction to your child is extremely difficult. If you tune into these strong feelings in yourself, using your parent Map perhaps, this can firstly help you to maintain a sense of control of your own feelings and reaction to your child's behaviour. And secondly, keeping your child's difference from neurotypical children in mind can help you to understand your own feelings of loss, particularly of the so-called normal things that you expect from your child. Lastly, thinking in this way helps to pitch conversations and structure the environment around these difficulties; in other words, keeping this difference in mind helps you to think about changes you need to make to fit with your child's needs.

In accepting your child as being different, not neurotypical, you will undoubtedly have to face some difficult feelings of loss (for the child you may have expected to have) as well as anger, sadness and other uncomfortable emotions. It can feel very difficult to accept that your child is not able perhaps to have the kind of to-and-fro reciprocal conversation you have with others, including perhaps your other children. You may feel frustrated and irritated when your child continues to talk to you about something, regardless of the many signals you've given off that you have something to say or to do yourself – a common trait in children with ASD. Noticing, naming and accepting these feelings in yourself are important as they are very valid. It's at these moments that it's particularly important to reflect on what the actual limitations are that your child faces. It's a balance between accepting their differences or limitations and adopting a stance that encourages more flexibility in both your approach and in how you encourage your child to think about other people's points of view. Accepting your child's differences from neurotypical children should not mean that you can't adopt an approach that seeks to develop the skills that they are grappling with, particularly the fundamental ability to understand themself and others.

It is also important to understand the impact that having a child with ASD is likely to have on your emotional state. There will be times when you undoubtedly feel frustrated, incompetent or inadequate, and you might also feel angry with your child for not seeing things through your eyes. If you have a non-verbal ASD child with additional learning difficulties, you will have the added challenge of not always understanding what your child needs, which will be extremely frustrating for both of you. The key to Reflective Parenting is not to always seek to fix these situations or to have a perfect solution for these differences between you and your child but simply to learn to regulate your own emotions around your child so that you can help him or her become calmer and more able to communicate their thoughts, feelings and wishes to you in a way that makes you want to help and understand, rather than leaving you feeling frustrated or wanting to reject or ignore them out of anger or upset.

Difficulties experienced by fathers of children with ASD

Generally, fathers have fewer outlets than mothers for both everyday interaction with other parents or for their feelings about their children. Being the parent of a particularly challenging child with ASD can lead to feelings of alienation, and I know of one father who said that he felt so angry at seeing other dads enjoying 'normal' activities with their sons, such as football on a Saturday, that he avoided other parents, choosing to retreat into the safe world of his work instead. Another father described a difficult interaction with his son with ASD and then said that afterwards, as he sat on the train going to work, he had had a strong mental image of his child 'floating away in space in a space suit, out of my reach.' Talking to other fathers of children with ASD and sharing experiences can be helpful for dads. The father I've described found that sharing their experiences with another dad of an ASD child and talking about their feelings of anger helped to normalise the experience of parenting his child. He also found that trying to imagine what this feeling of being disconnected might feel like for his child helped him to feel more empathic towards him. Of course, feelings of loss and sadness apply to both dads and mums and can often get overlooked or suppressed as the pressure on parents to be achieving and enjoying every experience is strong.

Feeling disconnected from your child

The feeling of disconnection between parents and children with ASD is a common experience. Just as important as the impact of you as a parent on your child's ability to regulate his own emotions is the impact your child will be having on you and your own capacity to regulate your emotions in his presence. Parents can experience a profound lack of emotional connectedness with their ASD child that feels qualitatively different from the experience of being with a child without ASD. I was working with a family recently in my practice where I assessed a 17-year-old boy and diagnosed him with ASD. As part of this assessment, I always interview parents about their child's early development and ask about their experiences of their relationship with their child. This young man's mother broke down in tears as she described feeling her son wanting to withdraw from her and her longing for just one hug. She found it helpful to understand that he found physical contact uncomfortable – and to understand this wasn't necessarily just about his ASD but also about being an adolescent boy. It was important to give her space to acknowledge and express these feelings and to feel validated in her profound sense of loss and disconnect. It also raised another underlying worry about whether her son was depressed. The sense that you are not being related to on an emotional level as a human being, with feelings, thoughts and emotions of your own, can be experienced as alienating and unsettling. With these strong parental feelings in mind, let's look at the example from a parent of a child with ASD who came to see me.

Keisha is a young mum who has two daughters, Aleisha, aged 6, and 18-month-old Ruby. Keisha recalls in her first assessment that in the relationship she has with Aleisha, she feels as if there is a 'black cloud hanging over us.' In taking an early history, I learned that Aleisha's dad died, and that there had been a less than ideal relationship with him before this, as he came in and out of Aleisha's life. Keisha also said that she had suffered from postnatal depression. I started to think with the family about the origins of their difficult relationships, which started in the first few years of their life with their children. The history of Aleisha's early development, and the observation of Keisha and Aleisha in a ten-minute play session, revealed a striking lack of emotional response from Aleisha, despite the number of times Keisha initiated interaction with Aleisha and the number of invitations she offered to enjoy some close, warm time and physical contact with her. When I asked more about the relationship, Keisha acknowledged that well before Aleisha had lost her dad, she had felt that it had always been a struggle to feel a really strong emotional bond with Aleisha. I asked about everyday interactions and shared pleasures, and Keisha said that when they watched television, whereas Keisha would get involved in the relationships of the characters and their lives, Aleisha only noted the superficial details, such as how they looked, and appeared to miss, or completely fail to understand, any of the dynamics between the characters. Keisha became upset when talking about the experience of being with her daughter and said, 'I feel guilty, but when I'm with Ruby, even though she's much younger, I just feel as if she's more with me, if that makes any sense?'

This feeling of being with your child, but somehow still feeling alone, is an important one to note if you are working towards trying to be a more reflective parent to a child with ASD. It is not as straightforward as simply mirroring how your child feels. For example, you may think they are feeling lonely because they've left a play situation, but they may very well not feel that lonely at all for much of the time and may in fact feel much more comfortable when they are on their own. Working with Keisha, I encouraged her first, by using the Parent APP, to tune into this state of mind both in herself, and in relation to how her daughter might feel, which helped her to shift from looking at what Aleisha does to looking at how Aleisha feels and relates. In this complicated dynamic, there are different feelings to attend to. First, Keisha needs to accept her own feelings of being emotionally disconnected from her daughter. Whereas she wants a shared moment of connection, her daughter Aleisha wants just to watch TV and isn't too concerned about this being a shared experience. The fact that Aleisha isn't concerned about this being a moment to share with her mum leaves Keisha feeling even more isolated. However, if she can pay attention to her own feelings and recognise that they are simply different from how Aleisha is feeling, it can help her to feel less isolated. After all, Aleisha may be enjoying having her mum present but not able to express this to her. If Keisha can make the shift to thinking about how Aleisha feels, this becomes an important one in helping Keisha think about how the world might be perceived from Aleisha's point of view. Although this shift might be uncomfortable, because it is often difficult to think about our children's deficits, it might start to have an impact on how Keisha understands and responds to her daughter. Ideally, this would eventually lead to Aleisha starting to observe her mum and to slowly pick up the skill of taking an interest in other people's perspectives and learning the social skills that come with this, even if this does not always come naturally to her.

Using an enhanced Parent APP with an ASD child

Being the parent of a child with ASD is likely to have a greater impact on your capacity to manage your own emotions than having a neurotypical child. Therefore, it is essential you devote a good amount of time – more than you would usually do – to understanding your own responses, thoughts and feelings, what I refer to as having an 'enhanced parent APP.' If you are well regulated and in a calm, mentalizing space (we would also think of this as in the 'warm' range on the emotional thermometer), this will allow you to consider the very different (usually much stronger) emotions your ASD child is experiencing.

Before you think about your child with ASD, it is worth asking the question, 'Is how you are feeling much more intense than how I am feeling about . . . ?' I often hear parents saying things like, 'I can't believe he's so upset about that pair of shoes he has to wear for school,' without asking themselves, 'I wonder *why* he is upset?'. It is very common for parents to tell us that their child doesn't just get mildly annoyed but is furious because a flickering light can feel like hot needles being stabbed into their eyes. It is important not to underestimate the very real discomfort they feel and instead note to ourselves that the experience is not exaggerated but is really experienced much more intensely. If, with your child, you try to think, 'A bit itchy to me is an unbearable termites' nest to you then you are on the right track to being more mind-minded. Using an enhanced version of the Parent APP with ASD children, as with looked-after children, will mean that you are focusing more than usual on trying to take their perspective. It might require a bit more work but bear in mind there is an accentuation of experience, be it sensory, emotional, or behavioural, and so taking your child's perspective on this becomes even more important, not only in helping them but also in bringing down the temperature of your own emotional response.

There are multiple examples of this that you may be familiar with as parents, such as noticing that mild irritations felt by you or another child may be experienced and exhibited as volcanic fury

161

by your ASD child. Again, these feelings are real and experienced with the intensity in which they are described. Finally, in the case of Jacob and his mum, notice that when Jacob was feeling more in control of his own emotions, he was able to see that he had had an impact on Laura's and had enough insight into this to say 'sorry.' Many parents in clinical sessions have commented that their child will seem to express remorse after an outburst, but that they are never sure if this is really meant or not. I would encourage you not to doubt this and to try to use this instead as a springboard for getting into a more mind-minded conversation about both how great it is that they must have noticed their behaviour was having an upsetting effect on you and also how much you appreciated that they want to try to change the feeling you are left with for the better. This can be said in really simple, straightforward words. Keeping in mind again that you are using an enhanced Parent APP, providing empathy also needs to be done at these critical points with an extra emphasis, as this helps to bring the emotional temperature of the situation down and make it more likely that your child can then go on to reflect on his behaviour. It is also important to tell your child when you think you got it wrong about what they were really thinking and feeling or why he behaved in a particular way. This helps to model your mind to your child and the difficulty everyone experiences – not just children with ASD – in getting to the heart of what is really going on in someone else's mind.

There will undoubtedly be differences about your child with ASD that should be celebrated instead of focusing only on a perceived deficit. For example, many children with ASD have great imaginations and will often rely on their imaginative world for comfort and stimulation when the challenges of relationships in the outside world become too much. Equally, their attention to detail and precision can be extremely useful in many situations. As long as you can understand your child's need for precision, by taking their perspective, then you will hopefully be able to get alongside your child and support them in using this strength to their advantage in life. Some children with ASD are very good at being able to see both viewpoints in an argument, without becoming emotional about either perspective – this can be a strength in adult life. And the ability to focus on an issue, without getting distracted from it, is a huge strength, particularly academically. There are many other strengths and differences from neurotypical children that can be celebrated, and one of the consequences of being a reflective parent with your ASD child is that you will start to pay attention and to validate their different perspective on life, which will not only enhance your child's self-esteem but will also increase the feeling of connection between you.

How to help children with ASD expand their awareness of themselves and others

Once you have been able to accept the limitations of your child, and very importantly your feelings about these, the next step to take is to start to help your child to learn how to appreciate other people's minds and to feel more connected to you and others. After all, the target for most parents of children with ASD, as well as to feel more connected with their child, is to help their child to feel more comfortable in the world, in their own skin, and in their relationships with others.

A common misperception is that children with ASD are generally poor both at recognising and naming emotions. Interestingly, ASD kids are able to identify well the emotional state they are experiencing themselves – in fact, if you are a parent of a child with ASD, you are no doubt very familiar with strong expressions of emotions from your son or daughter – but they are much less able to identify an emotional state in another person or to identify the complexity of thoughts and triggers for their own strong emotions. One practical way to tackle this issue, if you are a parent of a child with ASD, is to name emotions constantly in yourself and also in the world around you. This can be done in the most mundane of moments and doesn't have to be anything too complicated. Watching something on TV or on a device with your child offers lots of opportunities for commenting on the emotional states of others. For example, catching up on an old episode of the Simpsons together, you might say, 'I think Bart's feeling embarrassed by Homer again because he walks around the house in his pants!' or watching a drama about a child separated from their family, you could say, 'It must feel really lonely at times for Tracy, living in a home without her parents.' These statements or reflections demand nothing of your child, other than just to note what you've said, and hopefully start to notice that there is more to Bart Simpson than a skateboard and spikey hair, and that he actually has a set of emotions, related to the people and things happening around him. The more you introduce this 'mind-minded' approach to everyday conversations in the family, the more familiar your ASD child will be with commenting on what's happening on the inside as well as the outside of people. You can of course use this method when observing other members of your family and your child's friends at school so that you frequently and quite naturally comment on the states of mind of other people. At the start of the book, I talked about reflective functioning (RF) and how people who were high in RF were good at supporting their child's mentalizing skills because they commonly referred to mental states (thoughts, feelings, and wishes). Through repetition and rehearsal, over time, you can start to see real changes in how your child talks about people, which begins to include statements about people's states of mind as well as what they look like or behave like on the outside.

Mind-blind or mind-short-sighted?

Clinical psychologist at Cambridge University Simon (before Baron-Cohen) Baron-Cohen (6) coined the term 'mind-blindness' in the context of research he carried out called Theory of Mind in ASD children, and it is important to keep this concept in mind when thinking as a parent of an ASD child how you can be more mind-minded. Baron-Cohen and his colleagues described mind-blindness as a cognitive disorder, where an individual is unable to attribute mental states to themselves and others. In other words, the person is unable to think about their own thoughts and feelings or another person's. As we have talked about throughout this book, the understanding of your own mind and those of other people's is one of the key elements of Reflective Parenting. If you have a child who is not capable of seeing or understanding the beliefs and desires of others, you might wonder if being reflective can really help.

What would happen, though, if the environment the child lived in was constantly, rather than intermittently, providing perspective-taking training, or to put it another way, if there were to be a parenting environment created where the child's mind is at the centre and sitting right next to that is you, the parent, with your own thoughts about your child and the world? Within this kind of reflective environment, it seems perfectly possible that a brain that struggles to be social could become more so. Take the following example of a 12-year-old child with ASD and his parent, where the mum is trying to create this kind of environment.

Mum:	'Dan, did you remember to pack your stuff for Rugby later? You've got that after school remember? And there's a drum lesson at 3.20. Hang on, come here, are you wearing the same shirt you had on yesterday? I can see a stain down the front. Can you go upstairs and change that please before school?'
Dan (holding his head tightly and making a noise):	'Arghh, too confusing. Can you just stop talking mum? I'm not going to Rugby. I don't like Rugby any more. And I had drums yesterday. I can't change my shirt now, I'm going to be late. Arghh (holds his head again, covering his ears). You're making me really frustrated. Why are you shouting?'
Mum:	'I'm sorry. That was too much information all in one go wasn't it? It's confusing for you when I ask you about more than one thing at a time. And I shouldn't ask you just as you're getting ready to leave the house.'
Dan (taking his hands away from the side of his head):	'You were saying it in an angry voice.'

Mum: 'Was I? Well, sorry I didn't mean to sound
                          angry. I think I get a bit stressed in the
                          morning when there are so many things
                          to remember and I'm trying to get your
                          brother to put his shoes on, and listen to
                          him, too. I should tell you these things the
                          night before probably. We could have a
                          chat about it before bedtime. You know
                          what? The shirt doesn't matter either, it
                          might make you feel more confused and
                          rushed if you change that now. Have a
                          good day at school, love.'

Some people argue that if a child has 'mind-blindness,' as is thought
to be the case with autism, then trying to help that child to think
about himself and others may not be beneficial. So, in your relationship with your child with ASD, are you trying to be more
mind-minded with a child who is completely blind to your mind
and his own? I would suggest here that it is not mind-blindness as
such, but instead mind-short-sightedness. With this more hopeful
conceptualisation of the ASD mind, I would like to set out how as
a parent you can try to develop a more clear-sighted view of your
child's mind, from both the parent's and child's perspectives. I am
encouraged by my work with young people with ASD who, through
having an approach that focuses on the key elements of Reflective
Parenting (attention, perspective taking and providing empathy),
have been able to develop a greater capacity and skill in understanding that other people have thoughts and feelings appreciably
different from their own. I should stress again that perspective taking and providing empathy in particular need to be emphasised so
that the communication to your ASD child is clear. There is growing evidence that teaching perspective-taking skills to people with
ASD, using interventions such as video modelling of social skills
and interactions that encourage these skills, is effective.

One of the first things I noticed in my work with children and
young people with ASD is that during the initial assessment, they
were able to talk clearly about how they felt and how they felt in
relation to other people. As one ten-year-old said, prior to diagnosis, at a stage when he was feeling particularly unhappy, 'I know
there's something different about me. I'm just not like everyone else.
And I don't really 'get' other people.' This kind of statement is not

uncommon when assessing young people for traits of ASD, and it is this kind of insight that belies a greater capacity for reflecting on feelings, both in themselves and in others, than we might have previously thought possible. It's the foundations for this type of perspective taking that we want to help you build on if you are parenting a child with ASD and are feeling frustrated about how to help them develop better social relationships and insight into others.

Building up an understanding of emotions

So how can these networks in the brain for understanding the meaning and intentions of others be exercised so that an emotion-understanding 'muscle' is built over time, and other people's intentions can be better understood?

British psychologist Tony Attwood (7), an expert in the field of autism, comments that when a young person recognises that they are different from other children, a constructive response to this realisation is to observe people in order to try to analyse their behaviour and motives or to become an expert mimic of emotions in order to be accepted and included. If you spot your child or teenager with ASD behaving in this way, it's a very good sign indeed. One way of encouraging this is to try to persuade your child to take up a drama class, or if they can't face this, to mimic somebody they have seen on TV or in a film, or read about in a book. All aspects of pretence are great for the development of the skills you are trying to introduce them to, because they are all about entering into the mind of an 'other.'

Strategies for tackling an ASD child's behaviour

As a parent trying to communicate with your child in moments of high emotional arousal, you might find yourself unable to think, and your focus is on how to manage and control behaviour, as opposed to understand, empathise, and reflect back to your child. It will feel hard to apply the Parent APP in these particularly intense moments. However, if you think back to the idea of the emotional thermometer and striking when the iron is warm, you will hopefully be able to see that a good time to apply the Parent APP is when your child has managed to calm down a little. Although this is true for all children, if you again think that there is the need to use an enhanced Parent APP with an ASD child, it is even more important to mark out those times when you are waiting for your child to calm down and give them the feedback that you are doing this. For example, you might say,

> I know it is easier for you to think about what you want to do or say next when you are calm, and it all feels too confusing until you've done this, so I'm going to leave you alone until you feel a bit calmer and less confused, and then we can talk.

If you think back to the strategy of giving your child time alone, discussed in Chapter 5, it is important that you introduce this to your child and help them practise it at a set time of day perhaps, before you can suggest to your child that they use it to help them calm down or to regulate their feelings a bit better in the moment.

Trying to be more aware of how things look from your ASD child's perspective needs to be coupled with behavioural strategies that can be learned and rehearsed over time by your child until they become embedded in their skills, eventually enabling them to develop an unconscious understanding of the rules of social interaction. It's not actually as complicated as this sounds, and really amounts to helping your child to figure out when someone has good intentions and how to please people.

Behavioural methods such as showing your child safe ways to express and manage their anger, and rewards for not exploding with rage and keeping calm, are all helpful. You may find, though, that for your child there is a secondary gain in explosive anger, in that they may actually feel more in control at these times. As well as trying to manage their behaviour, try to name for your child what you think is happening, that is, try to help them understand this need for control.

Your child might have the need for control when they are feeling insecure or experiencing a sense that they don't feel connected to others, so it can be helpful to act and speak in a way that makes your child feel more secure at these times. Of course, our instinct at times like these is just the opposite. Parents find themselves, often to their regret, shouting at their child when their child is exploding, and if our understanding is correct, that it is at these moments that the ASD child is probably feeling a lack of security, this will only compound the feeling. Referring back to the Parent APP, using an enhanced version of this means that not only will you have to first get your own feelings under control, but then you will also have to work harder to see things from your ASD child's point of view, in order to help them feel better connected to you and less isolated.

Again, thinking back to the concept of striking when the iron is warm, it is nearly always better to step back, allow your child to calm down and, with a focus on keeping calm as your specific goal both for them and yourself, think about their feeling of insecurity and reflect this back to them, with a clear statement about how it must be; for example, tell them you can understand that it is very frightening and confusing to feel that you don't have control over things that happen.

Advantages of being reflective with your ASD child

Some might argue that we are trying to force children who are naturally more solitary to become something that makes them uncomfortable. Children with ASD may state a preference for being outside of a social group, without friends or close confidants. They may tell you, much to your concern, that they prefer to be alone. However, one of the reasons for promoting Reflective Parenting even more with this group of children is that there is a heightened risk that ASD children will be exposed to the kind of problems other, more social children may be naturally protected from. For example, they may be more likely to be bullied, get lost when going somewhere new when they are a bit older, or feel depressed and anxious. While it is important to respect your child's need for time on their own, time with their routines, comforts and moments where they are free from the confusion of interacting with others, I also want you to encourage a more relational existence because there is good evidence that being connected to and interacting with others offers some sort of protection from the harsh realities of life.

It is a common concern of parents with children on the autism spectrum, and parents with a child who is fostered or adopted, that their child struggles to make and to maintain friendships. Using an enhanced version of the Parent APP, particularly when it comes to helping your child learn to see things through someone else's eyes, is then especially important when it comes to helping your child to develop and maintain friendships.

In addition to helping ASD children develop relationships with others, Reflective Parenting also offers advantages to their educational placement. One large-scale study (8) found that where parents of children with ASD were able to see things from their child's point of view, and where the attachment between parent and child was secure, these predicted children's educational placement in inclusive programmes (an environment where individual educational needs are met) 4.5 and 8.5 years later, over and above the prediction offered by children's IQ and their interactive competence.

Connection not correction

I talked about the importance of connection not correction earlier in the book, and this is possibly even more critical for both the parent of a child with ASD and the actual child. Cast your mind back to the father who pictured his child floating in space in a space suit, far away from him and cut off from Earth. This image came to the father on his way to work after a particularly difficult argument with his son that morning. His son had been extremely agitated about going swimming and not being able to find his goggles. He then escalated this to feeling that they were the 'wrong goggles' because they were too tight on his head, until eventually he was curled up in a ball in the corner of his bedroom screaming and banging his own head because he didn't want to go to school at all. He couldn't articulate what he felt other than anger at this point, and his dad shouted back at him that he would be late for school and to get out of the house with his swimming kit. This exacerbated his son's feelings further.

We might try to understand his feelings a little better if we turn to his father's experience on the journey to work, and his vivid image of his son floating away from him in his space suit. Our understanding of this might be that his father was accurately reflecting on his own feeling of being unable to reach out to his son when he is distressed but also accurately tuning in to his son's feeling that he is alone in the world – feeling as if he is somehow detached. Connecting to this feeling at times when you might otherwise get angry can not only increase your empathy for your child but also, crucially, actually get him to do what is needed, or socially expected, at this particular time. Connecting in this way may be more successful than simple behavioural strategies and outright bribery. As I have said many times in this book, the impact on your child of your use of your attention, empathy and perspective taking is very powerful in changing the way your child behaves.

When your child is really angry, it can feel like they are being totally unreasonable and out of order, and you may feel as though your feelings and point of view are ignored. At these times, it is easy to slip into methods of parenting that are centred around controlling your child's behaviour. Feelings of resentment can quickly build when the behaviour we see is so difficult to manage, which does not naturally lead us to feel empathic.

Emotional overload

Try to imagine your ASD child as a can of fizzy drink. Each time you ask a question that is about emotions or relationships, you are giving the can a little shake. The drink gets a bit fizzier every time you ask another question, make another statement or introduce a seemingly complicated emotion into your child's mind. Eventually, the can becomes too fizzy and explodes. You've given it too many shakes. Try putting the can down on a nice, flat table and just letting it sit still. It stays fizzy but is much less likely to explode. A word often used by people with ASD in conversations about emotions or relationships is 'confusing.' This is actually a very accurate reflection and shows some capacity for thinking about other people's thoughts and feelings. Connecting with this confusion rather than trying to unravel it is probably the best place to start. After all, children with ASD don't benefit from explanations while they feel confused or 'fizzy'.

Learning to be more aware of other people's minds

Sarah, mum to a boy with ASD, was feeling sick and tired of coming in from work and being 'bombarded' by her son with ASD, along with her two other children, with the details of things they had done with their days, with no regard for her own feelings or thoughts on her day. Sarah's son with ASD, Harry, was particularly vociferous in relaying every detail about his day. Sarah decided to get him to practise asking her about her day when she got inside the house (and had taken her coat off) after she came in from work. Sarah noted that at first Harry only asked her a question in order to be able to then tell her about his latest progress on his favourite computer game. After a while though, she noticed that he began to ask her a bit more detail about her day, and seemed interested in whom she had spoken to at work. He even started to contribute ideas about how she might handle certain situations at work.

It is an interesting question whether Harry's questions were a socially learned behaviour. Or did he learn that there was something inherently rewarding and interesting about having a social interaction simply for the sake of it? A reciprocal to-and-fro conversation, simply for the sake of enjoying the conversation and finding out about someone else's mind? It leads us to reflect on whether in fact all social skills in childhood are initially learned behaviours that become gradually embedded and incorporated into children's understanding of and curiosity about other people's mental states? What Harry's mum noticed over time was that he started to generalise this 'How was your day?' question to asking other people about their lives, thoughts and eventually feelings about things. In other words, he started to become curious about the workings and inside story of other people's minds.

Young people in care with early developmental trauma

Where ASD children have an underlying neurodevelopmental reason for their difficulties in mentalizing, children in care often have similar difficulties due to a history of developmental trauma. At the start of this book, I looked at the origins of mentalizing and how a secure relationship in which the caregiver mirrors the thoughts and feelings of her baby helps them to develop an understanding of their own, and other people's, minds. What then is the developmental trajectory like for children who haven't had this experience in their early lives? This part of the chapter is for anyone looking after a child who has had an early experience of deprivation in their relationships. I have developed a model of Reflective Parenting for foster carers with the needs of this group of children specifically in mind (Reflective Fostering). Caring for a child who struggles to trust and understand other people, particularly in close relationships, is extremely challenging for any parent or carer, but the results from our clinical trial with foster carers show that offering this mentalizing approach has proven not only that foster carers can improve their relationship with their children but also that they can regulate themselves and feel more committed to the role and less burned out.

The number of children in care in the UK has been increasing, with an 8% rise in the last five years. There are currently around 104,000 children and young people in care in the UK. This includes approximately 83,840 in England, 12,596 in Scotland, 7,080 in Wales, and 3,801 in Northern Ireland. Many children are looked after away from their parents' home because of concerns about how their parents cared for them, and it's unlikely that these children would have received any degree of Reflective Parenting during much of their formative early years. For many different reasons, parents may find it difficult to keep the needs of their child at the forefront of their own minds. For example, they might find it hard to manage their own emotions around their child or struggle repeatedly to see their child's perspective, instead becoming fixed on negative perceptions of them and why they do things, which in turn might lead to punitive parenting. Or parents may continually overlook their child's needs, too preoccupied by events going on in their own lives. Essentially, what connects these scenarios is that the parents struggle to understand and truly connect with how their actions impact on their children.

Of course, it's unrealistic to expect parents to be constantly aware of how they impact their children; however, when this lack of awareness becomes chronic and extreme, children may be exposed to everyday situations that are traumatic, for example where there are high levels of violence in the parental relationship, or where children's basic needs for food and warmth are neglected. These experiences impact significantly on how children develop and continue to affect their behaviour even when they live in permanent alternative care. This section of the book is for the parents of these children, whether this be their foster parents, adoptive parents, special guardians or grandparents or other relatives (often known as Kinship carers) who take on the care of children in their families.

There is a great deal of extremely helpful research that informs adoptive and foster parents on how they can help their children, and really I am just touching upon this area here. However, the ideas around Reflective Parenting discussed throughout the book are highly relevant to carers looking after children who have been mistreated. A number of studies have identified how adoptive and foster parents can help their children work through earlier traumatic experiences. Interestingly, how well children adjusted in adoptive families was found to be dependent on how sensitive their adoptive mothers were to their thoughts, feelings and perspectives (9). In other words, the more reflective an adoptive mother was, the better the child appeared to recover from earlier difficult experiences.

As a note of caution, for children who are significantly struggling to overcome past trauma, there may be a clear role for specialist help and I would certainly advise an assessment or advice from a mental health professional.

What makes these children's lives more difficult?

In many cases, children who come into care have been constantly overlooked or misread by their parents, who consistently failed to notice or think about what was going on inside their child's mind. The parents would also have been unaware of their own emotions and how they came across to others. When a child has had such flawed relationships in their past, this can lead to frequent misunderstandings between a new carer and the child, hence the need to devote space specifically to consider this group of children.

> *One-year-old Suzie had developed a painful ear infection that was especially aggravating at night. She cried often. Her mother found the noise irritating and could not stand being woken up. She felt got at, as if Suzie was fussing and annoying her on purpose. When Suzie needed comfort and nurture she instead received anger and negative messages from her mother.*

Such negative interactions can involve direct harm and maltreatment, such as neglect, abuse and abandonment, and some children witness traumatic and terrifying situations at home, such as parents being hit or sexual abuse of someone in the family by an adult. These traumatic experiences come from the very people – the parents – a child would typically depend on to get through such difficult times. Ideally, parents help children feel safe and contained. Children can then concentrate on developing an awareness of their feelings. In a safe parental relationship, they can also learn about how to relate to and connect with other people. However, in harmful situations, when a parent is a confusing mix of a source of safety and fear, the child finds themself in an environment where they are unable to develop the skills necessary to enjoy healthy relationships. Instead, children like Suzie can be stuck in a highly emotionally arousing and distressing environment at developmentally vulnerable times. Remember the emotional thermometer? It is as if Suzie's mother's is stuck on high, and, inside, Suzie's thermometer is, too. When children experience life in this way, there is a complex difference to how their brain grows and the structures within it are formed. A child's development of the orbitofrontal cortex (an area in the front of the brain) is influenced by interactions with their parent and this is critical to his future capacity to manage emotions, to appraise others' emotional states and manage stress. These traumatic family situations show how critical the role of the parent–child relation-ship is in developing emotional, psychological and neurobiological abilities.

How do challenging and traumatic early experiences affect children later on?

Adoptive and foster parents can often find their children's behav-iour confusing, hard to deal with and persistent. If you are one of these parents, or know of a child who is in care, it is so important that you understand and recognise some of the ways your child has been impacted by his previous experiences.

Stress and how children experience emotions

Chronic stress affects certain structures in the brain that are linked to the ability to think rationally and make good choices in stressful situations. So when a young child is exposed to the chronic stress that comes with insensitive and traumatic parenting, their mind is maturing at a time when they are feeling unsafe and they are preoc-cupied with survival. They will therefore have higher levels of stress hormones, even when their body is at rest. It is as if the stress from the trauma causes their brain to be 'rewired' to function as if it is in a constant state of high alert, and they remains ready to protect themself from danger in an instant through aggression, withdrawal or zoning out. The important point here is that their mind will con-tinue to work in this way even when they move to a loving and sensitive family; they will still get easily stressed and emotionally aroused, more reactive and take longer to calm down.

> When Suzie was four years old, she moved to her adoptive family. Her parents were puzzled as to why she became dis-ruptive and hyperactive when people came to visit. Suzie would hit out and seemed constantly to seek her mother's attention. Rather than jumping in and dealing with the behaviour as it happened, her parents stood back from the situation and realised that Suzie became stressed when there was a change in her environment, when she would become excitable and disruptive. They decided to limit the number of times people visited until Suzie became more settled and they saw progress in other areas.

If you are an adoptive or foster parent reading this, you may feel puzzled and frustrated by patchy progress in your children. One month it can seem that they have settled down only for things to regress the next month. However, thinking about these ups and downs in a child's behaviour as normal can help adoptive and foster parents to cope with difficult behaviour and not become downhearted when things aren't going well. Specific spikes in your child's difficulties can often be traced back to stressful events, such as a transition to a new school, holidays, birthdays, peer difficulties, puberty, the start of a meaningful relationship, stress in family relationships or moving house. These times of change can be especially difficult for looked-after children as they are less able to cope with instability and uncertainty. Persevering and pushing through stressful situations is a challenge and your child will need help to identify that stress is affecting them. Sometimes, the triggers can be much less obvious and subtle, such as a touch, smell or even a feeling associated with previous trauma.

I outlined in Chapter 1 how babies and infants rely on the adults around them to help work out how they are feeling. When an infant feels upset, they look at his parent's face for an explanation of how they feel, a bit like a mirror being held up to reflect an image of their internal world that says, 'You are upset!' Feelings become understandable and linked to events. But what happens when parents are not interested in holding back a mirror? Research has shown that children who had been neglected found it harder to discriminate different emotions in the faces of other people (10), which meant

that understanding other people's emotions was much harder, and it was harder to connect with others in meaningful ways.

What if a parent holds back a mirror that distorts and reflects different feelings than her child, feelings that are angry or hostile? How and what does a child learn about their feelings then, and how do they develop an ability to manage feelings? Imagine that when an infant feels upset, instead of seeing this feeling reflected in their parent's face they see aggression. In other words, looking at their parent can be scary! When children experience this, they become emotionally aroused and distressed and might either turn away from their parents, or look at their parents but zone out, or look right through them. Once a child witnesses their parents' unhealthy ways of expressing their emotions, trusting their own feelings becomes difficult and they become harder to understand, which can make emotions feel scary and overwhelming. The knock-on effect of this is that children who are exposed to overwhelming experiences can feel unable to cope with their emotions or lack the ability to understand them. There is a strong link between how much young children can use language to talk about their emotional life and the quality of their relationships with caregivers. Language delay is common in preschool children coming into care.

Earlier on I looked at how being able to understand emotions gives us greater control in how we behave. It follows that a child who has difficulty understanding emotions may find it extremely hard to manage their behaviour during periods of stress or intense emotion. Their ability to understand their own mind, to link together how they think and feel and to be curious about who they are is underdeveloped. No one has helped them with this before.

How can you understand misunderstandings together? A child would rather jump from one event to another without much reflection. They have limited curiosity about themself, why they do things, the impact they have on others and how emotions help us connect.

How children with traumatic histories see and 'do' relationships

What would it be like to grow up in an environment where you had to be alert and vigilant all of the time? It must be a bit like the difference between swimming in a shallow swimming pool and being in shark-infested waters. If you see a black shadow under the water, you would probably have two very different reactions: in the shark-infested water, you would probably feel certain that the shadow is a shark, a threat to you, even if you cannot see under the water. Your brain would slip automatically into the 'fight-flight-freeze' response, a physiological response to perceived threat whereby the body releases a combination of a neurotransmitter called epinephrine and various hormones, which work together to create a boost of energy. Well the same goes for children in chronically traumatic environments. They become hypervigilant to threat and danger, although in their case the threat is their parents.

This exaggerated response to a perceived threat, which, to your child, has been an adaptive and helpful way of functioning in the past, is brought into your home. Just as you cannot see below the water to see what the danger really is, they cannot see beneath your actions and understand what your intentions are when, for example, you ask them to stop doing something. People have been hurtful and punitive before to your child, and just as you wouldn't question what the shadow is under the water, they won't question your motives either, certain that they are negative. Their perception of you at times may become fixed and guided by previous situations in previous homes. This will be the case however kind and loving you are being, as this past experience of trauma is powerful and has become their 'script' for how adults will behave towards them.

> *Billy an eight-year-old boy in a foster home, was being told, 'No you can't go out on your scooter without your helmet.' Billy immediately reacted, saying, 'I hate you, you can't make me wear it! I hate you, you are mean!' Billy thought his foster parent was being horrible and didn't like him. He stormed off upstairs.*

I have discussed how children are sensitive to their parents' feelings. Well, your foster or adopted child might have become hypersensitive, especially to signs of negative emotion. Research has showed that children who had been physically abused interpreted and understood emotional signals in facial expressions differently from children who had not been abused (10). They actually over-rated anger and aggression in faces, seeing danger and threat where there was little evidence of these things. What would this be like for children? It is likely that a child would go into either a fight, flight or freeze mode. Figh-flight-freeze shows just one reason to be even more aware of how you are coming across. It is well established in the research that children who have experienced past traumatic relationships become hypervigilant to threat and also perceive threat, even where it doesn't exist. What might appear to be an irritated facial expression to one child is more likely to be experienced as angry to the child who has experienced early trauma, causing them to spin into a fight-or-flight response.

A child's ability to trust other adults is also compromised when they experience ongoing abuse or neglect at the hands of their primary caregivers, or when their caregivers are unable or unwilling to protect them from ongoing abuse or neglect. Children learn fear and self-reliance instead of safety and trust. This makes it doubly hard for a child to work through misunderstandings as they may not trust why you are asking them to think through situations.

A deep mistrust of adults skews how a child in care will experience your parenting.

How these children see themselves

In Chapter 4, I looked at the helpfulness of a small amount of shame in helping young children learn about acceptable and unacceptable limits. Experiencing shame motivates young children to not behave in a way that they predict will upset their parent. When being told off, the impact of shame is reduced when parents reconnect quickly with their children so they can still feel loved and valued. For example, a child has been told off for grabbing the pudding first before their playmate can help themselves to their serving. The parent reprimands them and says, 'It's polite to let your friend choose first.' Not wishing this feeling of shame to be a big deal, though, the parent then goes on to sit down at the table for tea and gives the child a reassuring hug. Unfortunately, some children are not given the opportunity to reconnect to a parent and instead can be left in a state of prolonged shame. Additionally, children tend to blame themselves for any negative events that happen in their lives and perceive that direct messages from parents back this up, for example 'If only you didn't cry everything would be okay!' or 'If you were a good boy Daddy wouldn't send you to your room.' What would this be like, how would you make sense of these experiences? Unfortunately, children can internalise this experience of shame, in turn affecting their psychological development: remember shame is an overall sense of being bad. A child is likely to conclude that they are unlovable, ineffective, helpless and worthy of rejection.

A child will then carry this negative perception of themself into their new home. So, getting told off, being disciplined or lectured all have the capacity to lead them into a state of shame. Children will avoid feeling this if possible, acting tough, getting angry, lying, denying, blaming others or refusing to talk about something that happened. Again, this makes understanding misunderstandings very difficult, as, for the child, an exploration of a situation and their behaviour feels a bit like getting them to admit what an awful person he really is.

What can you do to help your fostered or adopted child?

How can you parent a child whose mind has been so affected by past experiences? What are the challenges and how persistent can their difficulties be? Fortunately, there is good news: your child is not limited by their past traumas. They have strengths and toughness that can be built upon. Many children are able to recover and lead positive lives as adults. Also, through your care and Reflective Parenting, you are giving them the best possible chance of progressing to a satisfying and fulfilling life. You can offer a nourishing environment for them to grow and recover. Here are a number of specific things that you can do to help them recover. The ideas here essentially are the ideas explored in the rest of this book, just modified and with various aspects enhanced. They are:

1. Always keep in mind your's, your child's and the family's emotional thermometer
2. Create a shame-free zone
3. Use an enhanced Parent APP
4. Remember that two perspectives on the same thing can be entirely different
5. Create an environment of curiosity
6. Celebrate resilience

What do I mean by the family's thermometer? Well, this is thinking more generally about the rhythm of your house. How loud is it, how predictably do things happen? Do people shout down the stairs? Do random friends drop in without notice? Do you have set routines? Asking yourself questions like this about how your home functions and how things might impact on your child can really help you to consider what the best environment is for them. You might find that periods of quiet are actually harder for your child, and make them feel more anxious and stressed, in which case thinking about how to help them with these particular times becomes more important. Again, if you keep your child's sensitivity in mind, it will be easier for you to see that the environment needs to adapt to them, certainly at first, and not the other way round.

Some of the best ideas when you are holding in mind the idea of lowering the emotional temperature in the home come from thinking about the everyday parenting of toddlers. Toddlers thrive on predictability, structure, the authoritative parenting styles I described in Chapter 5 and a matter-of-fact approach to behaviour – just the things that your sensitive child needs to feel secure.

Chapters 2 and 3 discussed the importance of being aware of how you feel. This is so very important for children recovering from traumatic experiences, whose thermometer is sensitive and set on alert, and who are watching you and expecting negative things to happen. This may not be obvious at all in some situations or may present itself with a sudden outburst or refusal to follow a direction. So being more aware of how you are coming across is vital, as when a child's emotions are highly aroused, this can overwhelm them and spin them into a fight-flight-freeze response.

Some additional ideas to help you lower your emotional thermometer include

- Remind yourself that you are not to blame for your child's problems.
- Create links with other parents in similar situations, whether this is through fostering networks or adoption support groups. You can not only hear about other people's struggles but also share their joy and pleasure in their experiences.
- Be realistic – change does not happen overnight, or in a week or a month.
- Redefine your role. Sometimes I encourage adoptive parents to see themselves as co-therapists, who are not only offering a loving home but who also have a task at hand – to help their child to recover and be able to make trusting, healthy relationships. Love on its own is not enough to make a child with a traumatic history suddenly trust you.

As well as your own emotional thermometer, remember your child's. Strong feelings and flight or fight responses can cause them to have even more fixed and skewed ideas about you. It's easy to reflect, sitting on a beach afterwards, that the black shadow in the sea was most likely a rock or seaweed. However, thinking like this while swimming is more difficult. When your child is angry and upset at you, it is extremely unlikely you can help them see things differently in that moment so this is not a great time to ask them to reflect on events. Instead, giving space, using humour, doing something wacky or using distraction may be more effective. Or, in extreme cases, sitting outside a door while a room is being trashed might actually be more helpful. Pick your timing carefully and accept that this is the way you need to handle your relationship. It's important not to lose sight of how extremely sensitive a child like this can be, and that this sensitivity will underlie everything they feel and do.

Create a shame-free zone

Shame is an experience we all want to avoid. However, if you have a generally positive sense of yourself and you have felt accepted and valued by people in your life, you will be more able to withstand shame and get past the feeling. However, children who have experienced trauma in their lives find this feeling too much and, because they cannot fall back on a positive view of themselves, will avoid feeling shame at all costs. Negative behaviour can escalate and parents in turn can become more frustrated and disappointed, which then impacts more on the child and an escalating cycle of negative exchanges begins.

With this difficulty and sensitivity in mind, Table 7.1 suggests what common parenting practices you might choose to avoid and which you might choose to use.

The concept of 'Two Hands' managing behaviour on the one hand, and seeking to understand it on the other – discussed in Chapter 6 is really important for the children described in this chapter. Daniel Hughes, a clinical psychologist based in the United States who has written a number of books on parenting (11), came up with this concept as a way to help children who struggle to learn from their behaviour, who need support and the experience of parents trying to understand them. However, these children also need boundaries to get used to the idea of parental care. Your child will be much more likely to accept a consequence if they see that you understand why they have done something, and this is less likely to make him feel shame.

Use an enhanced Parent APP

The main modification of the Parent APP for this group of children is to place an exaggerated emphasis on the 'P' for 'perspective taking' as this aspect becomes especially important. Try really hard to

Table 7.1 Common Parenting Practices to Avoid or Choose

Avoid	Choose
Conveying personal disappointment in your child's behaviour 'I'm so disappointed in you. You know I don't like it when you do that!'	Using empathy and support 'This is tough for you I think. We will get through this together, I think you need my help to do that!'
Questions and language that might suggest blame e.g. 'Why did you do that?'	Language of gentle exploration 'That seemed hard for you, I wonder what was going on there?'
Punitive responses , such as Time Out – telling your child to sit somewhere, alone, for a determined number of minutes, withholding attention	Supportive responses such as Time In – asking your child to sit somewhere, nearby, to express their feelings and cool down. During this time, validation of their feelings and often just connection is all that is needed.
Using illogical consequences 'You didn't go to bed on time. That means you can't go to the park tomorrow'	Using natural or logical consequences 'Well, it's hard for you to settle at night. I think that means you need help to calm down a little. We are going to try to shorten your play time before bed and have some relaxing down time'
Showing how invested you are in him changing his behaviour	Showing how it is in their best interest to think about their behaviour
Insisting on discussing something when they are aroused and/or demanding prolonged direct eye contact	Finding ways to discuss things, rather than letting an issue slip through unresolved When situations have calmed down, talking through problems during car journeys when your child is looking out of the window can be helpful, or at bedtime, when you are looking at a book together
After a misunderstanding, leaving him to dwell on it on his own	After a misunderstanding, reconnecting as soon as you can and as soon as this is likely to be successful
Not thinking ahead to situations where they are instead of he is likely to fail	Scaffolding situations so that they can succeed and increasing supervision making it more likely they will succeed

see things from your child's perspective and remember that how they see the world is often tainted by abusive experiences. If you are the parent of a young child who has suffered an early trauma, I know it must be hard on you to be viewed sometimes as someone who is unloving or untrustworthy, but bear in mind that it must be even harder for your child to overcome their feelings of mistrust.

They need empathy for how hard and unfair the world can feel through their eyes.

> *One meeting with Billy and Jan, a 15-year-old boy and his foster carer, involved creating different coloured lenses to put over a pair of his glasses. The idea was to highlight how we can all see situations differently; we filter different parts of the same situation without realising it. The colour of the lens related to what kinds of earlier experiences we had. Billy made his red and he realised that if he wore his glasses with a red lens for long enough, he would start to not notice that the world was red. He got used to it. He chose red as he felt it reflected the danger that he remembered at home but also how he often saw people's intentions as hostile and abusive. This gave Jan a helpful language to use with Billy, asking for example if he had his red glasses on today or whether he could see that she was not letting him go out late because she cared about his education, not because she was mean.*
>
> *In this example, Jan was accepting her child as he was. His difficulties were a result of past abuse, but she knew that if she didn't take care, she might interact with him in a way that contributed to these difficulties. By finding a different way of communicating with him, she could separate out her actions from his past and help him to see her more from the inside – to understand what her real intentions were.*

Your child needs to develop a sense of why they keep behaving in ways that make their life difficult. However, when you help them in this exploration, this must be done with a genuine interest in their perspective. They might not actually have a clue about the why, so gaining an insight into their actions is very much work in progress and work that you will have to start for them. Parenting a child who has had difficult early experiences can't just be about giving consequences to actions. You must try to understand what is going on inside their mind.

I visited a children's residential home recently. The home was fully embracing taking the perspective of their children. Staff were repeatedly encouraged to see the world from the children's perspective, from thinking about who was on shift to who should wake up a child, and that ideally the child should know in advance about what would happen rather than feel like it was a random event in an uncertain life. Staff were prompted to think about what would be the experience for a child of having an unfamiliar voice outside a bedroom door. How might this experience set them up for the day?

Create an environment of curiosity

The Parent APP encourages parents to be attentive to and curious about their children. For children who have not experienced a parent who has been interested in their developing minds or whose parents misread their minds, this aspect of the Parent APP will be difficult. However, it is imperative for children's long-term development that they are able to reflect on themselves and others in a way that does not feel dangerous or confusing.

Do try to encourage your child to be curious about you, in a way that is positive. You can help them see your intentions more clearly. If for example you are handing them their lunch for school, why not say gently once in a while, 'I gave you that because I care for you!' Your tone of voice and body language can help your child to receive your intention more easily.

Try also to encourage your child to explore their own mind, why they do things or thinks in certain ways. Be mindful, though, that this is likely to bring a strong sense of shame, so pick your moments and be genuine in your attempts. This exploration might be around positive as well as negative feelings – 'Hey, how come you gave Rashid that toy? Did you want him to play with you?'

Celebrate resilience

Children who have faced adversity and have difficulties in their lives as a result of this also have strengths and resilience. Sometimes this may not be obvious, but the difficulties that they display pale into insignificance in comparison with the difficulties that they have had to cope with in the past. They have survived these experiences.

It is really important to identify your child's qualities. What do you like about them? What are their strengths? Think of a quality you feel they have, for example kindness. Take note of every time you see them acting in a kind way and make a positive comment about it. For example, 'That was really kind of you to give Mason your toy!' As their everyday experiences are so tainted by how they see themself and the world, by pointing out their good qualities, they can begin to take note of them themself. It can take a conscious effort to do this, to label positive qualities and successes, and even as therapists we can often forget to do this, but it can be invaluable. I talk more about this in Chapter 9 where I look at mentalizing during good times.

Continue to help your child build a more positive view of themself and gain more confidence in their strengths and abilities. What are they good at? What are their skills and how can they be challenged positively? Think about your use of praise. Over time, carefully used praise will help your child respond to what you tell them, so if you don't regularly point out positive actions, your child might struggle to notice when they do something positive! What different messages would you like them to hear and start to believe? How can these messages be given effectively? Praise is useful only when it is linked to something specific, rather than general like, 'You are a good boy.' Why not praise a skill like problem-solving or good communication? To really surprise your child, why don't you write a special note and put it under the pillow for them to find; for example 'I thought the way you handled the situation with Dad was great yesterday, you really tried hard to see things from his point of view,' or for a younger child, 'I love you, you are so special' might go down well!

Finally, it is important to celebrate your own resilience. Try looking back regularly on your parenting progress and celebrate small achievements and goals. As well as being good for your self-esteem, this will also make you resilient when you come up against the next parenting obstacle. Attribute your successes to your own ability or parenting qualities. You could think, 'I am making a difference to their life, I have the ability to be a top parent.' Attributing even small successes to things you've actually done and choosing to see them as evidence of your ability or potential is important to give yourself credit for.

REFLECTIVE PARENTING SUMMARY

What do I mean...

Applying the principles of Reflective Parenting, and enhancing certain aspects, to help children who particularly struggle to understand the minds of other people/struggle to relate.

It helps you by...

Perhaps nowhere is it more important to be able to step back and realise that how your child sees their world is very different to yours. Remembering this will help you a great deal to remain calm and to bring the qualities of the Parent APP to your communication with your child.

It helps your child by...

Children with difficulties in understanding other people and how they work need an enhanced Reflective Parenting stance in order so that they can begin to learn to appreciate the thoughts, feelings and intentions of other people through parental guidance. Your child needs help, support, understanding and encouragement to be able to relate to other people and lead positive and fulfilling relationships. When you clearly state your thoughts, feelings and intentions to a child with ASD or a history of traumatic relationships, you are greatly supporting their future emotional development.

It helps your relationship by...

When you are caring for a child who finds it difficult to understand and control their own emotions, and also understand other people's minds, adopting an enhanced Reflective Parenting stance will reduce your feelings of being isolated from one another and not understood. You and your child will gain a better connection and understanding of each other from your using a reflective approach with him.

Keep in mind...

1. Be aware, as much as possible, of your child's sensitivity and how they see relationships and situations differently – particularly during challenging times. Be aware that it's not as obvious to your child as it is to others how you or other people think and feel.
2. Hold your child's emotional thermometer in mind – it reacts differently from yours and other children's. It could take your

child longer to cool down from an emotion that might be more intense than one you, or another child, experiences.

3. Make your intentions clear – don't assume your child understands why you do things. It is important to be explicit about what is going on in your mind and why. Mentalize yourself out loud if you can, for example 'I was a bit slow to understand what you meant there.'

4. Even if you find it hard to relate to their experience, make sure you validate your child's feelings – they are real and strongly felt. Use an enhanced APP, where the emphasis is on perspective taking.

5. Be as clear and open with your own state of mind as possible so that your child doesn't have to struggle trying to understand what you are thinking and feeling. It is harder for sensitive children to understand the intentions behind your actions.

6. Notice your child's strengths and times when your child is less sensitive to how others act.

7. ASD children or children with a traumatic history may have an 'Inside Story' that feels hard to understand. It takes time, patience and lots of empathy.

8

FAMILY, SIBLINGS
AND FRIENDS

As children grow and develop, their social world becomes broader and other relationships become important. So when your baby becomes a toddler, you will find yourself becoming increasingly concerned with how they get on with siblings or with friends when they start nursery and then school. And the multiple relationships that your child starts to develop both inside and outside the home are dependent on their understanding of how relationships work in general, an understanding that has been built up over time from the countless exchanges within their very early relationships with you and other important family members. These interactions are also based on their observation of your relationships; particularly the one you have with their other parent. These everyday, frequent moments between you create a model, or blueprint, held in their mind, and although your child is not aware of it, the blueprint shows them how to relate to other people and what to expect from others when they relate to them. So how members of the family interact with each other around key events and situations is important and models to your child what they can expect from people outside of the family. If they see their family appreciating the thoughts and feelings of each other during good times and difficult times, they will learn over time that doing this is important for relating to others. Family life gives your child exposure to many other people's thoughts and minds so, in the context of their family, your child starts to see things from three, four or five different points of view, which provides a fruitful environment in which to learn about relationships generally. At the same time, the family environment is where mentalizing is most difficult as relationships are at their most emotional and intense, so the capacity to be reflective about other people's thoughts and feelings is lost on an almost daily basis.

In this chapter, I will look at how you can be a reflective parent both in the family and through your guidance on your child's wider

DOI: 10.4324/9781003483762-9

social world. I will look at how, as well as using the principles of the Parent APP yourself, you can encourage your child to use them too, to have a positive impact on their relationships both inside and outside of the family. A Reflective Parenting stance can directly influence your child's ability to socialise in their ever-expanding social world. I will also look at the impact of the world of social media and online activity on your child's emotional and behavioural development and the importance of adopting a mentalizing approach to try to understand this world.

A Reflective Parenting stance applied to the whole family, as opposed to being geared exclusively towards your child, means trying to understand more than one person's point of view at the same time. It can be quite a challenge to hold in mind a number of perspectives and how they all might link together and affect each other. We all find this a struggle much of the time. However, research shows that when families do this, communication and the ability to solve problems together will improve in the family. The outcomes for families where this approach is used in a clinical setting, using something called mentalization-based treatment for families, show encouraging signs of improvement in family harmony when members of the family start to appreciate more the viewpoints of each other (1).

Naturally, over the course of their childhood, your child will have an increasing number of chances to practice the skills they have learnt from you. Just as your child's ability to understand others and take their needs and views into account develops over time, so does the widening of their social world – increasingly they are introduced into new and more varied social situations. And as their exposure to a more social world increases, they will become more and more affected by the experiences they have, and other people begin increasingly to influence your child. In the past decade, we have seen a rapid rise in another influence over your child's social world; the impact of social media. Increasingly, social media and online platforms and apps have an impact on how your child learns about other people, and many parents are understandably concerned about the lack of control they feel they have over these influences. However, your support is essential still. By being reflective in your approach to your child, they are able to continue to learn about social relationships and their role within them. By helping your child to name and understand their emotions, you are helping them to regulate, including in the frequently dysregulating world of social media influences. Crucially, I come back to the point that how your child learns to interact in the social world stems from their understanding of how relationships work – which they have learned from you.

The parental relationship

Parents may be in a relationship together, or have a parenting alliance, whereby they co-parent their child, even if they are not partners. If you are a single parent and have no contact with your child's other parent, this section of the chapter may or may not be of interest. It can be helpful, though, even if you are parenting alone, to think a bit about how the exchanges between adults that are witnessed by children can impact the children's understanding of you and of other people.

Using the Parent APP in your relationship with your partner means modelling to your child that it's important to pay attention to what your partner is saying, to try to see things from their perspective, and to provide empathy when it feels appropriate. After all, if you are working hard at trying to be more reflective in your parenting, but simultaneously using none of these ideas in your relationship with your partner or co-parent, this is going to be very confusing for your child. There is strong evidence to show that when parents are in conflict, this has long-lasting damaging effects on children (2).

Parental conflict

Since studies carried out in 1971 by the eminent child psychiatrist Michael Rutter on antisocial behaviour and depression in childhood, researchers in the field of child psychology have understood the damaging impact parental conflict has on children. In Rutter's seminal study, he compared the risk effects of divorce and bereavement. He found that the risks of antisocial behaviour in children were far greater where they had experienced their parents' divorce or acrimonious separation than where they had experienced bereavement or an amicable separation (3). In other words, this early research pointed to the importance of the *quality* of the parental relationship, with the impact of an unhappy separation being even more severe than an actual bereavement for the child's longer term mental health. Since Rutter's research, subsequent studies have expanded on this finding and underline the negative effect of conflict in families on children's wellbeing. These later studies stress the

191

importance of the family environment and that it is not separation or divorce per se that damages children's development, but more the quality of the relationship between two parents.

In 2020, child psychiatrist Eia Asen and Clinical Psychologist Emma Morris set out their model of assessing and working with parents where children have become 'triangulated' in the acrimonious conflict between their parents (4). This triangulation process refers to children becoming involved in adult disputes and forming problematic alliances with one parent against the other. I have worked clinically very closely with Asen and Morris and can see how traumatising this dynamic is for the children involved. It's also evident that when parents are so consumed with their own grievances against each other, they are largely unaware of the damaging impact they are having on their child.

A Reflective Parenting, mentalizing approach is extremely helpful in this type of parental dynamic. If you find yourself in a similar situation with a current or ex-partner, taking a step back and recognising how your actions are impacting your child is a helpful first step. Then it can be extremely helpful to start a process of learning to mentalize yourself, perhaps using the Parent Map tool in Chapter 2. Start by thinking about your own experience of being parented and the impact it had on you. Reflect on your own mental health and the current stresses and pressures you feel in your life. To what extent are these past and current influences impacting how you act towards your child and interact with your partner? While you may feel your dissatisfaction and grievance with your partner is entirely justified, for example by their behaviour, it is also important to take note of whether, in the maelstrom of this conflict, you have lost your ability to mentalize your child. As we know from this book, it is entirely normal and understandable to lose one's capacity

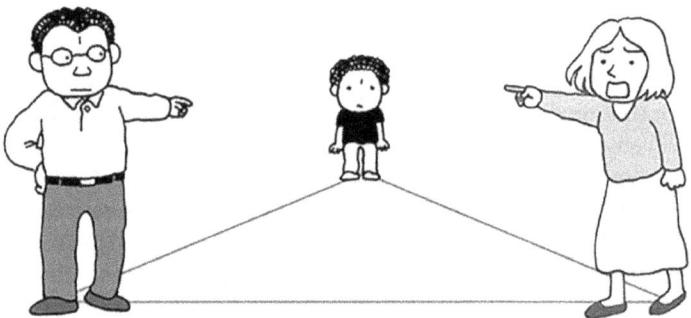

to reflect on the thoughts and feelings of other people when we feel highly stressed. However, if the level of conflict in your relationship is so all-consuming that you have lost your capacity completely to mentalize your child, then it is likely that they are suffering the fallout from your relationship. If you are currently involved in a high-conflict relationship, you can help your child greatly by taking some time to reflect on the following:

- Your current ability to meet your child's basic needs, for example to feed and clothe them.
- Your ability to talk about the importance of your child having both parents in their life and, if you are separating, your ability to make plans to enable this, including agreeing some goals with your partner for how to achieve this.
- Your child's need to have a relationship (of some sort) with both of their parents.
- How your past behaviour may have contributed to your child's suffering, including your own negative views of your partner or ex-partner.
- Your willingness to work in partnership with your ex-partner/ the other parent for the benefit of your child.

One of the main characteristics of Asen and Morris' model for dealing with parental conflict, which, like Reflective Parenting, is based on the theory of mentalization, is its emphasis on helping parents to mentalize themselves, each other and their children more effectively. The bottom line in Reflective Parenting is to try to separate out your own state of mind from that of your child's. There are many negative consequences for your child if you don't, at least partially, succeed in doing this. When one or both parents appear to be blind to the separate needs and experiences of their child and instead relate to their child as if they are an externalised part of themselves, their child may struggle to develop their own separate identity, complete with their own thoughts and feelings. These children can experience a 'self' being reflected back that actually represents the parent's thoughts and feelings rather than the child's own. In 2002, psychoanalyst Peter Fonagy and his colleagues referred to this as the 'alien self,' which can be very problematic for a child when, for example, they want to form their own relationship with one parent, but they have become alienated from them by their other parent (5).

Verbal abuse of children by adults

Professor of child and adolescent psychiatry at King's College, London, Andrea Danese, said, 'The sticks and stones rhyme is wrong. Words can harm a child's wellbeing and development and leave lifelong psychological scars.'

We have long understood the negative impact of physical abuse and maltreatment on children but, until relatively recently, less has been understood about the impact of verbal abuse. This can involve anything that shames a child, including shouting at children, shouting at others in a child's environment, laughing at a child, shaming or ridiculing a child. Some parents post videos of their child on social media where the child is shamed and the parent thinks it is humorous.

Today, we know much more about the impact of verbal abuse on children's development and this topic is much discussed. Recently I was part of an interesting event in the House of Commons involving experts in children's mental health such as clinical psychologist Eamon McCrory and Peter Fonagy, discussing the impact of verbal 'violence' on children's brain development and subsequent emotional and behavioural development. Jessica Bondy, founder of 'Words Matter,' a charity that aims to improve children's physical and mental health, has recently highlighted the impact on children of verbal abuse by adults – which affects a shocking two in five (41%) children – noting that it can cause profound and lasting damage to a child's mental health and wellbeing.

By this point in the book, you are hopefully getting to grips with the idea that well-regulated children are the result of calm, Reflective Parenting. At the same time, it would be unrealistic to think you will never lose your temper and/or never shout or have an argument with your partner or child. It's important to stress that shouting as a common everyday part of parenting is not only ineffective but also actually damaging to your child's sense of self and whether they feel lovable and confident. Shockingly, recent research informs us that harsh verbal abuse from adults to children, as well as underpinning so much of their later anxiety and distress, also actually changes the structure of their brains. Research carried out by McCrory (6) that involved taking MRI scans of children's brains showed that sustained exposure to abuse during childhood, including verbal abuse, leads to significant biological alterations in the brain's structure and function. It can alter both the 'threats' and 'rewards' circuits in a child's brain, which play a key role in helping children to navigate the world and also in building and maintaining relationships. McCrory's imaging studies show how abuse, both physical and verbal, can alter a child's brain so that they perceive the world as a more dangerous place. Children subjected to verbal abuse can start to misinterpret neutral jokes, glances or facial expressions as threatening, and this can lead to them withdrawing from social contact or lashing out to protect themselves. The verbal abuse of children is widespread in our society, with not just parents, but also teachers and activity leaders using verbal abuse indiscriminately; as a result, verbal abuse is the most prevalent form of child maltreatment.

Verbal abuse is not just about shouting directly at children but also about the effects of shouting in their environment, even when not directed at them. Let's look at the following scenario involving Rachel and Matt's family:

Six months before Rachel and Matt decided to separate, and before Matt set up his own furniture-making business, he worked for a large furniture store. Matt's boss was often critical and after one particularly annoying day at work, Matt came home late. Rachel had already fed baby Jack and given the twins their dinner. She was slumped on the sofa in front of the TV when Matt came in. He slammed the door loudly and Rachel knew instantly he was in a bad mood. 'Hey! Don't slam the door like that, I've only just got the kids to bed.' Matt exploded immediately, 'Thanks for the warm welcome! I've had enough of being got-at all day you know. I don't need more from you.' Rachel shouted back sarcastically from the living room, 'Well, sorry you've had a bad day! I've only been up since 4.15 with the baby, sorted the whole house out, AND done dinner, bed and bathtime! You might have warned me you'd be late. Thanks a LOT for the help!' A long and loud argument ensued about who had had the worst day, done the most work, was most tired, and so on. Upstairs, baby Jack stirred and grizzled in his cot and twins Grace and Lilly lay awake in their bed with their eyes scrunched up tight and their hands covering their ears. When the shouting got louder, Grace jumped out of her bed and hopped into Lilly's, only getting out to go back to her own bed when she felt the dampness of the sheet. Lilly had wet the bed. The shouting continued downstairs, climaxing in the sound of a glass being smashed in the kitchen.

What causes parents to shout?

Using all the tools you've learned about so far, and reflecting on Matt and Rachel's conflict, we can see that the tension arose at a point where they were both at the high, or 'hot' end of their emotional thermometers. Matt returned home late after a particularly stressful day, having not communicated with Rachel. At the end of a long day of childcare, Rachel was feeling exhausted and possibly unappreciated by her partner. The baby had woken up early and, as the non-working parent, Rachel had done the heavy lifting at home, looking after a young baby, getting the twins to school, back home, fed and all three bathed before doing the nighttime story routine. It's highly likely and extremely common in such situations that neither parent is thinking much about the thoughts and feelings of the other. They are both stuck at their own emotional temperature, possibly feeling preoccupied with their own state of mind and uncared for by the other. When both parents are in this highly aroused emotional state, neither is even able, never mind willing, to mentalize. Feeling criticised and unappreciated at work, Matt arrives home already very wound up and in 'fight' mode, and Rachel, if not feeling criticised, very likely feeling invalidated for all unpaid childcare work, is on a short fuse. With little or no capacity for any mentalizing (of themselves and each other), both Rachel and Matt act out rather than reflect. Matt shows his anger and frustration first by slamming the door, to which Rachel immediately reacts, seeing this as an aggressive attack on her and the calm house she's worked hard to create, and immediately retaliates with a criticism of Matt. Without any reflective capacity, the couple let out their anger on each other, which escalates to the point that their children upstairs are disturbed, and Lilly is made so anxious by the shouting that she wets the bed.

Matt and Rachel eventually decided to separate. Matthew subsequently started his own business and in doing so realised that his job had been a major source of his unhappiness and failure to mentalize others in his family. Matt left the family home, leaving Rachel as the primary parent, with the twins staying with Matt alternative weekends. Although this situation might not sound ideal or even desirable, the impact on the children has been positive. When the children heard their parents shouting downstairs after they had gone to bed, this clearly made them feel unsettled and anxious, and even frightened.

How can Reflective Parenting help?

While verbal abuse of children is the most prevalent form of damage to a child's development, it is also one of the most preventable causes of mental health problems. Peter Fonagy explains, 'Harsh words can actively weaken the brain's foundation during development. Children need kind, supportive communication from adults. It's vital for building their identity and emotional resilience.'

In the introduction, I discussed how attachment theory forms the foundation of Reflective Parenting, wherein parents mirror their young child's emotions and feed them back to them in a calm and regulated way, using encouraging language to inspire their child to learn and recover from setbacks. The language of Reflective Parenting helps a child to understand who they are, in their relationships and in the world in general. It's hard to overstate how beneficial this is to a child's development, and throughout their entire life.

The first step in addressing the issue of verbal abuse would be to go back to your Parent Map and think about whether there are factors there that make you shout as a parent – say, a past history of being shouted at yourself, or stressful events in your life right now, as was the case for Matt with his job and for Rachel with the load of parenting a young family. Once you have figured out how these things affect you as a parent, then you can start to make some changes to your approach to conflict and hopefully stop shouting as much.

Secondly, use your parent APP to try to take the perspective of your child. What does it feel like to hear your parents arguing with each other? How does it feel to be shouted at yourself? If you imagine that your child is scared and anxious when you shout at your partner or at them, would this modify how much you shouted, or even help you to stop? If you use your perspective-taking skills, a key part of mentalizing your child's perspective, you can start to step into their shoes and imagine what you look like to them when they see you shouting at your partner and losing control. Your child is likely to be confused about why you're falling out with their other parent and will also start to feel confused about emotions more generally. If you can't control your emotions, how can they learn to regulate theirs in any other way than shouting or acting out?

Imagine your child is shouting at you. Perhaps you've denied them a later bedtime or not allowed them to watch something you don't trust on their device. They might shout at you, 'You're so mean, you're so mean, and you don't let me do anything!' Rather than punish your child for shouting, or shouting back at them, if you deployed the Reflective Parenting stance you might just reflect back what you imagine they are feeling like (the feeling behind the shouting) and say empathically, 'I'm very sorry I've got to set that rule for you. It's really hard and I can see it feels unfair to you.' Feeling understood in this way and seeing that you care about how they feel can have a dramatic effect on your child. Your anger can dissipate and the situation just stops without you having to punish your child at all. Whereas if you use a punitive behavioural strategy such as 'time out,' because you feel your child is being rude and because you also feel angry and out of control of your own emotions, this can make your child feel resentful and angry; it might diminish the behaviour in the moment, but it can actually increase negative behaviour and disconnection in the long term.

Over time, as parents practice Reflective Parenting, it's extremely heartening to see them become more interested and curious about their children and to see their children become more curious about other people and what's going on in their minds. Observing this with multiple families I've worked with, I notice how quickly conflict and disconnection are replaced with warmth, communication and connection.

In adult relationships it is easy for us all to become entrenched in our own views of the world and a lot harder to be curious and attentive to the different perspective of our partners. This might be particularly true when we are trying to manage difficult behaviour in our children. It's hard to let go of the view that as parents we know best, and in many parental relationships there can be a dominant voice of the parent who believes that they know best of all. Where there is either a strong parental character, or a particularly vocal and expressive child or teenager, it is easy for this family member's perspective to dominate over all others, and for the other parent and child to feel that their opinions don't count for much. Being a reflective parent means being curious about *everyone's* perspective and not about giving a disproportionate amount of attention to one particular person's view. Often we are so preoccupied with our own lives, making it hard to be empathic and mind-minded towards each other.

We know that children observe their parents closely, and that their appraisals of how parents behave towards each other strongly determine how children expect their parents to behave towards them.

If then, in your relationship with your partner, you are showing interest, empathy for how they are feeling and an appreciation of what is going on in your partner's mind – and that they
hold a different perspective to you – then your child is much more
likely to expect that you will be similarly curious, empathic and
mind-minded in your approach to parenting them.

Some practical take-out tips for parents on positive ways to handle conflict in front of children

- Try to be aware of children during arguments with your partner rather than wait until the argument is so bad that your
  children become upset.
- Acknowledge how horrible it is to see people arguing. In this
  way, you take on the perspective of your child, recognising the
  impact you are having on them, which also helps you move
  away from being preoccupied with your own feelings.
- Explain to your child that parents, like children, sometimes fall
  out. If there is an opportunity after the fall out, once emotional
  tempers have come down, show that you are interested in what
  the other parent had on their mind.
- Model and explain to children that arguments can be resolved and
  that coming to an understanding of each other (sharing perspectives and validating them) is an important part of any relationship.
- Show your child that it is possible to feel distant and annoyed
  with your partner but then, after resolving the argument, to go
  back to a place of safety, closeness and security.
- If these kinds of arguments and misunderstandings can be
  explained and resolved in front of children, they are immediately both less threatening and valuable opportunities for
  learning about other people's minds. A lot can be learned from
  repairing a rupture.

Sibling relationships

One thing that is given if you have more than one child is that you
have to hold in your mind the needs of at least two children, as
well as maybe a partner, a job, bills, meals and friends and other
extended family members. The demands can feel relentless, and
sometimes it can feel that there is a desperate need for a space of

your own in your mind because there are so many demands being made of you. This can be especially true if you have younger children who seem to need constant stimulation and attention. With older children there is a different, but equally difficult dynamic involved in trying to keep the needs of more than one child in mind, particularly when they want to be more independent from you. It can be really hard to meet the demands of everyone, you can end up not only giving no time to yourself, but you might be unable to step back and see what is going on for your children.

Whatever the nature of a sibling relationship, it is often strongly ambivalent. It may not be a surprise to hear that research shows that communication between siblings often contain both greater warmth and greater conflict than those found in relationships with parents or friends (7). Children are not born with the skills to work out differences, so get into conflict at some point or other. As a result, these relationships hold far more opportunities to deal with conflict and to understand misunderstandings. Just as when you discipline your child, sibling difficulties can actually be useful opportunities to help your children work through disagreements, to turn competitiveness into cooperation and resentment into appreciation. As a great deal of siblings' time is spent interacting with each other, with your support, they can gain much from each other.

Managing and supporting sibling relationships

On some days, it can seem siblings argue about just everything. They might argue about a toy being theirs, about whose turn it is to clear up, who watches what, who is the best player in the Premier League, who does better in school and any number of issues some children seem to have personality clashes, or one or more children may have reactive temperaments that make compromise and adapting to change difficult. Alternatively, siblings might clash because a big age difference means they want different things or because they are close in age and compete for the same things.

Your children are sharing space and resources as well as sharing their parents.

What do you think siblings need from their parents and from their home environment to help them develop positive relationships? Try to imagine planting two seeds in the same pot. They are going to grow together, sharing the pot until they are strong enough to be planted separately in the garden. What do you think they need to be able to thrive together and not compete for the same resources? What conditions will help and how much might you need to help their growth? Just like seedlings, siblings need individual attention and nurture, an environment in which to grow up together where they do not have to compete for resources and where direct attention is given to how they might be affecting each other.

Rest assured that if you have been following the ideas in the book so far you will already have been creating an environment where your children will start to get on better with each other. Not only will you have been enhancing the skills they need to relate to each other, your children will also be feeling more appreciated and understood by you. Feeling appreciated makes it less likely to perceive a sibling as a direct threat. Giving loving guidance instead of punishment raises children who are happier and emotionally healthier, so they get along better with their siblings. Please also bear in mind, however, that it is normal for siblings to not get on all the time, and that this is not a result of bad parenting. In fact, learning to problem solve an argument can be one of the most useful skills that siblings can learn from their disagreements. Helping them work through disagreements and see the benefits of cooperation provide useful skills for life. Having a sibling even increases a child's ability to understand other people's perspectives.

Attention

It can be really helpful to have an overall positive mindset when it comes to family relationships. Expect kind and cooperative relationships in the family, state these expectations and pay close attention when this is not happening and be curious about what has gone wrong.

> *In Lisa's family, her and her partner put a lot of emphasis on building relationships in the family and wherever possible expected a culture of being supportive. Lisa, with this strong view, would be very interested when she felt these expectations were being broken. When she noticed her two children being spiteful and mean she saw this as an opportunity to explore what this was about.*
>
> *'Hey kids, what are you fighting about? Do you think you can work out a solution all by yourselves without a grown up?'*

Some interesting recent research on bullying between siblings shows that being bullied regularly by a sibling can increase a person's risk of depression when they are older (8). So it's important that parents pay attention to sibling relationships, and if they think a sibling is being bullied, intervene early to stop this continuing and to model healthy relationships.

There are other ways to encourage an atmosphere of cooperating other than expressing this directly in words. For example, siblings can be encouraged to pay more attention to one another's lives so they have a better appreciation of the one another's personalities, likes and dislikes. Encourage them to recognise each other's achievements and offer each other congratulations for doing well at something. The positive effects of paying more attention to each other and appreciating each other's qualities are noticeable. Families can easily drift apart from each other when kids are ferried to and from a lot of separate activities, and a sibling group can lose the sense of being a unit and become instead a group of individuals. Why not play games or be active together? You could make room in the weekend for group activities. Having shared family traditions and rituals are important, too. This might be a special meal once a week or a regular Sunday trip, spending time with extended family or creating your own way to celebrate traditional days – all these experiences create a bond and a shared identity that helps children feel closer. This needs to be balanced with giving each child some individual time, which in itself can lend perspective to thinking about another person's needs when you all come back together.

To really encourage your children to work together, why not every now and then set an incentive for them to cooperate with each other? For example say:

> *I love it when you two get on together. If you can manage not to bicker with each other during this drive I will let you both stay up a bit later tonight.*

We all tell children when they are not interacting well – this seems to come easily. You could turn this on its head and pay attention to moments that go well. You might want to give your children a special message when they resolve conflict well or even a little reward very occasionally when you see them working things out together. You could go further and make an effort to point out whenever one sibling is having a positive effect on the other. 'Look, you made your brother so happy when you let him borrow your toy!' or 'Look how you were so funny and now he is smiling!'

> *Finn and his two children came home and found that Lisa, his wife, had left some chocolates on the table for them. Charlie picked them up, took them to Ella and said 'Why don't you take one first Ella?' Finn noticed this and said to Charlie, 'That is so thoughtful and kind, Charlie' and ruffled his hair. A few minutes later he went back to Charlie and Ella and said 'I feel touched at how kind Charlie was back then. I'd like you both to have another chocolate!'*

Do you remember when I encouraged you in Chapter 4 to try watching and waiting when it comes to paying attention? Perhaps you can try this, as sometimes staying out of the way and noticing can be helpful if you have a tendency to get too involved in your children's misunderstandings. Obviously there might be times you must intervene, for example if there's the possibility of physical injury or there is cruel taunting. But learning cooperation and problem-solving is an important skill in life, and siblings can learn this skill early on by working out problems together without your intervention. Watching also gives you time to see what is really happening in a disagreement, rather than assuming you know what has happened. Your children may need help to reach a resolution, but given a few seconds they might manage this between themselves. It also allows you to look at each child's viewpoint and ask yourself, for example why are they arguing? Siblings are in close proximity to each other a lot of the time. They have to share resources such as space, toys and your attention, and arguments usually revolve around variations of one or other of these themes.

It's quite common for people to have experienced the feeling that another sibling received more parental attention and love. Perhaps this was relevant for you when you were thinking about your Parent Map, as this isn't uncommon for everyone at some point to remember feeling that their brother or sister was favoured by their parents, whether because their sibling was more intelligent, a boy or a girl, or sportier. As a child you probably did not blame your parents for this but instead grew up to resent your brother or sister, making the likelihood of conflict greater. A simple way of avoiding this happening is to try to avoid comparing your kids to each other or to any other child. Love each one best. If they feel as loved as their sibling, they won't feel jealous very often. That said, when comparisons are made between siblings with a friendly, good-humoured tone, children can often rise to the challenge of the competition with their sibling and try to behave their best.

> *Why can't you put your pyjamas on like your sister? She's only 4 and she can do it.*

How often does this sort of interaction happen in numerous homes across the world? It is so tempting to say this sort of thing, especially when it feels like for the last year you have been tearing your hair out in a constant battle to get your child to get changed without a fuss. Most parents say things like this at times; it's inevitable. What does it feel like, though, to receive such a comment? And how much harder would it be for the child when his three-year-old sister comes up and says happily:

> *Look Mummy, I've got my pyjamas on, he hasn't has he!*

With older children, you might choose to focus on the positive aspects of their relationship with each other as a sign of their growing maturity. For example, 12-year-old Maddy getting on well with her younger sister or brother could be framed as *'It's great that you don't get into squabbling with your younger brother and little sister any more. It's really nice for me and dad to hang out with you now you don't get into arguments all the time with your brother and sister.'*

Finally, children are more likely to fight when they get bored. At times, why not try to pay attention to when they are likely to start to get bored, intervene early and keep them occupied? It would be unrealistic to be able to do this all the time and would not give them a chance to learn to occupy themselves. However, you might find that when you are unable to give attention before they start to fight, you will have to give your attention anyway when they do fight but in a more stressful environment. An example of this is on a long car journey going on holiday, or a rainy day when the weather is too bad to go out anywhere with young children. A combination of giving attention to children in anticipation of these times, and setting aside time to play but balancing this with supporting children in having to create their own activities and use their imaginations are strategies that can prevent boredom from escalating into conflict.

Perspective taking

You can also encourage your children to use perspective taking to see things through another person's eyes. Evidence suggests that having a sibling can be an advantage when it comes to having knowledge and understanding of your own thoughts and feelings and those of another person. In a study of young children's perspective-taking skills, it was found that children with older siblings performed better on tasks where they were asked to take the perspective of another person (9). These children appeared to become more socially skilled through interacting with and learning from their older siblings. If you think about it, having a sibling with thoughts, feelings, and desires that are different and separate from one's own offers an excellent opportunity for a younger child to reflect on the impact of their own thoughts and feelings on others, and vice versa.

Sibling misunderstandings are perfect opportunities to help instil the idea of taking another person's perspective in order to understand why people act in particular ways. Teaching children how to put themselves in someone else's shoes helps them to relate better to others and manage conflict more effectively. It promotes caring, respect and fairness. Research shows that children who have learned to value the views of others are more likely to include and appreciate children who are different from them or who are viewed negatively by others. Of course, all children can be taught the value of taking into account other's thoughts and feelings, but having siblings gives a great platform from which to highlight these things and provides a natural advantage. If you have just one child, you can have these discussions through friendships and other family relationships.

To help your child practice perspective taking, you could ask questions that encourage one child to step into their sister's or brother's shoes. Questions like 'How would you feel if . . . ?' can help your children learn skills for perspective taking. Asking questions in a supportive way helps children to think through situations and encourages them to take others' feelings and perspectives into account. Similarly, praising your child when they notice that their sibling might feel differently from them can do a lot to instil these perspective-taking skills, even if the comments are made in a moment of upset. For example, a child says,

> *I hate Sam, he wants to play on his Play-Station, but I want to watch my programme.*

And a parent could respond by saying,

> *Yes, Sam wants to do something different to you, it's hard when you can't both get what you want, you can have your turn in 20 minutes.*

Perspective taking can occur during conversations and family discussions – perhaps over dinner or in the car – that allow family members to talk safely and comfortably about problems or conflicts that they have with their brothers or sisters. Try to set expectations that family members listen to each other. You might find also it is easier to talk about other people's perspectives when it involves thinking about positive achievements rather than negative feelings. These family talks are good opportunities to practice the aspects of the Parent APP, which will help everyone feel that their opinion and view on things are equally as important as others. If your children cut across each other during these discussions, this presents a further opportunity to encourage perspective taking. For example, you could acknowledge the child who has interrupted and say:

> *I know what you are saying is important, too, but we are just listening to Ella. She's also got something important to say and might feel upset if we don't listen to her. Let's listen to her first and then we can come and listen to you.*

Provide empathy

All of the aforementioned tips will probably be less effective unless you spend time to validate properly and empathise with how annoying it can be to have a brother or sister sometimes. Remember how important it is to provide empathy if you wish to be a reflective parent? Without this final quality in your interactions, your children may feel that you do not really understand them and will be very likely to continue to feel resentful of their sibling. You need to make both children see that you get each child's perspective and appreciate why it is hard for them to always get along well together, as only then can their resentment of each other decrease and your children can feel better about their relationships with each other.

> *Grace (aged 7) was playing in her room on her own and was engrossed with her arts and crafts materials. She had a great idea to make her Uncle a card because he had been poorly recently. Her younger cousin Freddie (aged 4) came charging into her room running over her materials, shouting and whooping. Grace's stuff was scattered around the floor, and she got angry and hit Freddie. Freddie screamed and ran out crying, telling Grace's mum that his cousin had hit him.*

In this example, Grace's mum had a number of different ways in which she could deal with this situation. She knew that Grace was going through a phase where she was struggling with her twin sister, and so when her cousin was round her house, she felt that he often got in her way. She also knew that it was not acceptable for Grace to hit her cousin. After comforting Freddie for a little bit she went up to speak to Grace, deciding to start by expressing what she thought might be Grace's perspective and calling her by her affectionate nickname to help Grace realise she was not about to get scolded.

> *'I'm guessing Freddie got in your stuff again Gracey?'*
> *'YES, he walked right through my stuff and mucked up my card.'*
> *'Oh no, after you had that great idea too! Is it ruined?'*
> *'YES!!'*
> *'I'm sorry Gracey, it can be really tough having a little cousin that doesn't take care and gets in the way. I know that it's hard for you Gracey.'*

'It is Mummy, I hate it! Why does he do it?'

'Well, he is quite young I guess. I'm going to remind him again to not get in your way and I might get him to help you clear a few things up. I think he just gets too excited sometimes and just forgets what he's doing.'

'Well he's so annoying.'

'I bet. I'd like to help you make your card if you want me to?' 'Yes I would.'

'Ok great. You probably don't feel like saying sorry right now, but it would make Freddie feel better, and you really must never hit anyone. I'm going to go and see if Freddie's ok now and I want you to stay here and tidy. Then I will come back and we can make that card together.'

Grace would be more likely to want to reconnect with her cousin if she felt understood by her mother. Timing can be crucial as if your child does not feel you have taken their perspective into account first they are unlikely to be willing to think about their sibling. Just telling them off or telling them that they cannot hit is likely to make them more resentful.

Friends

Lisa picked up 6-year-old Charlie and his friend from school and took them to the park for a run around before teatime. Sitting on the bench chatting with some other mums, her friend Kate asked, 'Where is Charlie's play-date then?' Lisa replied, 'Oh, that'll be the boy standing over in the opposite side of the playground – the one that Charlie's not talking to.' The other mum let out a knowing laugh – this was a typical playdate scenario.

Getting to grips with your own child's moods and behaviour is one thing, but trying to negotiate your child's relationships with others, and particularly when they are under your care for playdates, parties or sleepovers, can be a minefield of emotions. As well as the responsibility of looking after someone else's child, you will also no doubt be very concerned to see your own child behaving themself, getting on well with other children, and generally being what we think of as socially skilled.

Building friendships and negotiating these throughout childhood into adolescence and beyond is one of the main areas of concerns of worried parents. This is completely understandable as our children's ability to get on with other children, and adults, is one of the markers for their general development, and also a marker for how we feel we are doing as parents. Parents often express great worries that their child doesn't have many friends, or is always getting into trouble and fights with friends, or finds themselves frequently upset or confused by their friendships. Reflective Parenting is not only a useful approach for helping your child to resolve some of these struggles and understand friendships, but it's also great at helping them to find it easier to make friends in the first place.

As your child grows older, so does their social 'map,' where their world expands and other relationships in it become more and more important. Just how does a typical child's world change? When your child is young, their world is you and their immediate family. However, from toddlerhood, where you notice and celebrate independence, through to five and six years of age they become more assertive as they reach out to others for friendship. Then, increasingly to adolescence, they will become much more aware of how popular they are and will increasingly spend time at friends' houses or get invited to more selective parties. Their relationships with you and their immediate family, although still important, become less and less of a focus as their friends become more and more at the centre of their world.

The Parent APP is just one of the tools you can choose to use when thinking about how you might help your child to develop, and then nurture, their friendships.

Paying attention

When I talked about paying attention in relation to your child, I considered how this would have an immediate impact on your child's sense of being understood by you. The interest and curiosity that you show in what's going on inside your child will start to be reflected in the way that they behave on the outside. This includes how they start to take an interest and curiosity in what others around them are thinking and feeling. For example, in the playdate scenario, Lisa might start to express curiosity in what felt so hard about playdates for Charlie. You are a really important influence on helping your child become interested in other people, and as they get older they will start to learn this from their teachers and other respected adults too. School-aged children will often comment that they like certain teachers because they are 'fair,' and when they elaborate on this, it usually means the type of teachers who let each child take a turn and show interest and curiosity in what everyone in the class has to say at particular times.

Like a teacher then, helping your child to be interested and curious in what their friends have to say, and what they think about things, is a great way of teaching your child to be more reflective and cooperative and will undoubtedly have the advantage of making them more popular amongst their friends. Imagine the following conversation and think about what it feels like from Charlie's point of view:

Charlie: *'I got a brilliant Star Wars Lightsaber for Christmas Isaac!'*

Isaac: *'Did you? Were you excited when you got that? Wow! What's it like? Did you play with it in the holidays a lot? Can I play with it with you next time I come to your house? What colour is it? Does it light up?'*

In this brief exchange between two six-year-olds, the curiosity that Isaac shows in his friend and his new toy is likely to make Charlie feel special and valued. Isaac, naturally, asks a lot about the toy as he is keen to play with it himself, but he is also curious to know whether Charlie was excited by getting it. The experience for Charlie of having his friend show curiosity in how he is feeling will be a factor in strengthening the bond they already have between them. Here is a conversation between two older children showing the same kind of attention and curiosity to each other:

Sam: *'So, what did you get up to in the holidays, Jamie?'*

Jamie: *'Not a lot, it was a bit boring after a while. We went away with the family, but there was no Wi-Fi at the place we were staying so you can imagine . . .'*

Sam: *'Blimey! What was that all about? What did you do then? Did you have to do loads of stuff with your family all the time?'*

Jamie: *(laughs) 'Yeah, lots of healthy walks and stuff, you know how they love all that. I missed seeing my friends, but still, it's boring being back in school too.'*

Sam shows his interest in both his friend's experience and how he felt about it, and this elicits a warm feeling in Jamie towards his friend and his school friends in general. In this exchange, the attention and curiosity of one friend in another also has the power to make them feel close to one another and importantly to feel understood. One of our jobs as parents, then, is to help our children to show interest and curiosity in others; we have shown you how this can be practised at home with siblings, if they have them, and can then be extended to their wider social network. The overall aim is the same: to increase a feeling of connection and harmony between friends.

Perspective taking

Perspective taking is an important factor in children developing social skills. There is an established link between children who have poor perspective-taking skills and social anxiety. This isn't that surprising – imagine your child for example going to a party for the first time, where they know some, but not all, of the children and put yourself into their shoes for that moment when they first walk into the room where the other children are gathered. If your child has great difficulty in understanding what's going on in the minds of other people and really struggles to reflect on how they come across in relation to others, they will easily be overwhelmed by situations where there are other children, and where there are games with rules and consequences. On the other hand, if you have been able to model to your child that it is important to think about different perspectives, and to accept that others may have an entirely different way of seeing the world, including different rules for games, then your child is more likely to enter into the party with a natural degree of trepidation, but with the social skills to be able to join in the games and play according to the 'rules' of the occasion.

One of the key factors in helping children to form a secure attachment to their parents is the parents' ability to reflect on what is going on in their own minds, and their child's. I have emphasised this throughout the book. Where children have had an early experience of feeling securely attached to their parents they are therefore better at being able to appreciate that other people hold different perspectives (10). This link goes even further to children who have these advanced perspective-taking skills being more 'popular' or well-liked by their peers. Moreover, the relationship between children's perspective-taking skills and their social skills appears to become more significant with age. So, for children over the age of 5, this relationship is even stronger, as children who have a good understanding of the way that other people think and feel, and who understand other people's intentions, do well in their interactions with potential friends in their peer group (11,12).

Your job as a parent then, through using a Reflective Parenting approach, is to help your child to develop these perspective-taking skills, which are so vital to their developing social skills. By doing this you will not only be helping your child to have successful friend-ships, but you also help them to be able to negotiate some of the more tricky aspects of relationships with friends. So, in your every-day interactions with your child, the more you can show an inter-est in and curiosity about how things look from your child's point of view, and how things look just generally from other people's perspectives – walking in another person's shoes – then you will be helping your child with a whole range of skills, from learning to manage one's own emotions through to managing relationships with friends. I hope I have shown you that this can be done dur-ing the most mundane of everyday moments with your child, from watching TV together, having a chat about what went on in each other's days, and playing and reading together. Here is an example of how you might do this in relation to your child's friendships:

> Sam had one of his best friends, Ollie, round to his house to play in the garden and stay for tea. Sam's mum Karen sat outside with Ollie's mum chatting over a cup of tea while Sam and Ollie were bouncing on the trampoline. Ollie thought it would be fun to bounce in just his t-shirt and pants as it was a hot day, so he took off his shorts and went to get back onto the trampoline when Sam blocked his way. 'You're not coming on the trampoline Ollie, this is my trampoline, and there's only room for one person at a time to bounce on this. AND, the rule in this house is you're not allowed on the trampoline if you're in just your pants!' Ollie said to his mum, 'Mum, Freddie's not letting me play on his trampoline.' Sam shouted to his mum, 'It's MY trampoline, and MY house, and I don't want him on it. Not when he hasn't got his shorts on.' Karen, embarrassed by her son's outburst and apparent meanness towards his friend called to him, 'You will let Ollie on the trampoline RIGHT NOW. He's come to play with you, and you have to share.' Sam became more stubborn, and zipped up the enclosure to the trampoline, shutting Ollie out, who was starting to cry by now. Karen, becoming more exasperated

and embarrassed by him, told him off further, saying, 'Right, well maybe Ollie won't want you back to his house if you're going to be so mean, and he won't let you play with his toys and trampoline.' At this, Sam got cross and angry and started to kick the sides of the trampoline enclosure. Meanwhile Ollie, shut on the outside of the trampoline, started crying and shouting at Sam to let him on.

What is going on for each child? And how might the elements of the Parent APP help Karen to resolve the difficulties between her son and his friend during this playdate? Her command to Sam to let his friend on, followed up by a criticism that he is being 'mean' and the subsequent threat that he won't get to go to his friend's house and play, are all exacerbating the situation, as Sam continues to dig his heels in, and Ollie gets more upset and feels left out. Uppermost in Karen's mind is no doubt the feeling that her son isn't being a very nice friend, and she is probably concerned about what her friend thinks of her son's behaviour. What she isn't able to do because of these intense feelings in herself is to think about what it might look and feel like from Sam's perspective, or what might have led up to his behaviour towards his friend. Let's go back and replay the scene, this time with some perspective taking thrown in:

Sam had one of his best friends, Ollie, round to his house to play in the garden and stay for tea. Sam's mum Karen sat outside with Ollie's mum chatting over a cup of tea while Sam and Ollie were bouncing on the trampoline. Ollie thought it would be fun to bounce in just his t-shirt and pants as it was a hot day, so he took off his shorts and went to get back onto the trampoline when Sam blocked his way. 'You're not coming on the trampoline Ollie, this is my trampoline, and there's only room for one person at a time to bounce on this. AND, the rule in this house is you're not allowed on the trampoline if you're in just your pants!' Ollie said to his mum, 'Mum, Sam's not letting me play on his trampoline.' Sam shouted to his mum, 'It's MY trampoline, and MY house, and I don't want him on it. Not when he hasn't got his shorts on.' Sam's mum asks him, 'Is it bothering you that Ollie isn't dressed in his clothes?' Sam shouts, 'No! I just don't want to share my trampoline with him. It's mine!' Karen says, 'How about if you take it in turns to go on, then you can each have it to yourselves for a bit?' Sam says, 'I'm going first though, it's MY trampoline.' Karen, trying to stay calm, says, 'Well, how about you show Ollie one of your star jumps, and then he can show you what he can do, while you come and sit with me? Do you want to check with Ollie if he's okay with that?' Sam excitedly says, 'Ollie, want to see my star jump then you can have a go?' Ollie's mum says, 'It's more fun if you can show each other your moves isn't it?' Within minutes Ollie and Sam are laughing at each other's tricks on the trampoline.

Providing empathy

Karen tried to see what was going on from his point of view and encouraged him to see that it would be more fun if he involved his friend. Had she gone the whole way and used the full Parent APP, she might also have been empathic towards Sam about his worry about his friend coming onto the trampoline without his shorts – however ridiculous this might feel to her, it was something clearly quite important to Sam. Of course, it is every parent's instinct to get their child to behave according to the social norms in this type of situation. We all want our children to share, be polite and considerate of other people's feelings. The problem is that how we go about trying to achieve this can involve making our children experience feelings of shame (telling Sam he's being mean) and threatening to take things away from them (Sam not being allowed to go to his friend's house). And all the time we are led by our own feelings of embarrassment, anger, irritation and desire to have our children do what we want and expect them to do. Making a small shift from this focus, to first being attentive and curious, and thinking about what's really going on inside the mind of our child, though, can help to de-escalate the situation much quicker and lead to greater cooperation. Also, by showing Sam that she is trying to see things from his point of view, Karen also modelled to him that this is an important part of relationships in general, making it more likely that Sam will want to see how things look through his friend Ollie's eyes in the future. When children like Sam learn to apply the same rules of curiosity, perspective taking and empathy towards friends, they in turn are becoming more socially skilled and well liked.

Empathy can be used in two ways. In the previous example, Karen was able to get Sam to be kinder to his friend Ollie by empathising with how he felt about his friend sharing his trampoline, and not being, as he saw it, properly dressed. Another way of using empathy to help your child develop and nurture their friendships is to get them to openly express feelings to their friends. Of course, with young children you will need to model this for them by saying things like, 'Oh, Ollie must have felt pretty left out when you closed the zip on the trampoline.' With an older child, you can encourage them to express their feelings by modelling this in your conversations with them, your partner if you have one, and their siblings in the home. You will soon see if you demonstrate how to express feelings your child learns to do this spontaneously and this becomes an important part of their developing social skills. In the example with Jacob and Jamie, Jacob's ability to empathise with the boredom of a family holiday when he would rather be with his friends, brought them closer together through a shared understanding. This feeling of being understood is of course one of the cornerstones of all relationships, and friendships are no exception.

Friendships and the impact of online life and social media

It is impossible in today's social media-saturated age to talk about parenting without talking about the online world and children's access to social media and online apps. These are the statistics according to a UK government research briefing from February 2024:

- 99% of children spend time online.
- Nine in ten children own a mobile phone by the time they reach the age of 11.
- Three-quarters of social media users aged between eight and 17 have their own account or profile on at least one of the large platforms.
- Despite most platforms having a minimum age of 13, six in ten children aged 8–12 who use them are signed up with their own profile and companies aren't checking up on this.
- Almost three-quarters of teenagers between 13 and 17 years old have encountered one or more potential harms online.

- Three in five secondary school-aged children have been contacted online in a way that potentially made them feel uncomfortable.
- There is a 'blurred (without the speech mark) boundary between the lives children lead online and the "real world."'

I could go on and on, listing the known and potential harmful effects of the online world on children's development, but I'm confident that you already know many of these from your own reading and conversations with other parents. The argument for banning phones from schools and limiting children's access to online platforms altogether until they are over 16 is growing momentum fast. In November 2024, the Australian Prime Minister passed a law in parliament that bans children under the age of 16 from accessing social media. Prime Minister Anthony Albanese says the legislation is needed to protect young people from the 'harms' of social media, something many parent groups have echoed. I was particularly struck by this quote from Albanese: 'We want our kids to have a childhood and parents to know we have their backs.' Equally striking is a statistic reported by Ofcom, the communications regulator in the UK, that over half of under 13's and 38% of five to seven-year-olds are on social media.

In his book, *The Anxious Generation*, psychologist Jonathan Haidt (13) makes a strong case for suggesting parents should not give their child a smartphone before the end of secondary education, at around 16. Haidt highlights the sharp spike in anxiety and depression levels among young people, which he states is strongly correlated with an increased access to social media during puberty for today's generation.

Given these statistics, I wouldn't be surprised if you felt powerless to do anything. After all, aren't all your children's friends on smartphones, or planning to get a smartphone too? What would it mean if your child was the only one of their friends who didn't have a phone with social media access? Would it mark them (and you) out as different or weird? From my observations working with young people I agree with Haidt's research that the more time children spend on social media, the more anxious and depressed they become. Children are not able to regulate their use of these platforms because they are so instantly rewarding and addictive. It is important to state, however, that as yet there are no studies which demonstrate a *causal* link between social media use and mental health problems, only correlational ones.

Social media and building self-esteem

The culture of comparison in young people – obsessively counting the number of 'likes' to social media posts and constantly comparing themselves to other, perhaps more popular teens – can lead to despair. I was working with a young person who felt intense pressure to be liked by everyone. She obsessively counted the number of 'likes' she got for her posts on her social media accounts and constantly compared herself to other, more popular, girls in her immediate circle but also notably in the online world. It can be bad enough comparing ourselves to our immediate peer groups, let alone to the social media following of people such as Taylor Swift or the Kardashians. As parents, we can start by understanding that comparison is the 'thief of joy' as Theodore Roosevelt reputedly said. While it's true that we can't instantly stop children from comparing themselves to others, we can certainly have a big impact on their capacity to value themselves above others.

Self-esteem stems from a number of intersecting factors, but mainly from the relationships children have with their parents or early caregivers. Consistent support, positive reinforcement and unconditional love can foster healthy self-esteem, while criticism, neglect or abuse can negatively impact it. Equally, the way your child talks about themselves reflects their beliefs about themselves; if you are a validating, empathic and warm, reflective parent, this can encourage your child to focus on their strengths rather than perceived deficits, which will enhance their self-esteem. This will make them far less vulnerable to negative comparisons than a child whose parent continually criticises and punishes their behaviour, making them doubt their self-worth.

> *Karen and Tom's eldest children Maddy and Sam have smartphones. Maddy didn't get hers until she started secondary school, which seemed to be the rule among Karen's parent friends at the time. By the time Sam came along, the conversation among her parent group was all about what type of phone was 'safest' for them to have and how it was 'part of the boy culture' to let boys have smartphones so they could play games and communicate with each other. Karen became convinced that Sam would be more sociable through having a phone as he tended to be a bit of a loner and she felt some relief when she started hearing sounds of laughter from his room when he was playing a game online in the evening after dinner. At the same time, she had noticed recently how Sam seemed more combatant with her and sometimes quite aggressive towards his sister. She was worried about what he was accessing online. One evening after dinner when Karen passed Sam's bedroom, she overheard him laughing on his phone and talking with a group of friends about a girl at school. She startled when she heard him call the girl a 'bitch' and more derogatory, aggressive comments followed. She hovered outside his room until the conversation was over, then knocked on the door and said, 'Can we have a chat, Sam?' Sam looked flushed and shoved his phone into his school blazer inside pocket. He seemed agitated and clearly wanted his mum to go away. 'What is it you want?' Karen was shocked by the aggressive way he spoke to her and said, 'I don't like your tone, and I didn't like what you were saying on the phone just now.' Sam snapped back at her, 'What are you doing, listening in to my private chats. It's got nothing to do with you, and you don't get it anyway. Get out of my room, will you?' Karen snapped, 'Give me that phone now! You're banned for 48 hours!' Sam angrily grabbed*

the phone from inside his pocket and hurled it at his mum.
It caught the side of her head and she screamed in pain as
Sam pushed past her, marched towards the bathroom and
locked the door behind him. As he slammed the bathroom
door, Karen heard him say the word 'bitch' again under
his breath.

How do you think Karen feels? What is she thinking about Sam
and his conversation on the phone and subsequent behaviour? How
would you react and do you think it's effective to ban phone use?
What about Sam? Can you imagine what's going on in his mind?

We might imagine that Karen is feeling shocked by the way she
heard Sam speaking on the phone with his friends. It seems as
though, in this moment, Sam is behaving like someone she doesn't
recognise. Her usually quiet and fairly withdrawn son is laughing
and speaking aggressively about a girl in his year group, and then
he uses the same aggressive tone and even violence towards his
mum. Karen's mind starts racing to all the possible things she imagines Sam might be involved in. Is he part of the 'manosphere' she's
heard about, where toxic masculinity and 'alpha male' behaviour is
lauded and girls are belittled? What does this mean her son thinks
about her she wonders? She is feeling shocked, upset and angry
about Sam's behaviour but doubts her threat of the phone ban and
taking this off him will calm him down. Did he really just hurl a
mobile phone at her head?

Sam is furious meanwhile. It's taken him ages to get in with the
group of boys in his year and to feel like one of them. For him, it's
jarring that his mum listened in to his phone chat and she knows

nothing about the girl in his year who refused to sit next to him in English last week. He feels unattractive already and doesn't need it rubbing in by a girl.

A Reflective Parenting approach to social media

So how does being a reflective parent support you in working out a way to protect your from the potentially harmful effects of social media?

There is clearly a lot to consider in the scenario with Karen and Sam; some of the issues may be familiar territory or at least represent some of the fears you have about the largely unknown online world your child engages with. One of the key aspects of Reflective Parenting is keeping a close connection with your child via the use of active attention and curiosity about your child's perspective. Karen might have started a more open and curious discussion about Sam's phone conversation, rather than starting off from a confrontational stance about the way he spoke on the phone. This leads Sam to immediately be on the defensive and, worryingly, it potentially reinforces any prejudice he has about girls and women. The scenario also highlights the huge gap that exists between parents' understanding and knowledge of the digital online world and her son's, leading to a confusing area where meaning can be easily misinterpreted and parental fears are projected onto the child, without any exploration of possible alternative perspectives. A recent television drama, highlighting the dangers of online life for young adolescents, highlights how digital communication can create gaps in understanding, particularly across generations.

One of the best aspects of Reflective Parenting is that it's always possible to go back to a moment just before a misunderstanding or dispute happened with your child (or partner for that matter) and to think about what was going on in your own mind in the moment just before emotions erupted. In the scene with Sam and his mum, we can see how Karen jumped quickly to a worse-case scenario, no doubt influenced by things she has heard and read about boys and online male-dominated sites, which target and try to influence vulnerable young men. She probably feels ill-equipped to understand the complexities of her son's online life as well as his difficulties and relationships with his peers. We might wonder if she has had a conversation previously with Sam where he's expressed any doubts or insecurities about his friendship group at school. The good news is that it's not too late to rewind and revisit these types of situations.

Rewinding back to the moment before she had the argument with Sam, Karen might reflect that she was already quite worried about her lack of insight into her son's social life. He spends a fair amount of time in his room, mostly on his phone, and she realises that she has never asked him what he does on his phone. When she hears him use the word 'bitch' in relation to a girl at school, she remembers watching a programme about a young boy who was so heavily influenced by the online world of 'toxic masculinity' that he murdered a girl in his year. She can't get this out of her head as she walks past Sam's room and so when she confronts him in her state of high anxiety and upset, she completely ignores any other potential reasons for Sam's comment and goes to the worst possible place she can imagine. Failing to mentalize herself, she reacts strongly. Also, failing to mentalize Sam, she mixes up her own strong emotions about a fictional character with his (seemingly one-off) behaviour. Had Karen been able to regulate her own emotions first, to understand that she was being heavily influenced by things she had seen and read, she might have been able to be more curious and open-minded about Sam's words on the phone. She could still have taken the line that she didn't want him to use the words he used, but she might have tempered it with something more mentalizing such as, 'I know you speak differently to your friends than you do to your family, but I was shocked when I heard you.' This could have allowed Sam space to realise that his mum didn't see him differently from how she usually does but that she wasn't aware of how different he is when he's with his friends.

The importance of reducing shame

Sam may be feeling a degree of social shame, in not having a solid group of friends or lacking social media presence. Another type of shame is familial, such as having well-meaning but non-understanding parents: where is Sam's dad in this scenario for example? Does he provide the role model Sam needs at his age? There is also an element of personal shame, brought on by feelings of unattractiveness, weakness and social rejection. Looking out for feelings of shame in your child and trying to minimise these is extremely important. Shame is a powerful and deeply social emotion that significantly influences thoughts, behaviours and mental health. Shame is internalised and impacts an individual's self-identity. At ten years old, Sam is on the cusp of adolescence, where young people are most vulnerable to shame. At this age, young people are starting to develop a sense of identity. When shame is compounded by social rejection or failure, it can contribute to depression, anxiety and maladaptive coping mechanisms, including risky online behaviour.

In this alternative scenario, where his mum took a more mentalizing approach, Sam would most likely have felt less shame. He might have experienced a degree of guilt instead, but he would be able to recover quickly from this, knowing that his mum cared about him. In this more emotionally regulated environment, Karen and Sam might have been able to have an open conversation to address his worries about not being accepted into the group of boys at school.

Identity and self-worth in the digital space

There is no doubt that there is an external negative influence in the form of media and online interactions that needs adult monitoring, supervision, censoring and selective blacklisting. For a vulnerable child who is trying to negotiate their sense of self from an already flawed perspective, escaping online provides solace and the potential to seek validation and engage in risky behaviour. The fact that most adults know little of the online world means that they are unable to offer protection, in the way they would usually do.

The biggest risk to young people from digital platforms is that when they seek validation online, they are susceptible to unrealistic comparisons and external criticism. The absence of adult guidance in navigating these digital environments, often interacted with frequently, in the quiet of a bedroom, further compounds vulnerability. Research into the effects of screen time on wellbeing in young people from American psychologist Jean Twenge and her colleagues suggests that online interactions can intensify feelings of inadequacy, particularly when young people rely on social engagement for self-worth. In addition to knowing more about the online world, parents and influential adults must actively engage with and understand the role of digital landscapes for their child and provide the necessary supervision and support.

Something can be done: Reflective Parenting can help!

While the digital world places a huge burden on young people, there are, of course, a whole range of reasons why young people struggle with issues such as identity and self-worth. Using your Reflective

Parenting tools and embracing the positive influence and role you have in your child's life, *including* the influence you can have over their use of the digital online world, can make a big difference in how they are impacted by social media. Some proactive, Reflective Parenting steps you can take to mitigate the risks of social media and digital use include:

- Cultivating a respectful environments in the home and through your child's school and community.
- Emphasising mutual respect through positive role modelling and consistent guidance; model reflecting on your own thoughts, feelings and vulnerabilities, creating an environment where no feelings are shameful.
- Establishing clear boundaries with clear expectations and consequences to support your child's emotional and social development – use the 'Two Hands' approach.
- Educate yourself about digital risks so you can openly and effectively monitor, supervise and support your child online.
- Most importantly, be available to address your child's emotional needs, speaking openly about thoughts and feelings (mentalizing yourself) and being attentive and curious to what's going on inside your child's mind (without adopting an 'expert stance', where you seem to have all the answers, as being a Reflective Parent is all about adopting a more curious, not-knowing stance).
- Communicate clearly to your child that you are interested and want to learn what things look like from their perspective, without judgement.

REFLECTIVE PARENTING SUMMARY

What it is . . .

A Reflective Parenting stance when you are with family, siblings and friends is a way of reflecting about the many different relationships in your life, including your child's wider circle of family and friends and their online life where they have contact with people you don't know.

It helps you by . . .

Being a reflective parent helps you to become more aware of the different thoughts, feelings and intentions of more than one child and more than one member of the family. It helps you to see that everyone in the family and in your child's wider circle has a different perspective and allows you to reflect on these different views of the world. It also helps you to consider the influence of unknown people in your child's life and to be curious about the level of contact and impact they have on your child.

It helps your child by . . .

Reflective Parenting in the family helps your child learn to be curious and interested in the thoughts, feelings and intentions of their friends and siblings. Through this curiosity, it also helps your child to learn about other perspectives, and this helps them to manage their relationships with friends. In your child's online world, it helps them to reflect on the emotional impact social media has on them. Using the Parent APP in your adult relationship means that you will model attention, curiosity and empathic skills to your child.

It helps your relationship by . . .

Being more reflective in your parenting helps you to communicate better as a family and appreciate each other's points of view. Giving each of your children equal attention in turns will help siblings to feel equally valued and bring them closer to you, reducing competitiveness between them.

Keep in mind . . .

1. Your everyday conversations and behaviour with your partner are closely observed by your children and are how they will expect you to behave towards them.
2. Listen to your children with your full attention one at a time – encourage turn taking but show each of them that you

are interested in hearing what each has to say/seeing what each wants to show you. Practice 'parking' – so you let one child know you are interested in what they have to say, but let them wait while you pay attention to the other child, then make sure you come back to the first child.

3. Helping your children to see things from other people's perspectives will help them to be socially skilled and get on more easily with friends and family.

4. Notice and pay attention especially to times when siblings are getting on well but also help them to problem-solve differences. Working out a solution will train them in taking each other's perspective more.

5. Remember that in family life, it's not going to be possible for everyone's thoughts and feelings to be taken into account at the same time. Practice being aware of, but learning to manage and hold on to, your own feelings – trying to understand several minds at once is really hard work!

6. In relation to your child's online activity, pay active attention and curiosity to the type of activities your child is involved in online; ask questions about what they are interested in, ask them to reflect on how they feel after being online and help them to understand the difference between 'in real life' relationships and activity and the unreal world of people online.

7. Being reflective about what you think is going on in your child's mind will help them to learn to be curious about other people, and this will help support their friendships and relationships.

9

MENTALIZING DURING GOOD TIMES

When you start to think about what your child is doing and reflect on your relationship with them, it is easy to focus on what isn't going so well, on the negative behaviours and on the difficult times, because these are the things you want to change. Now I'd like to shift your focus towards thinking about the good times that happen between you and your child, when you feel close and warm, and to highlight the times when your *child* is thinking about what's going on in other people's minds (mentalizing). So much of Reflective Parenting is about creating a relationship with your child that is positive and supportive, and which by its very nature reduces negative behaviour patterns in your family – those patterns that occur when a lack of thinking about our own and others thoughts and feelings leads to ever-increasing misunderstandings. Reflective Parenting is equally as important when you are enjoying good times together. When you adopt a reflective stance during enjoyable times with your child, they will notice your interest and curiosity about what they're doing. This will not only enhance their experience but will also increase the likelihood of these interactions happening again. Reflective Parenting can also be extremely helpful when you notice your child using those same reflective qualities in their own relationships, for example when they are showing an interest in how things look from another person's point of view and connecting with this. Sometimes, you might see the benefits of Reflective Parenting almost immediately when you notice your child is feeling appreciated from being thought about from the inside, particularly in their relationship with you. There are many long-term benefits of Reflective Parenting, though, that you might not see until your child gets a bit older and starts to become reflective in their relationships away from you. You might notice your older child be reflective about some of the feelings that seemed so hard for them to manage when they were

 DOI: 10.4324/9781003483762-10

younger, and this will be a nice bit of evidence that your Reflective Parenting has paid off. Equally, you might start to see how your ability to regulate your own emotions (perhaps through reflecting on your Parent Map) leads to your child regulating their emotions. This might include them noticing, for example, the impact that playing on a device has on them, and they might even start to self-regulate by taking digital breaks to go and do something more calming.

Training ourselves to look for the times when things are going well doesn't come naturally always. Sometimes, we can find ourselves following up positive comments with a negative or critical one. For example, one parent, on being told by her seven-year-old son that he had made his bed said, 'That's wonderful Jack. Now why can't you do that every day?' It's all too easy to focus on what is not going so well, without even realising that you are doing it.

Being reflective during good times

You might walk into the sitting room, see your children playing together and as you sit down on the sofa say to them, 'Great to see you two playing together so nicely.' Or perhaps if you notice your child putting their phone aside and meeting up with a friend to play, you might say something like, 'You have such a good laugh when you play with Savi. It's good you can have breaks from your phone.' When you are trying to be reflective in your parenting, all times can be meaningful and offer important training opportunities. Each family interaction helps you to think about how you have approached a situation and to recognise what is going on inside your mind, and allows you to help your child to understand why they are feeling a certain way. Of course, it would be unnatural to be doing this all the time in every moment of family life. However, try to make a conscious effort to think about what led to a positive feeling or a positive sequence of behaviour. What was this moment like for you and for your child? Was there anything you did to encourage the positive behaviour?

At these times, try asking your child the question, 'What does it feel like when you play with your brother/sister like that?' and 'What do you like about doing . . . ?'

At the same time, you can try asking yourself the question, 'What do I feel about . . . ?' and 'What is my emotional reaction to . . . ?' during these good times.

Joining in your children's play can be a perfect time to help develop their reflective abilities.

Often we miss these opportunities within our adult relationships, too; failing to tell our partners or friends when they do something that we really like or that makes us happy and pointing out their mistakes instead. Yet we all know how good it feels when we are told that we've done something really well, or that we look great when we've dressed up to go out. On a superficial level, these compliments make us feel good, but they also go deeper, building up our self-esteem and our understanding of how others see us. It's exactly the same for your child. We may sometimes feel it's too embarrassing or awkward to say when we are really happy or pleased with someone, to *name* when something is good, and yet it really is worth getting into the habit of doing this, as it has a powerful positive impact on your child.

> *Matt came out of the kitchen and saw his children Grace and Lilly talking about their days, taking turns and listening to each other. He sat on the sofa and thought, 'Great, I can get two minutes rest!'*

How do Grace and Lilly know that what they are doing is helpful and positive? What is the impact when you consistently notice when your child misbehaves but take their good behaviour for granted? Of course, it is absolutely fine to take time out for a rest, but it's worth marking good behaviour and positive moments together before you do so. Behavioural techniques that you may be very familiar with, such as praising appropriate behaviour and ignoring disruptive behaviours, can be used here, by adding statements that mark what you see going on inside your child. For example, if we think of Grace and Lilly talking about their day and listening to each other, Matt might say, 'It's great how you two really listen to each other. It feels nice to have someone interested in your day, doesn't it girls? It's lovely to hear you chatting and getting on.' Or Matt could ask one of the children how they felt when they were asked about their day. Sometimes, reflecting on your own state of mind can be just as useful in accentuating the good times your child is having. For example, Matt might say, 'I'm shattered, but I wish I had half the energy you kids have. You're having much more fun than old dad! Lovely to see.'

When you make these kinds of observations to your children about both what they are doing, and how you think this might make them feel inside, as well as telling them how you feel about their behaviour, you are modelling for them how to notice good times in relationships and take an interest in another person's perspective. In everyday situations, it's good to get into the habit of asking questions and having conversations where you note and think about positive interactions. For example, in a conversation about a classroom activity you might ask your child about something that happened between him and his teacher, 'Why do you think she picked you first?' Or when you take your child round to a friend's house for a party you might ask, 'What do you think Jamie will feel like when he sees you arrive with his present?'

How can I make the best of good times?

Just as when you deal with challenging behaviour, to make the best of good times it is important to separate out things in your mind and ensure first that you're not being distracted by other strong emotions. This will enable you to have a good experience with your child, and you can be explicit about how you feel – let your child know that you are enjoying being with them and doing what you are doing together. This may feel a bit odd or unnatural at first – it's something that most of us aren't really used to doing, but once you start to get into a habit of doing this, you will quickly notice how your child appreciates it, and how much it encourages them to think about what certain situations feel like for them, too. For example, at bedtime, you might comment on how lovely it feels when you read together and kiss each other goodnight, or express how happy you feel when your child hugs you and you hug them back. Or you might tell your child how good it makes you feel when you watch them play, or what a great time you had when you went to the football match together. It doesn't have to be a comment on something you did together, but simply something that reflects your positive interest and curiosity in their experience. I recall one parent I worked with saying that when she saw her daughter was soaking wet from splashing in puddles on her way home from school, her first thought was to tell her off because she immediately thought about the extra washing. Then, using her Reflective Parenting tool, she paused and thought about what the experience must have been like for her daughter and said, 'It must have been so much fun jumping in the puddles with your friends.' This parent said it led to a lovely evening where the two of them snuggled on the sofa, and she acknowledged that the evening would have been stressful and probably involved an argument had she failed to see things through her daughter's eyes. The list of ways in which you can capitalise on good times is endless but be reassured that you can't really give your child too much positive feedback. Children really love it when parents talk in a complimentary way about them, particularly because these conversations encourage a strong affectionate bond and show commitment of your interest in and appreciation of how they think and feel when you make these comments. Even after difficult moments you can say, 'I still really love you, even though we had a difficult time earlier.'

Good times in the family

Family life can be hectic and chaotic at times, but within this chaos there can also be a lot of fun. As well as noticing when things are going well with your child, it's as important to notice and comment on when your whole family is having a good time, and particularly when family members are mentalizing each other well.

Karen sits down to a family meal and notices that her three children are asking each other about their day at school. Her eldest child Maddy says to her brother Sam, 'So, what did you do in food tech today? Are you making Thai food the same as us?' Sam replies, 'No, we're making pasties. Thai sounds a bit more interesting. Did you have a laugh

*doing that with Ilsa and Sharni?' Molly laughs and tells a
story of them putting too many chillies in the food, which
makes Sam, his mum and their younger sister Molly fall
about laughing. Karen comments, 'That was really lovely
of you Molly to ask about Sam's day like that. It's nice
when you take an interest in each other isn't it? I love having meals like this with you three.'*

Not knowing and being curious

It's very important when you are reflecting on good times with your
child that you make it clear that you don't know exactly what's
going on inside your child's mind, but rather suggest how you think
they might be feeling, and allow them to take the lead. You might
express this by saying something like, 'Let me check if I've got it
right . . . you want to play with the cars today because you found
it too boring drawing last time?' In this way you express that you
don't really know for sure what your child is thinking, and you give
your child the opportunity to tell you what is *actually* going on in
their mind, as well as showing them that you are very curious about
whatever it is they are thinking/feeling at that given moment.

You can also practise this on your partner in front of your children so that you model the same idea for them – that none of us
can know what's going on in anyone else's head at any given time,
but that we are going to have a stab at guessing, and certainly show
that we are curious to find out. So, for example, you might say
something like this to your partner in front of the rest of the family, *'I can't imagine what that was like for you (when your brother
left you out of his birthday celebrations). Are you really bothered
by that or is it not a big deal?'* In this statement you show that you
don't know what is going on in your partner's mind, but that you
are interested to learn, and this has a powerful effect on how your
partner will feel.

With children on the cusp of adolescence, showing them that you
are curious about what's going on in their minds, while also validating their positive emotions might look something like this:

> *Karen, noticing that Maddy has been sitting at the table for
> over an hour after school, working on her French home-
> work, sits next to her and says,*
> *'I can't imagine what it's like to have the amount of
> homework you kids get at the moment. I really felt for you*

*last night when you had so much French homework. You
spent ages on it; I was really impressed by how much effort
and concentration you put into it. You deserve to do well
on the test after all that hard work . . . '*

Equally, when your child is getting great pleasure out of something
and is showing you how they feel about this, try validating this feeling, using an expression and tone that matches their experience. For
example, when you see your child bouncing on a pile of cushions,
and they look at you and grin and laugh, a validating response
would be, 'That looks so much fun, you're really enjoying bouncing
on those cushions, aren't you?' Or for an older child who comes
back from a trip to the shopping centre with their friends in a good
mood, adopt a warm and friendly expression and tone to tell them,
'Great to see you've had such a good time with your friends. You
seem really happy, love.'

Being reflective during play

Why is play so important to your relationship with your child? All
children love to play, and play is fundamental to how they learn
and develop skills in the early years. One of the most obvious areas
where you can experience good times with your child is when you
are engaging in play together. However, playing together does not
always work out exactly how you would both like it to go, as illustrated in the following example:

> *'Mummy! Will you play cars with me?'*
> *Six-year-old Charlie arrives at the bottom of the stairs
> carrying a large box with around 30 toy cars in it and
> looks up expectantly at his mum. Lisa was about to start
> preparing the evening meal, and do a bit of tidying up
> around the house. She had done a half day in the office
> that morning and left at 2pm to pick up Charlie from
> school.*
> *'Maybe in a minute Charlie, I've got to do a few jobs
> first. You get them out and start playing. I'll be there in a
> minute.'*
> *Charlie tips the cars from his box all over the floor and
> in a huff says, 'You never want to play with me Mummy!'
> then stomps off in search of his dad's iPad so he can play a
> game on there on his own.*

If this scenario sounds familiar to you, don't worry, you are not alone. Many parents find it hard to make the time to play with their children, for lots of different reasons. In Lisa's case, she felt she had other things that needed doing – she had to get some food prepared for the family, and was feeling that the house was a bit of a tip. She was possibly also still holding on to some feelings from her morning at work, and so her mind was already a little preoccupied. From Charlie's perspective, being told 'in a minute' was a phrase that he'd obviously heard many times, and which he had come to learn often meant that playing together wouldn't happen. So, somewhat dejected, he reached for the iPad, which he could play with on his own.

There are some other possible emotions that might have been playing out here, too. As adults, we sometimes find it extremely hard to get interested in the type of play our children want us to join them in. Many parents find it hard to admit to themselves, never mind others, that pushing cars around the carpet for up to an hour or more is something they find fairly boring. Other parents may not have had parents who played with them when they were young. I've often worked with parents like this who long to know how to play – and how to enjoy playing – with their own child, but they lack this experience in their own childhood. The important thing is to find a way that play can be both engaging for you, the adult, but also feel interesting for your child; in this way you will create a better connection between the two of you, and play will become something that is mutually enjoyable and that also helps in your child's development. Play doesn't have to be a particular toy or game even. It's surprising how much fun a younger child can have helping you load the washing machine or cook the dinner, if you inject humour, playfulness and some energy into these everyday chores. Older children can also be involved in cooking and gardening for short bursts of time. However rarer, child-initiated and child-led play can be a real treat for a child and an opportunity for special connection. One way Lisa could have responded to Charlie would be, 'How about we play cars for ten minutes and then you can help me cook the dinner super fast?' This shows that you value both activities, and both of your priorities matter.

Respecting a child's autonomy during play

When you play with your child, it is important to let go a little of the normal parenting need for control. One study (1) found that when mothers were highly controlling of their children's play, those children were less likely to want to engage with them. When you are playing with your child, if you can respect your child's need for autonomy, you will also create a positive relationship with them as your child will view you more positively.

In later childhood and into adolescence, they will be more likely to respect and respond to your view and to respond better to your setting ground rules and boundaries, which still need to be in place.

Importance of pretend play for children's development

Interesting research into the psychology behind children's play has identified an important link connecting the ability to engage in pretend play to the extent to which a child develops an understanding of other people's feelings and beliefs (2). Studies showed that the more parents talked to their children about the feelings they had during times together, the more likely the children were to get involved in pretend play and vice versa, so children's involvement in pretend play also led them to be able to understand other people's perspectives and feelings about things. This research suggests that talking about the way you imagine your child is feeling when you are playing together leads to a broadening of their imaginative play, which will undoubtedly be more enjoyable for the two of you.

Just as watching a television programme with your child might provide an opportunity to talk about other people's perspectives, so imaginative play opens up the possibility of talking about others' thoughts and feelings. For example, when you and your three-year-old play with their dolls together, you can talk about what the dolls might be thinking and feeling, as well as what they are doing; you could think of a game where the dolls are all, say, pretending to be magicians who have come to your child's bedroom to turn it into a magical kingdom. Your child will not only get an enormous amount of pleasure out of seeing you get involved in their world of imagination, but also you will be helping them to learn something about how they understand people, which will assist them in their social life now and in the future. With an older child, a game of darts, or pretending to do karaoke in front of the TV, might lead you into pretending you are both famous celebrities competing against each other for fun. You could adopt the mannerisms and accents of these people in a playful way, if your older child doesn't find that too embarrassing. Parents often find it harder to play with older children, and vice versa. Many older children love to play online games with their friends and parents can feel excluded from this world – often lacking the technical skills to play the game or even use the device. Don't be afraid to suggest your child teaches you how to play one of these games as it will not only allow you a window into their world, but perhaps also offer some reassurance in terms of their online life. Most importantly, you will be meeting your child at *their* level of interest and showing genuine curiosity in the games they love to play. This will help you and your child develop a stronger connection.

How play is both fun and beneficial for your child

When you think about your own childhood, can you recall times when you and your parents played together, whether hide-and-seek, a board game or some other game you all enjoyed? Or perhaps your parents didn't get very involved in your play, instead leaving you to your own devices? If you have the advantage of remembering playing with your own parents, you will also no doubt recall that these occasions helped you to feel close to the people you loved. Whether playing in the sand on a family holiday, or playing trains with your mum and dad, these shared moments are the kind of childhood memories that stand out in our minds as adults. Play also allows us to make fun of ourselves and, often, when we make jokes about ourselves and our behaviour, we diffuse tensions and enhance positive feelings towards each other.

There are so many other benefits of play, one of the crucial ones being its role in children's development. Play acts as a catalyst for learning as through play children make sense of their experiences and express their ideas and emotions. Play also gives children the opportunity to develop and practise skills such as self-control, turn-taking, following rules and developing their memory skills. Rehearsing and exploring adult roles, such as cooking or fixing cars, helps children move towards independence and rehearsing and exploring these things are an opportunity for them to explore how being someone else might feel. And when children engage in interactive play, it helps them to build relationships. The many different types of play – whether outdoor play involving lots of physical activity, indoor construction play, pretend play or creative play – help children to develop a variety of skills, from the ability to climb, balance, run and jump, or hold a pen, to cognitive problem-solving skills. A major benefit of parents and children playing together – whether the play involves a simple board game or game of cards, a quiz on a long car journey, getting down on the floor and engaging with your child's toys, or enjoying a physical activity together – is that relationships are enhanced and family bonds are strengthened. If you find playing games with your child challenging, something like a family camping trip, involving other families, is a great way of facilitating your child's play. Encouraging your child to join sports teams is another great good way to observe their play and encourage their connection with other children, without involving you directly. Another big advantage of play is that it offers the opportunity to rehearse and rethink something that might be anxiety-provoking or upsetting for your child. For example, playing school together might help your child to explore their feelings of stress or any problems that might be arising for them at school.

The benefits of play then are well known, but it seems that the opportunities for joint play have diminished over time as children are more likely to be involved in scheduled and structured activities, or plugged into digital devices. Indeed, with your older child, you may have the reverse experience of being with a toddler and find yourself wanting to play with your child more than they want to play with you, as they sit engrossed in a solitary game on a device. Although it can feel like a losing battle trying to involve your older child in interactive play, there are ways you can get both younger and older children involved. For younger children, it's more about ensuring you do certain things with them, whereas for older children it might be scheduling a family half hour, watching a favourite programme together, having a meal out together or playing a game that spans the ages and is fun for everyone. Or it might involve inviting some of your child's friends over to the house so they can all hang out together, with you simply facilitating this.

Online play

Spending time online on devices is now a seemingly inevitable part of family life. You might have to set a time limit around the amount of time or times of day (avoiding meal times, or last thing at night perhaps) that your child is on a device. When this time is over, try asking your child about what they were looking at or playing on their device. It's possible you could learn something important about their interests and, at the same time, reassure yourself about their online safety. Doing this also helps debunk the notion that adults know nothing about the world of technology while simultaneously allowing you to be truly curious about things that your child knows more about than you. Actively listening to your child and finding out what they are interested in when they go online is extremely important as the alternative – staying uninformed and detached – drives disconnection rather than connection. It's easy to demonise everything about your child's online world, but taking this stance is likely to lead to fall outs between you. I would advocate instead finding ways to encourage your child to reflect on the emotional impact of their online activity, for better and worse. For example, after they've been on their device for a while, try asking your child, 'How do you feel, after coming off your game?' If your child seems angry or agitated, instead of taking a judgemental tone and saying something like, 'Well I told you it's not good for you being on your device too long', try saying something like, 'It's a really helpful skill if you can notice what makes you feel good and bad when you're on your device.' Maybe you might add a self-reflection such as, 'I've noticed I get a bit anxious when I scroll on my phone too long, so I'm giving myself a long break and going for a run now.' Dropping small observations and curious questions about their online life, where you listen and express curiosity in how they feel about this part of their world, will encourage your child to reflect on their mood at these times and will hopefully lead them to learn to self-regulate and give themselves digital breaks. The concept of a 'digital detox' is becoming more popular and you might choose to use a phrase like this so your child starts to see breaks from their device as a positive.

The following tips give practical suggestions for how you can approach play with your child, helping make your playtime together successful and enjoyable for you both:

- Schedule play in advance – tell your child, for example, that you will play together after dinner, at 6 pm. Check if there is a clear time when it can happen.
- Try to do what comes naturally to you, so that playing together doesn't feel like a chore.
- Play to your own strengths. For example, if you are good at arts and crafts but not noisy play, don't feel pressured to play in a way that doesn't fit your style, but try your best to join in.
- Try letting your child take the lead and tell them, 'You can be in charge of our play for a while.' This takes the pressure off you and can give your child an important sense of control and responsibility as well as a sense of how you trust and respect

REFLECTIVE PARENTING

them. With an older child, this might entail you asking them to teach you one of their online games.

- Follow through on your promises – if you've said something will happen, make sure it does, even if it's just for a modest amount of time.
- Stay in the moment and think about what might be going on in your child's mind. For example, if you are sitting with your child playing a game together, you could consciously try to shut out all other things going on around you and all other thoughts, and focus just on the moment of enjoyment between you and your child, and all the details of the game. Or, for example, if you're making a sandcastle on the beach, put your mind to the play, shutting out all external influences.
- Your child will take note of your expression and general demeanour, and when you are both involved in a mutually enjoyable bit of play, their excitement at your enthusiasm will make you feel good as a parent and valued by your child.
- If you really do find it hard to enter into your child's world of play, bear in mind that it takes practice. Try starting with straightforward activities, such as reading together, getting out a few toys that your child really likes or simply doing something outside that you both enjoy, such as kicking a football around. If you're struggling in the game, try naming your own feelings, saying 'I'm not very good at this, you'll have to train me up.'
- Start with ten minutes of play, then, just as you might in the gym, build up the time you spend playing together so you increase your stamina for play.
- Don't try to fit in play time when you're mentally preoccupied, unless you can manage to set your feelings aside for a short time. In other words, manage your own emotions before commencing play with your child, and explain to them that you need to 'cool off' from whatever is taking your attention before you can play

Playing successfully with your child

As it can be quite hard to engage children at times, the easiest way to make the experience enjoyable is to take cues from what interests your child and follow their lead. Playing together will help you and your child to build a strong connection that they will rely on as they grow and quite possibly will provide your child with memories

238

that will last a lifetime. One dad noted that it felt difficult to 'snap into play' at weekends when he had had a busy week at work or been with adult friends. He reflected that what helped him to play in an enjoyable way with his children was to feel in a positive and calm frame of mind, to have time to play, to feel prepared and to be able to manage his own emotions. In fact, what he was articulating are all the elements that I've talked about throughout the book and, importantly, how being aware of your own emotions first puts you in the right frame of mind for entering into the world of your child, and makes you able to pay more attention to them, see things through their eyes more and, finally, empathise with their experience. As discussed earlier in the book, the increased use of devices, by all family members, can increase the distance between parents and children and result in everyone inhabiting different, solitary, spaces within the home. It's good to think about ways you can initiate more joint activities or time together in the family, even if this involves you spending time hanging out in your child's bedroom playing an online game with them sometimes.

So, how can you make play work for both you and your child? If you think back to the Parent APP, making sure that you are in a calm enough frame of mind will ensure that you can pay attention to what's going on in your child's world. This isn't always easy, of course. For example, imagine you are walking your child to school and they are telling you that they have been made the 'eco' monitor in their class and they want to count spiders' webs together on the way to school. Just five minutes previously, though, you had read a text from your mum that has made you feel really irritated. How likely are you to feel like playing a 'count the spiders' webs' game on the way to school? Play can often feel easiest when it's something that you are prepared for in advance – it can be hard to snap into it, even though you know it would make your child happy. However, if you can recognise how you are feeling and manage to put this feeling to one side for even five minutes, your child will benefit from you entering their world, and the walk to school will be much more enjoyable than the subsequent sulk or difficult behaviour that is likely to result if you ignore their request.

There are also ways that you can avoid play pitfalls:

- Uninterrupted playtime with your full attention, even if it's only for ten minutes each day, will be more beneficial than ignoring your child most of the time and trying to engage intermittently for several hours. So, set yourself a realistic goal of how much time you have to play together, but then when you've set this, stick to the commitment and put all other things to one side.

- There are times when your child will be happily playing alone or with other children. At these moments, it's important to resist interrupting or taking over, to check in with your child that they are okay with doing this.

- If your parents didn't play with you much when you were growing up, you may find that playing with your own child doesn't come naturally to you, and it is actually quite hard to engage in play, a bit like trying to do a 10-km run when you've never trained. Just as going to the gym and practicing is important for your fitness for the run, so practicing playing will help you to find playing easier over time. You could start by introducing play into daily routines, perhaps play peek-a-boo when you're changing your toddler's nappy, play a guessing game when you're making breakfast for your preschooler, make a game of being mechanics with your primary-school-aged child when you're putting oil in the car and cleaning it, and make words out of license plates on car journeys with your older child.

- Sometimes children will disengage from play. Tuning into your child's interests, concerns and needs when they are playing is all about taking their perspective and seeing things through their eyes. When your child experiences you doing this, whatever they're playing at the time will feel intrinsically more interesting to them, because they've got your full attention, and they will feel that you see the game in the way that they do.

- Games can often involve losing, feeling that things aren't fair or getting frustrated when toys don't work in the way your child wants them to. Provide empathy at this point and make a point of naming how bad this feels; equally, empathise with how great it feels for your child when they have got all their teddies dressed up for a teddy bear party, or with their excitement about playing a pretend game with their friends.

Trying to do too much

One of the curses of modern parenting is feeling as though you always have to be entertaining your children, filling their evenings with extracurricular activities and weekends with trips, playdates, sport, music, drama and so on. As much as these activities are important to some extent for your children, so is learning to play and use their imagination; actually, doing nothing is also quite good for them, too.

When you are with your child, does it seem like your child's mind wanders and they just zone out sometimes? We tend to get a bit too agitated about this, worried that our children aren't listening to us, have poor concentration or aren't doing anything constructive with their time. In fact, not only is this behaviour normal, scientists now believe it is also necessary. The brain has two 'attention' systems. One system is for focused tasks, while the second system is for 'mind-wandering', otherwise known as daydreaming. It is the second system that leads to creativity and also enhances your child's problem-solving ability. Too much activity can interfere with this. So it's important to make sure there is room in your child's day for doing nothing at all but letting their mind wander – you don't have to be doing things for or with your child all the time. The number of devices that children and young people have can mean that it is a real difficulty to let your child experience just letting their mind wander and doing nothing. Just like a toddler needs to learn self-soothing skills, a child needs to experience some down time, even boredom, to learn to manage this state and to self-motivate. It is important, therefore, to set limits around your child's use of devices and to feel assured that you are supporting their development by allowing them downtime, where there are no immediate distractions.

Picking up on your child being reflective

Your parenting helps to shape your child and teaches them how to be reflective in their own relationships. Your child is learning from you how to use the qualities of the Parent APP for themselves – how paying attention, taking alternative perspectives and being empathic to their own and others' thoughts and feelings helps them get on with others, as they are more able to understand others' actions from the *inside* – to understand the underlying reasons and motivations for their actions.

So how do you know your child is being reflective about themself and about others, and what is the evidence that your Reflective Parenting is rubbing off on them? These are golden moments and clues that your child is mentalizing and building up their ability to understand their own thoughts and feelings and those of others. When you do notice your child behaving or talking in a reflective way, how can you encourage and reinforce this ability in them and help them see how helpful this quality can be?

Noticing your child being reflective

The same qualities that are so important in your relationship with your child – attention, perspective taking and providing empathy – can help you to think through what you might notice your child doing when they are being reflective about their own mind and those of others around them.

A – Attention and curiosity

One of the first things you might notice when your child is being reflective is that they are paying attention to how they feel, and they are able to link their feelings to things that happen to them. In the following example, Sam is talking to his mum about a situation involving his dad and is getting very agitated and upset.

> Sam had been trying to tell his dad about what happened with his friends at the park when they were playing football after school. However, his dad focused on the fact that he had dumped his football kit and boots in the corridor and told him to clear them away. Sam goes to speak to his mum Karen about how this made him feel:
> Sam says to his mum, 'He is so stupid. He always does things to hurt me, he doesn't care about me. He's not listening to me, I HATE HIM.'
> Karen listens to him and looks sympathetic to the fact that he feels hurt by his dad not asking about the game, but waits without saying anything back to him.
> Suddenly, Sam hesitates, only for a second, and says, 'I dunno, it feels really confusing. I don't really know how I feel about him.'

What's important here is that Sam is indicating that, just for a moment, he is able to step back and pay attention to the fact that he is experiencing a complex set of emotions. Sam was able to pause and name just how confusing feelings can be about someone you are close to – that you can love a person and simultaneously find them infuriating and hurtful. This awareness might allow him to reduce the intensity of his feelings and realise that it is difficult for him to make sense of his father's actions.

In another example, Grace and her mum, Rachel, are recovering from the aftermath of a very difficult bedtime routine. Grace had become oppositional and defiant towards Rachel, reacting strongly to being asked to put on her pyjamas and brush her teeth. Rachel had had a difficult and long day looking after her parents and found herself becoming increasingly irritable. She knew that she was bringing negative feelings into her interactions with Grace and that this was probably making the situation worse. Grace eventually became uncontrollably upset and angry at Rachel, pushing and hitting her. Finally, Rachel managed to get Grace to settle in bed; sitting alongside her after a cuddle she asks:

'Are you feeling alright now?'
    'Yes . . . bit better.'
    'Well, that was all a bit hard wasn't it? I got stressed out there.' Putting her arm around Grace again, Rachel asks, 'Are you alright then? What was hard for you?'
    'I was really angry with you.'
    'Ahh, you were. I was as well.'
    'I was really angry when you said you were turning off the television.'

What's interesting in this scenario is that, with the warmth in the cuddle from her mum, first Grace is able to label an earlier feeling – that of the anger she felt when her mum wanted to turn off the television. She also seems to be genuinely interested in how she was feeling, expressed by the way she talks to her mum about what had happened. And she seems to be curious about her mum's point of view. These are all clues that Grace is trying to understand herself, especially her emotional world and why her feelings may have influenced her behaviour.

In both of the previous examples, children of different ages are paying attention to their own state of mind and voicing how they feel. It is Sam and Grace's curiosity about how their minds are working and why they feel a certain way that is important, not so much whether they are right or wrong in the conclusions they reach. This interest of your child in their own emotional state and how this links into situations is an important first clue of their emerging ability to be reflective. It might be as simple as one day your child saying 'I'm really upset', and they may not have much insight beyond this simple statement at first, but this shows that they are realising that emotions are important. Your child may also pick up on the family mood, say around the dinner table, and might make a comment like, 'It's a better atmosphere tonight. It felt really stressful last night at dinner.' This is a great reflection, and it's unimportant that there is a negative emotion, but rather more important that a child has noticed and named an emotion and feels safe to reflect on it with their family.

You might notice times when your child is genuinely curious about other people, too. For example, your child may ask a direct question about why someone acted in a particular way, or they might volunteer a suggestion that indicates that they are thinking about other people and why they do things, as we can see in this scenario.

> Charlie came home from school and talked about what had happened with Max, a new boy who had just moved to Charlie's school and started in his class. Earlier in the day Max had been very bossy to Charlie and his friends, insisting that they play his game by his rules! Charlie said to his mum Lisa, 'Mum, Max is just so bossy, I didn't want to play his game at all, but I did.'
> Lisa asks, 'Really, why did you play if you didn't want to?'
> 'Max is new in school, I didn't want to upset him. Why is he so bossy? I think he is being bossy because he wants to make friends.' 'Maybe Charlie, why do you think that would make him bossy?' 'Maybe he just wants to make friends and is worried he won't. That makes him more bossy.'

So Charlie is displaying curiosity about Max and has already thought about why he is being bossy. He is open to discovery about what might be influencing Max's behaviour in a way that goes beyond simply, 'He is just a bossy boy.' Charlie is curious about seeing Max more from the *inside*.

P – Perspective taking

You might also start to notice your child taking different perspectives on why they acted in particular ways or felt particular things.

Returning to the first example with Grace and her mum, where they were talking about their difficult moment together, Rachel decided to carry on this conversation and said:

> *'Maybe me saying I was going to turn off the television made you angry, but, thinking about it, you seemed quite angry before I turned off the television.'*
> *'Umm, I don't know why I got so angry then.'*
> *'Let's try to figure it out shall we? It's a Friday, so I guess this is the end of a busy week for you? Perhaps you're tired? Or maybe something happened at school and you still feel a little upset about it?'*
> *'I am tired.'*
> *'Are you?'*
> *'Sometimes I think I get more angry when I am tired, I think that's it Mum!'*
> *'Yes maybe, I know I'm more grumpy when I am tired.'*

Breaking down this scenario, there are lots of really helpful things happening. In her dynamic with her mum, Grace is experiencing that learning about feelings is helpful and important and it feels okay to do this with her mum. At the same time, her mum is showing that she's interested in how her daughter feels and why she feels this way; she isn't trying to *tell* her how she feels, or why, but helpfully suggests a few options. While it's important to let your children see you being curious, being a 'mind-reader' can be very annoying for children (and adults) as this can feel as though others are telling them what they think, and often this doesn't match how they really feel inside. In Grace's case, we can see that she is gradually changing her mind about why she got angrier than normal during an everyday routine – that she is developing a helpful ability to shift perspectives about her own thoughts and feelings. It's worth reflecting on this ability in your own life, thinking about the times when you are able to recognise that you may have overreacted in a situation with a friend or partner. It can be invaluable, but difficult, to notice times when your emotional 'temperature' became too high and consequently affected your behaviour. Over time, as Grace becomes more aware of how her thoughts and feelings have affected her behaviour, this will help her relationships. For example, she will find it easier in her present and future relationships to make amends after misunderstandings and ensure that her relationships continue through difficult periods, so that she can build connections that are stable and less likely to break up. For example, if Grace were to find herself disagreeing with a friend at school, she might be more likely to reflect afterwards on how she reacted to what her friend was saying, and go back to her friend and make amends.

Reflective Parenting will also start to have an impact on your child's ability to see the perspectives of other people and noticing this is as important as noticing their self-reflections. When you read books to your child, this is a great opportunity to begin to ask them about the characters in the stories and why they have acted in certain ways, so that they learn to see things from someone else's point of view and avoid jumping to conclusions about other people's actions. Simple perspective taking can happen quite early on in your child's development.

> *Ella is listening to a bedtime story about a princess and her father, the King. In the story the King forbids his daughter from dancing and going to parties with her friends. Ella's mother stops and asks,*
> *'I wonder why the King wouldn't let his daughter go to dances with her friends.'*
> *Ella replies, 'He doesn't like dancing!'*

While it is doubtful that this is the reason why a king would not let his daughter dance, this is however quite a typical response from a four-year-old, and indicates that she is able to think about the King and take his perspective. In another example, Lisa had asked her husband Finn to buy wrapping paper on the way home from work, as it was her mother's birthday. Her mother was coming over early the next day and Lisa needed to wrap her present. Finn walked through the door without the paper. Lisa asked:

> *'What happened to the paper?'*
> *'Oh no! I completely forgot about that!'*
> *'I can't believe it Finn' said Lisa, 'Just one thing I ask you to get and you don't get it! Do you not care about my mother?'*
> *Finn walked up the stairs in frustration. Charlie was listening to this interaction and, sensing that his mother was stressed, said,*
> *'I think Dad had a really busy day again Mum. He always forgets things when he has a busy day.'*

In this example, Charlie is both showing some awareness of his mother's feelings as well as offering an alternative explanation to why his dad forgot to bring the wrapping paper home. When you notice this ability in your child, it shows your child's growing awareness of how people see things in different ways.

P – Providing empathy

Imagine you have had a tough day, you felt very criticised by a close friend and you are feeling low. Do you feel you deserve comfort and support, either from other people or from yourself? Are you likely to get a blanket, a cup of cocoa, curl up on the sofa, switch on a favourite series on TV and feel sorry for yourself? Your ability to experience difficult feelings and tolerate them is learned mainly from your earlier childhood experiences with your parents. This self-supporting approach can be such a healthy way of approaching emotions – for these often everyday events to be less painful, you need to have low levels of self-criticism and an ability to soothe yourself. Just as you have learned the ability to soothe yourself, your Reflective Parenting communicates to your child that their feelings are important and manageable, that they deserve your empathy and support. You may then start to notice that your child is able to behave in a way that indicates that they have self-empathy and self-compassion, which is a sign of mentalizing. This is a sign that your child is able to look at their thoughts, feelings and emotions from the outside. Let's look at the following example. Lilly has come with her sister Grace to stay with her father after school and explained that her friends refused to play with her. She told her father that this made her very sad. At bedtime Lilly is lying in bed and Matt says:

> 'Well . . . I think you might have had a difficult day Lilly!'
> 'Yes Daddy. Can I have another big cuddle?'
> 'Of course you can Lilly. You need one probably!' Matt gave her a big cuddle and said,
> 'Tomorrow is a different day, I love you!'
> He saw Lilly deep under her blanket, snuggling up to her favourite teddy.

This ability to comfort yourself or let other people comfort you can really help deal with the adversities of life. With this ability to fall back on, we are more able to take ownership of our own thoughts, feelings and actions and have compassion for ourselves. And for your child, they will be more able to tolerate difficult feelings and not feel bad or guilty when relationships go wrong and instead be more able to take steps to make amends.

You might also notice that your child is able to be empathic towards others. For example, Charlie is speaking to Lisa about his 7th birthday party, who he wants to invite and what kinds of games he would like to play. His sister Ella is also in the room. Charlie suddenly says:

> *'I'll be getting so many presents, won't I Mummy?'*
> *'Yes you will because there are lots of people coming.'*
> *'But what about Ella . . . Can't you get her a dolly too? She would get upset otherwise.'*
> *'That's really thoughtful of you to think about how your sister might feel left out.'*

Impressively, here Charlie has managed to shift his attention from his own interest and excitement to consider his conversation from his sister's perspective. Not only this, but also he has been able to connect with how he imagines her to be feeling. Charlie is bringing the quality of empathy into his relationship with his sister – the same quality your child shows when they give you a cuddle a few minutes after you have said you have a headache, even though they are upset you aren't playing with them, or when they save you a sweet for when you come home from work.

> *Maddy was having a few friends over for a sleepover for her biirthday party and was running around the house, shouting with excitement about them all coming over, and what they were going to eat for snacks late at night, which movie they were going to watch, and so on when she saw Sam looking down and biting his bottom lip. Maddy said, 'Sam, I hope you don't feel left out 'cos we're staying up late? Do you want to hang out with us earlier on and then you could come ice-skating tomorrow with us? I don't want you to feel left out.' Tim, their father, told Maddy, 'That's kind, thinking of your brother's feelings when you're excited about your sleepover.'*

MENTALIZING DURING GOOD TIMES

Helping your child develop reflective capacities

Once you start to notice times when your child is interested in what is going on in their mind and other people's minds, what should you do? Although parents can't be expected to be therapists, there are some really useful strategies to help you respond well when you notice your child being reflective. How you respond depends very much on the situation, the age of your child and the importance of the situation. Bear in mind, if you are interested and curious about your child's perspective, these strategies, or prompts, should come quite naturally:

A.   Comment on what you notice
B.   Expand and be curious
C.   Explain what you liked or why it might be important

Comment on what you notice

By commenting when you notice your child being reflective, you highlight their behaviour, helping them to notice what they are doing and that you see it as important and helpful. There are plenty of ways you could do this:

> *'I saw you really think about how you feel there. And it was great that you told me how you felt, instead of shouting.'*
> *'Hey, you really thought about that, didn't you?'*
> *'When you did that, I was very impressed by how you tried to get your head around the situation and work it out.'*
> *'I was really interested when you asked me what I thought about that. You kind of paused and thought about me. I think you wanted to find out, didn't you?'*
> *'You seem to be getting a lot better at calming yourself down first and thinking about what you want to say rather than just exploding.'*

Expand and be curious

You can take your communication a bit further, continuing to use the qualities of the Parent APP. If you sense your child is happy to discuss a situation more, try asking a bit more about why they felt a certain way to try to see things from their perspective: what does the situation look like from their point of view, and what new insights might they or you have? Showing that you are curious, using an expressive, interested voice, can really help your child to open up more so that you can explore situations together:

> *'Oh, what made you think like that?'*
> *'Did things look different once you'd realised that?'*
> *'How do you feel now?'*

Explain what you liked or why it might be important

For instance, it might be helpful to your child to explain what you liked about them thinking in a certain way. You can explain why the way in which they dealt with a situation seemed important to you, and how this different way of thinking about things – that is, their ability to think about others – *might* help come up with different kinds of solutions when they find that they are in a troubling situation. Returning to Charlie talking about the new child in his class, Max, Lisa is impressed that her son was thinking about Max and what might have been going on inside his mind, why he was being bossy. She said:

> *'I really like the way you thought about that. I didn't think of it like that! So I guess if you are right he might get less bossy when he settles in a bit.'*
> *'Yes maybe.'*
> *'That's really interesting Charlie, thinking stuff like that.'*
> *'Why?'*
> *'Well you seem to get it that that's how Max feels. He might be trying to be the centre of attention because he feels worried. I really like that. You also carried on playing with him, I guess you were trying to help him fit in and feel better?'*
> *'Yes,' said Charlie.*
> *'Imagine if you just got angry because he was being bossy. Would you have stopped playing?' asked Lisa.*
> *'I would have walked off like Reece did. Max might have got more worried then!'*
> *His mother replied, 'He might get more bossy then! But you carried on playing with him; he might actually turn out to be a really good friend. You just need to wait and see.'*

'*He got less bossy at the end of the day. He asked me what my favourite game was, too.*'

So reflective parents, such as Lisa, search actively for examples of good reflective abilities in their children, positively frame them and make them more likely to happen. This brings meaning to these exchanges. In another example, Charlie tells Lisa that he would like to go bowling for his party.

'*That's a good idea love, do you think your friends know how to bowl?*'
Charlie replies, '*I'm not sure, maybe they don't all. But if they don't know how to play, they could just watch.*'
'*Do you think they would still have a good time if they just sat around watching?*'
Charlie seems to consider this a bit and says, '*I think, hmm, I really want to go bowling. No, I know. I want a football party, everyone in my class knows how to play football. Some people might not like football, but everyone knows how to play it. Hmmm, I don't know they might not like football.*'
Lisa replies, '*It's good you're thinking about your friends Charlie. So, what would be the best solution?*'
'*Football Party!*'

Here, the important point is not the solution that Charlie arrives at, but the reflective capacity he shows when thinking the situation through. This is what his mum notices and rewards with her comment that he is thinking about his friends.

Being reflective within your relationships means thinking about and reflecting on what you do and what you assume other people do. However, it is a skill to be able to do this well, one that you are helping your child develop. By noticing and highlighting these emerging abilities in your child, you are encouraging them to bring these skills into their everyday exchanges and enabling them to have more harmonious and stable relationships with you, your family, their friends and teachers.

REFLECTIVE PARENTING SUMMARY

MENTALIZING DURING GOOD TIMES

Mentalizing during good times

What it is . . .

Mentalizing during good times means thinking about the thoughts, feelings and intentions of others in your family and encouraging children to develop their own reflective skills through modelling Reflective Parenting to them, particularly when you are enjoying time together and experiencing positive behaviours in your child.

It helps you by . . .

Applying a Reflective Parenting stance and thinking about the mind of others in your family when things are going well will help you to have more enjoyable and harmonious times in your family and in your relationship with your partner and child. Having other members of the family notice something about you that you might be thinking or feeling that they like helps to build your self-esteem.

It helps your child by . . .

In positive interactions with your child where you express curiosity and interest in them, they will be more likely to increase their positive behaviours and interactions with others. Modelling a Reflective Parenting stance at these times helps them to feel close to you and enhances their self-esteem as the focus is on their ability to think about their own thoughts and feelings and those of others clearly.

It helps your relationship by . . .

Taking a Reflective Parenting stance with your child during periods of play and good times means that you and your child will get to appreciate the experience of being validated and held in mind and it will increase the likelihood of you wanting to enjoy these times together again. Seeing your child's world through their eyes will allow you to enter into their world of play and enjoyment with greater interest and enthusiasm, bringing you closer together.

Keep in mind . . .

1. Highlight when things are going well, particularly in everyday exchanges, and say this out loud to your child.

2. Show curiosity about what made things work well/feel good.

3. Model stepping into someone else's shoes and seeing things through their eyes and note aloud to your child how that feels, in a positive way.

4. Help your child or children to problem solve by asking how they might imagine someone else thinks or feels about something – with the focus on something positive.

5. The more you see things through your child's eyes and are curious about what is going on inside their mind, the more enjoyable and rewarding your times together will be as they respond to your attention and curiosity.

6. Try to always reward (with your interest and enthusiasm) times when your child is thinking through how things might look and feel for other people. It is not really important whether these are negative or positive feelings.

7. Start with setting aside time to play together – even ten minutes a day will feel great to your child – and find something you can both enjoy.

8. Playing doesn't come naturally to everyone. It can take practice.

9. Enjoying positive times can involve setting up activities for your child with other children, including young family members and your circle of friends.

10. Notice when your child is being reflective about their own thoughts and feelings and those of others – this is evidence that your Reflective Parenting is rubbing off on them.

11. Encourage your child to be reflective and reinforce this ability as it will help them build up their understanding of how they and others think and feel.

10

THE TRANSITION FROM CHILDHOOD TO ADOLESCENCE

Mentalizing in the 'tween' years

In this final chapter, we will turn to an important stage of your child's development and think together about how you can continue to be a reflective parent into your child's adolescence. For some parents, adolescence is experienced as an easier stage of parenting; after the seemingly endless years of sleeplessness and behavioural challenges you had to deal with in the toddler years, an older child might seem like a relief. However, for a large number of parents, the teenage years are by far the most challenging, particularly emotionally. How do you feel when you think about the prospect of your child becoming a teenager? What thoughts and feelings come to mind? Do you imagine there being lots of fun, laughter and shared good times together or do you picture a future fraught with problems and feel a sense of dread? I was doing a piece of 'life story' work with one parent I worked with, and when it came to drawing how she imagined her children as teenagers, she drew them with devil's horns on their heads and said she felt *terrified* of what lay ahead.

As we've focused in detail on how you can learn to regulate your emotions to help your child manage their own feelings and behaviour, let's bear in mind that the teenage years and beyond will often test your capacity to stay calm and in control more than at any other stage of your child's life so far. I'd like to help you prepare for this potentially tricky stage of your child's life, and will focus here on the pre-teen stage, or the 'tweens' as they are sometimes called. In this context, I will use the word tween to refer to children between the ages of 10 and 12 years. If you have older teenagers, you will find it helpful to look at the follow-on book, 'How do you Hug a Cactus?' where I set out some of the ways you can adapt your Reflective Parenting approach to tackle some of the typical

     DOI: 10.4324/9781003483762-11

experiences faced by parents of teenagers and young adults. If you can hold on to your mentalizing, Reflective Parenting stance into this next stage of your child's life, you will be much better equipped for the potential challenges that lie ahead during adolescence. As we've seen so far, an important part of Reflective Parenting is that it allows you to predict how you will react in particular situations, so being prepared for this next stage of your child's life will help you to manage your own emotions and behaviour and also help you to support your tween to manage how they respond to and feel about challenging situations.

How to use your Parent Map when thinking about parenting tweens and teenagers

Exactly the same tools apply throughout the lifespan of your parenting experience. If you have a child approaching the teenage years, it's helpful to start reflecting on some of the aspects of your parenting that might need to change, and to spend time, using your Parent Map, thinking about any specific factors that are likely to be more important on your map as you enter this next phase of parenting. In the same way the demands of parenting a baby then a young child influenced your feelings about being a parent, parenting a teenager will impact your approach and thoughts about parenting. For example, when your teenager moves towards greater independence, what do you imagine your feelings will be? Will you anticipate you will feel more anxious about your child's survival, for example, than you did when they were younger, or worry you will feel controlled by your adolescent as they assert their own will? Is there a risk that their dangerous behaviour could trigger hard to navigate feelings from your own history?

It's helpful to start by reflecting on your own adolescence, looking at what type of risks you took (or didn't), how the world was when you were a teenager and what your relationship with authority was at this time of your life. Were you a rebellious teenager who challenged the authority of your parents and other adults or were you compliant and risk-averse? What was your experience of puberty like and how did your parents help you during this time? Were you sexually active at an early age or did you pass through your adolescence fearful or cautious about intimate, sexual relationships? And were you aware of your sexual orientation and as a result secure in your identity? Some of you reading this may have your own history of trauma, perhaps including domestic violence and/or sexual abuse. How has this impacted your feelings about your own children as they enter their adolescence?

Where do you stand in relation to parenting your teenagers? Do you feel comfortable with being part of an older generation who doesn't always 'get it'? How do you think it will feel if your teenager doesn't want to share all the details of their life with you? How we approach this stage of parenting and understand our own emotional responses to having teenagers is such an important part of parenting adolescents. Without this self-reflection, or self-mentalizing, the risk is that we can either become too distant from our adolescents or get so close that we become intrusive and stifle their need for autonomy and independence. It's a tricky balance to strike, but one that learning to adjust your mentalizing for the teenage years can really help with.

Referring back to the Parent Map in Chapter 2, think about the current influences on your map and whether these differ from the ones when your child was much younger.

Have your own circumstances changed significantly since your child was very young? Perhaps financial pressures have eased as your child has got older and needs less childcare. Or conversely, perhaps your circumstances have changed and you are now parenting alone or on a reduced income or have higher mortgage or rental costs? These and many other factors are all significant in terms of how you parent, as they will impact your emotions and sense of confidence and competence. It's always helpful to keep in mind the relationship between emotional arousal (including raised stress levels and low mood) and your mentalizing ability. Remind yourself constantly that when you are either too emotionally aroused, or too low or cut off in your emotions, you will find it much harder to reflect on your own thoughts and feelings and on your child's. The teenage years can be very stressful for lots of parents; finding ways to manage your own emotions is vital to handling some of the challenges you might face in your relationship during the coming years.

Mentalizing your tween

When you had a baby, you no doubt spent a lot of time thinking about what they needed to grow and develop into a healthy child, from the basics of nourishment, sleep routines and stimulating play, to more complex needs, such as their need for friendships and understanding boundaries and rules. It's easy to shift our focus away from developmental needs when a child grows, and there's often a feeling of taking your foot off the pedal the older your child gets. Having worked with hundreds of teens and tweens and been through these years with my own children, I've learned that it's just as important to mentalize yourself and them during these critical years, possibly more so if you want to help support not just their physical development, but also their emotional development and, critically, their mental health. To mentalize tweens successfully, it's important to reflect first on the many physical and emotional changes taking place during this stage of their development.

What to expect as your child becomes a teenager

From a parenting perspective, the main thing you will need to prepare for when your child reaches their teenage years is a potential shift in their dependence on and closeness to you towards an emphasis on time spent with their friends and time alone in their room away from you and other family members. While this is not universally true, it's pretty much standard for parents to experience their teenager pulling away from them, and this obviously brings up some strong feelings. As your child moves further away from you, it is common to experience feelings of rejection, but it is equally important to recognise that this shift in their behaviour is not personal and their need to separate from you and forge their own identity is a vital part of their development. Ultimately, if a child doesn't go through an adolescence in which they learn to be somewhat separate from you, their parent, they don't learn the skills they need to survive in the world, or the skills needed to relate to their peers, which are essential to their social survival.

Changes during puberty

Puberty is when a child's body begins to develop and change as they become an adult. Signs of puberty include girls developing breasts and starting their periods and boys developing a larger penis and testicles, a deeper voice and a more muscular appearance. The average age for girls to start puberty is 11, while for boys the average age is 12. But it's perfectly normal for puberty to begin at any point between the ages of 8 and 13 in girls and 9 and 14 in boys.

Hormonal upheaval

As hormones flood your teenager's body during puberty in preparation for adulthood, their bodies begin to change and their emotions broaden, yet they don't have all the inner resources they need to regulate and manage how they're feeling. In other words, they need your help more than ever to make sense of themselves and the world around them but, conversely, they are often less willing to let you help. It's understandable therefore why this time can be so hard for young people and those around them. During puberty your teen becomes more sensitive to their environment and the stressors within it; they will begin to look different and act in new ways and they will also experience some completely new feelings. There will be days when their feelings seem to dictate their life and they feel a loss of emotional control. But all young people will have their own experience of puberty and so all need support in different ways.

Neurobiological changes in the adolescent brain

As your child enters puberty and the early stages of adolescence, their brain is going through some important changes that impact their behaviour so it's helpful, when mentalizing your tween's or teen's behaviour, to understand what's going on, not just in their minds, in terms of their thoughts, but also physiologically, in their *brain*. Mentalizing some of these changes might hopefully modify/impact your response to your child.

During puberty, our brains undergo their most significant development since infancy. As we get older, the prefrontal cortex, located at the front of the brain, responsible for planning, thinking and decision-making, is the last part to develop. This area continues to develop and mature throughout adolescence and into early adulthood, explaining some of the behavioural changes often seen during this period. It controls our impulses, yet this crucial part of the brain doesn't finish forming fully until around age 25. One of the common sources of conflict between parents and young teenagers is the parent expectation that their child should start to behave in ways that seem more adult-like, whereas in reality, teenagers are particularly self-focused and compromised in their capacity to reflect accurately on the minds of other people during this developmental stage because of their immature brain development.

During adolescence, three biobehavioural systems are being reorganised in the brain: stress responses, reward systems and mentalizing (1). Put very simply, the reorganisation of these systems leads to patterns of thinking, behaviour and responses to others, including parents, which may be difficult to understand and that seem illogical, highly reactive or self-destructive; however, I would encourage you to try to reframe your understanding of these behaviours and emotional responses as adaptive instead of disruptive. There are major developmental changes in adolescence and these are significantly related to the structural and functional reorganisation of these three systems. One of these three systems, the mentalizing, or social cognition, system is human specific and lies behind our capacity to understand ourselves and others in terms of 'intentional mental states' (i.e. as having feelings, wishes, desires and values). Psychologists Peter Fonagy and Patrick Luyten discussed how this mentalizing system is uniquely human and essential to our understanding of a complex interpersonal world (2).

Take, for example, an adolescent's typical lack of communication with parents or other adult/authority figures. From our adult parent perspective, we see this as rude, arrogant or self-centred. From the adolescent perspective, if they experience excessive stress in a relationship, the reward system in their brain is affected and this impairs their capacity to relate to others. Understanding your growing teenager's neurological reward is worth a moment's reflection.

This means that the adolescent brain has a heightened response to positive stumuli, which leads to increased risk-taking and impulsive behaviours. Combined with an underdeveloped prefrontal cortex responsible for decision-making and impulse control, this essentially means that adolescents are more likely to seek out rewarding experiences, even if they carry potentially negative consequence. An example of this might be smoking around friends because the reward of the social approval this brings far outweighs the negative (longer term) potential health effects.

Keeping in mind the following key points about the adolescent reward system in the brain and how it affects teenagers' behaviour can be extremely helpful.

Increased dopamine activity

During adolescence, the brain produces more dopamine, a neurotransmitter associated with pleasure and reward, which can amplify the positive feelings associated with certain activities. For your child, these activities might include online gaming or scrolling through social media posts, or it could be trying alcohol or substances.

Dopamine is sometimes called the 'chemical messenger' and it plays a role in how we feel pleasure. It's a big part of our unique human ability to think and plan. It helps us strive, focus and find things interesting. The changes in the adolescent brain result in a mini reward deficiency syndrome, in that teenagers need more stimuli to feel satisfied. What this actually looks like in adolescents and some preteens is something that may be very familiar to you: they are easily bored, and this can be coupled with frustration arising from their strong need to belong and/or achieve and the status these states are associated with. This experience often gives rise to intense feelings of rejection and failure, leading to subsequent further frustration and aggression. Such experiences can lead adolescents to engage in compensatory behaviours such as risk-taking, substance abuse and combative behaviour.

- **Ventral striatum activation**
  This brain region, right in the centre of the brain, is a key part of the reward system and shows increased activity in adolescents when exposed to potential rewards, making teenagers more sensitive to their possible positive outcomes such as positive feedback or anticipated pleasure and less likely to consider negative outcomes. This in turn can contribute to the increased risk-taking and reward-seeking behaviours that are typical of this developmental stage. For example the increased activity in this part of the brain when anticipating a reward makes it more likely an adolescent will use substances such as drugs and alcohol, which offer an immediate reward, because they are less likely to think about any of the negative consequences, which feel more distant.
- **Immature prefrontal cortex**
  While the reward system is highly active in adolescence, the prefrontal cortex, responsible for planning, decision-making and impulse control, is still developing, which leads to difficulty in weighing potential risks against rewards. This means your child is likely to act more impulsively and take risks, whether these are high-level risks, such as taking drugs and drinking alcohol, or a low-level risk, such as staying up late.

The mentalizing system in adolescence

So far in this book, we have looked at the positive benefits to children of mentalizing, but in the pre-teen and adolescent years, aspects of mentalizing that might have been helpful when your child was younger can become more problematic. Humans' unique ability to mentalize is necessary to enable us to communicate effectively within complex social systems and collaborate with others. Our capacity to mentalize also means that we can be self-conscious and gives us the ability to imagine situations. However, although these capacities can sometimes be helpful, for example, being self-conscious can mean we check our behaviour, they increase our vulnerability to mental health disorders. For instance, some self-conscious emotions such as embarrassment, shame and guilt can affect our ability to adapt to different situations when they become excessive. By the same token, imagination, which we think of as a positive characteristic, may cause preteens and adolescents to become negatively aware of the difference between their ideal self and how they actually are.

As with the stress and reward systems, the mentalizing neural system undergoes significant reorganisation as children enter adolescence. As your child begins the next stage of their development, the teenage years, you should expect their mentalizing skills to become temporarily disrupted. In fact, younger children are somewhat better at mentalizing than teenagers, which may feel contrary to your expectations of your older child. Naturally, we expect our children to become more sophisticated as they get older, particularly in terms of their relationships and thoughtfulness about other people's feelings. However, various theories suggest that teenagers experience a dip in their ability to mentalize, which manifests as a dip in social cognition, that is their ability to think accurately about what others might be thinking. What this looks like in real life includes scenarios you may already be starting to notice, such as your tween or teenager seeming over sensitive to your comments or feeling abandoned by friends when they don't get the response they expected to a text message. In other words, they are struggling to see situations from another person's perspective and, partly due to their increased self-consciousness, they default to assuming that comments are critical and others are judging them (in the same way they are judging themselves). This tendency of teenagers makes it all the more important to use some of the tools you have learned about in this book, albeit in a slightly modified way, to take into account the developmental changes your child is going through.

What does it feel like to be a teenager in today's world?

Being a teenager is not easy. If you cast your mind back to when you were a teenager, you will probably remember that it wasn't all fun. I wonder what your experience was like? Getting in touch with the type of teenager you were, perhaps by using the Parent Map you created in chapter two, will help you reflect on how you wish to parent your tween now. This self-reflection will help you to understand and empathise with your child as they enter this phase. It seems that being an adolescent today is harder than at any other time in recent history, if we look at the records of the numbers of young people referred to or seeking mental health support. This period of development presents such a challenge to young people because they are trying to establish themselves as independent and autonomous people with their own individual identities, separate from their parents. This inevitably presents a challenge to you as a parent, too. The child who once wouldn't leave your side, refusing to go to bed or let you have a minute to yourself, is now turning into the child who withdraws from you, spends more time thinking about their friends than you and wants to be different from you in every aspect of their personality and looks. It is extremely common and normal to feel very rejected by your child when they enter this stage of their development, and mentalizing yourself should include trying to understand that often this perceived rejection is nothing personal to you.

On top of this, the feelings that arise for your tween or teenager when dealing with relationships and other people in general can leave them feeling overwhelmed or hopeless. The complexities of relationships are difficult for adolescents to deal with, and this can lead to further feelings of self-hatred as relationships fill them with emotions such as anxiety and the fear of being rejected, not liked and/or not as good or attractive as other people. On top of this, overthinking the actions and intentions of others leads to further feelings of inadequacy, self-doubt and self-hatred. When these feelings become too intolerable and overwhelming, instead of keeping them in, which feels unbearable, they often respond with impulsive, acting-out behaviour. If your child has reached this stage, you will probably be familiar with sudden explosions in their mood, door slamming or overly argumentative and seemingly aggressive verbal outbursts. Although this behaviour is difficult to live with, it is how your teenager deals with feelings they can't tolerate (rather like a toddler might roll around on the floor, screaming and crying, when they can't fully process a feeling of frustration). If these strong feelings become more intense or intolerable and your teenager is struggling to mentalize, they might resort to behaviour such as self-harm or avoidant behaviour, such as missing school, avoiding forming other close relationships after experiencing a rejection, and staying in their rooms for long periods of time.

Social media and the digital world

As discussed throughout this book, today's preteens and adolescents have ever more access to people around the world via social media, leading them to compare themselves to this global audience. Of course, it is not just access to comparing with others, but the access to the most beautiful, successful and wealthiest. Recent evidence points to a strong correlation (although a *causal* relationship has not yet been established in the research) between rising anxiety and depression in teenagers since widespread availability of mobile phone devices among younger children. It has been noted particularly that the young people of generation Z, the first generation to have had constant access to social media and digital devices throughout their puberty, have shown the sharpest spike in mental health problems over the past few decades. I have personally seen a shift, even in the past ten years, in the age at which parents allow their children to have a phone. My youngest son attended primary school between 2012 and 2019 when it was commonly agreed among parents that no child would have access to a mobile until they started secondary school. In the five to six years since, I have noticed the majority of kids at the same primary school have their own mobile phone. The boundary between childhood and early adolescence seems to have been blurred, and the emphasis on free play in childhood is fast disappearing. The danger of spending less time playing in person with other children is that young people will lose the ability to mentalize themselves and others; indeed, much current research has focused on whether time spent on devices is increasing anxiety, loneliness and disconnect in young people. Our capacity to mentalize is the driving mechanism for us being different from other animals, as humans are social beings who rely on relationships to give meaning to their lives. Being aware of the importance of mentalizing in terms of enjoying meaningful connections can help us to prioritise supporting young children and teenagers to engage in the world around them as much as possible and think about the role social media and screen time plays in their

lives. Encouragingly, young people, perhaps through mentalizing themselves, are coming to understand the negative side effects of excessive phone use and the concept of a 'digital detox' is growing.

How to use your Parent APP when mentalizing a young teen

When talking to parents about much younger children, I encourage them to be 'detectives' and look for clues behind their child's behaviour, actively tuning in to the possible thoughts and feelings that have resulted in a particular. I hope that this stance of being actively curious has been evident throughout this book. However, when I am working with parents of teenagers, and having parented three teenagers myself, I am extremely conscious of the fact that this curiosity is often most unwelcome and intrusive and the last thing a teenager wants is to feel that their parent is looking to be the one who 'knows' and solves their problems. Teenagers need to feel that they don't *have* to depend on anyone else to solve their problems, but rather that they can experience a sense of control and agency themselves. It's important, therefore, to mentalize this position as part of using your Parent APP with your tween or teenager. There are some other basic rules that are helpful to apply when you're trying to work out the meaning behind your young teen's behaviour:

• Mentalizing your teenager helps you to understand that their thoughts and feelings are entirely separate from yours.

- Each time you mentalize your teenager – using the principles of the Parent APP – you are helping them to see you as someone who will listen, see their perspective and understand. This helps your teenager to feel more connected to you and more likely to trust you.
- Using your Parent APP to mentalize your teenager models to them a reflective mind, which will support the development of their capacity for reflecting on thoughts and feelings. This will help your teenager to make and maintain stronger relationships with others.
- As you seek to understand your teenager's thoughts and feelings, and validate and empathise with their perspective on the world, they will feel a greater emotional connection with you and an increased understanding of themselves.
- Being mentalized by their parents in a way that doesn't feel intrusive to your teenager is particularly important during adolescence, when brain changes make it harder to understand the intentions of others and harder to manage their own emotions. In turn, you will have better and more emotionally attuned conversations with your tween or teenager and feel a sense of increased security in your relationship.

Why is becoming a reflective parent important to your adolescent's positive mental health?

In mentalization-based therapy for adolescents (MBT-A), the aim is to increase the young person's awareness of the minds of others and help them to become more mindful of themselves so that they can make more accurate observations about their own and others' thoughts and feelings. In doing this, adolescents become less impulsive, less prone to risk-taking and more balanced in their thoughts and feelings about themselves and others. This mentalizing stance doesn't have to come from an MBT-A therapist, however. Your role as a parent is vital in supporting your teenager to learn how to mentalize, and you can model and even teach this by becoming a more mentalizing parent yourself.

Mentalizing an adolescent therefore requires a different approach to mentalizing a young child. While 'intrusive' curiosity might need to be kept on the back burner, the feeling of being understood as an adolescent is extremely important, and therefore taking the perspective of your teenager – stepping into their shoes and imagining just what it is like for *them* – is probably more important at this stage of their development than any other. Part of their feeling understood might involve you having to step back so your teenager doesn't feel as though you are trying to sort out their problems. This careful balancing act, between being available to your tween or teen when they need you, but sufficiently distant and separate when they need to feel more in control and independent themselves, is not always easy to get right. Start by accepting that you won't get this right a lot of the time, and just know that this is normal for almost all parents of tweens and teenagers, as we are all having to adjust to a new way of relating to our children.

As your child enters the preteen years, you may become much more conscious of their mental health than you were when they were little. Some things to look out for if you are worried your child's mental health is at risk or that they are not coping well with the changes of adolescence are:

- Has their mood or behaviour persistently changed?
- Have they become disengaged from their usual hobbies or interests?
- Have they developed obsessive or extreme behaviours?
- How are their eating, sleeping and exercise habits?
- Have they become withdrawn or isolated from others?
- Are they engaging in risky behaviours or self-harm?

While it may feel frightening to ask yourself these types of questions, it is important to reflect on any changes you feel particularly worried about while also keeping in mind that some of the changes your child is going through are entirely normal, and part of healthy adolescent development rather than signs of an impending mental health problem. Let's look at some of the normal changes you can expect at this stage of your child's life.

A secure base for your tween

As your child approaches adolescence, it's easy to fall into thinking that you as a parent are needed less, mainly because that's the message teenagers often seem to give as they shut their bedroom door on the rest of the family, taking themselves away both physically and mentally. Where in early childhood our relationship with our toddler then young child seemed to be the most important thing in their world and essential to their survival, as they enter this next stage of development, it can be quite confusing trying to figure out what our role and relationship should look like. It is still important, however, to offer comfort and protection and at the same time promote exploration, but just in a different form. For example, you might encourage your tween to go out with their friends without you being involved in the planning, but then show curiosity and interest in how they got on when they come home, giving a hug and warm welcome to show they have a safe base with you. For you as a parent, it is just as necessary to provide a secure base, even though it might feel at times as though you are the only one who wants this attachment. It is as essential to your tween's sense of security as it was when they were younger. When you take into account the social, cognitive and emotional changes your tween or teenager is undergoing and their need to be an individual, separate from you, you enhance both your own and your teen's capacity to redefine your attachment and enjoy a successful relationship.

The tween years are a time to reflect on how protective or facilitative you need to be of your child's growing need for independence from you

Threats to security

Tensions commonly arise when adolescents start to assert their individual identity, which in psychological terms is referred to as individuating. A crucial part of growing up is figuring out who you are and who you want to be. In doing this, the majority of teenagers will want to make a clear statement that they are separate and different from you and need you less; to parents, this can feel like a threat to the closeness of your relationship. If you are approaching the teenage years yourself, this shift in your relationship can come as a shock or a rejection. Mentalizing yourself and your tween is very helpful at this stage, so you acknowledge the sense of loss you're experiencing and also the normal developmental stage of your child. Another threat emerges where you, the parent, identify so much with your own adolescence that you can't sufficiently parent and then there are risks to the protection and development of your child. The real adolescent in the family does not want or need an adolescent parent who can't take on the adult authority role. An example of this would be a parent who is heavily involved in substance misuse of drugs or alcohol. Their own emotional needs aren't met so this void is filled through excessive use of alcohol or drugs to an extent that they are unable to take an appropriate level of responsibility for their children and instead focus on their own needs. On a less extreme level, a parent who is stuck in their own adolescence, just wanting to have fun all the time to meet their own needs, would also struggle to take the more authoritative position that's needed to parent well.

I come across a lot of parents who say they are their adolescent son or daughter's best friend, but is this what adolescents need from their parents? Yes, being on their side, showing you understand and take on board their perspective is important, but being a best friend implies being on the same level and being like them. It can be hard for some parents to take on a more authoritative, adult role. This is particularly evident where parents still need some of their own adolescent needs to be met. This could look like a parent who is quite focused on gratifying their own need for excitement, attention or entertainment, or one who wants to ally themselves with their adolescent by pursuing adolescent activities with them. The chief problem is that not only does this prohibit the adolescent from being able to separate out from their parent, which is essential to their development, but it also severely compromises the parent's capacity to offer protection and proper caregiving to the real adolescent in the family. In the most serious child protection cases I have been involved in, the parent who is stuck in their own adolescent stage of development neglects their children to the point that their child's very survival is put at risk. This very serious failure to progress through adolescence into adulthood and to be able to mentalize the real child or adolescent in the family in these cases can result in the removal of those children and young people from the family for their own protection and survival. I do recognise this is not the norm, as I work with a clinical population.

Influencing your teenagers' mental health

If we go back to some of the potential risks to adolescents cited earlier in this chapter, it's clear that there is a lot for parents to worry about. In fact, today's teenagers take *fewer* risks than in previous generations. As discussed in the introduction to this book, one of the biggest risks to teenagers today is their mental health, as research shows that they are less likely to engage in risky behaviour such as taking drugs, drinking excessively, having risky sex and criminal behaviour. Parents talk to me frequently about feeling confused around how involved they should get in trying to support their child's often fluctuating moods. I was personally very struck by something Professor Peter Fonagy, my former mentor and Director of the Psychoanalysis Unit at University College London, said in a talk on adolescence: 'Don't leave them alone in their bedroom for ages thinking they will be okay. They won't be.' He wanted to emphasise the importance for adolescents of feeling that their parents were available to them when *they* wanted them. In other words, even if your teenager closes the door on you, it's important that you give the opposite message: that your door is always open. This can feel particularly hard when you have a strong emotional reaction to their behaviour or if you are extremely worried about them, making it near impossible to regulate your own emotions. However, you will find that if you use the tools of the Reflective Parenting stance, you will be able to manage your own emotions and turn your mind to what your teenager is going through in a way that is useful to them.

The parents' relationship

Your relationship with your partner will also influence your tween's mental health so it's important not to ignore this. Studies show that parents often underestimate how important it is to their adolescent children that their parents get on well, mistakenly thinking that their teenager is so wrapped up in their own world that they don't notice what's going on in their parent's or couple's relationship. When there is tension in a couple's relationship, this impacts adolescents' mental health. Most children feel they have a responsibility to make their parents get on. I have talked in more detail about conflict in the parental relationship in Chapter 8.

Where teenagers do engage in risky behaviour, this can impact their mental health by bringing them into conflict with parents and other adults. The paradox of risk-taking behaviour among teenagers is that it takes adolescents in two directions at once: satisfying their need to feel big and adult in one direction but provoking adults to manage them as if they were much younger, either by parenting in an authoritarian way or, in the most serious situations, youth services may become involved. Here's a fairly typical example of how both teenager and parent can mishandle a situation with potential risks.

Karen comes home after a long day at work and, on entering the house, hears loud music coming from the bathroom. Maddy is in the shower, singing at the top of her voice to a Billie Eilish song while Sam is in his bedroom, gaming. Tom is already putting Molly to bed as it's nearly 7pm and Karen has missed the nightly routine. Karen's head is still full from the clinic staff meeting she attended before she left work. It went on longer than planned as the team had to handle a complaint that had been made by a patient about the alleged rudeness of one of the reception staff. This wasn't Karen, but she felt there was excessive scrutiny on her as a result of the patient's complaint and she was feeling extremely irritable with everything and everyone as she entered the family home. Maddy came out of the bathroom and brushed past her mum without saying anything. When Karen said, sarcastically, 'Well, hello to you, too', Maddy rolled her eyes and said, 'I haven't got time for this, I've got to be at Aliesha's in 20 minutes.' Karen had been expecting a family evening meal at what was nearly the end of a long week and was shocked to hear Maddy say she was going out after 7pm on a Thursday until she remembered it was the Billie Eilish concert. 'How are you all getting there? Is Dad giving you a lift?' 'No, we're all getting an Uber there, you don't need to do any-thing Mum. Stay out of it.' After the difficult meeting and feeling criticised already by her team at work, Karen snaps, 'Stay out of it? I'm not having a couple of 12-year-olds getting an Uber to a concert. What does Aliesha's mum have to say?' Maddy lets out a scream of frustration from her bedroom and shouts, 'Aliesha's mum is cool about it. She's not like you. Thank God!' At this, Karen storms into Maddy's bedroom where she finds her daughter dressed in an extremely tight dress, applying thick eye liner around her eyes at her dressing table. Maddy shouts, 'Get out of my room!' without turning to look at her mum, at which point Karen snaps and shouts back at her, 'Well you can forget going out. You're not going! You're not wearing that dress or make up and getting into an Uber. You're grounded until you can learn how to stop being so rude. You're 12 years old. You can stay in your room!' At this, Maddy screams at the top of her lungs and starts sobbing and smashing her hand down on her dressing table over and over again, 'I AM going, I hate you, I hate you. I want to speak to dad. DAD, DAAAAAD, come and tell mum that I can go. NOW!'

Mentalizing the parent – Karen's perspective

Have you had a scenario like this yet in your parenting journey? I wonder what feelings come up for you when you imagine being in Karen's shoes? Her emotional thermometer was already at the 'hot' end of the scale after her difficult meeting at work where she had felt she was part of an attack on the reception staff at her clinic and pos-sibly feeling very anxious as well as annoyed, among other strong emotions. In her mind, she was hoping and expecting to come home to the security of her family, perhaps expecting a familiar greeting as she entered the house that would ground her after her difficult and 'after her difficult day at work that had left her feeling sensi-tive and emotional. Instead, she found everyone preoccupied with their own worlds, apart from Tom, who was putting their youngest to bed, but still unavailable to her at the moment she might have needed a hug. Not only is her son Sam lost in his own world of gaming, not leaving his room to greet her, but also Maddy is openly hostile to her from the get-go and appears totally absorbed in her own rush to get to the concert with her friend, oblivious to her mum's current mood, even irritated by it as it threatens to distract her from her excitement.

Does Karen overreact to her daughter's rudeness and to her intention of getting a cab to the concert, or is she right to set a boundary around how her daughter speaks to her, then how she is dressing? I wonder if you feel it's normal and okay to wear makeup and older teenage clothing at 12 years old, or if your reaction would have been similar to Karen's? How might Karen have handled things differently if she could have, and avoided resorting to more authoritarian parenting, where she shouted at Maddy and grounded her?

Mentalizing the 12-year-old tween – Maddy's perspective

Maddy is clearly completely preoccupied by her evening ahead with her best friend, seeing her idol Billie Eilish in concert. She has probably been waiting a long time for this day to come, and her emotional thermometer is also up at the 'hot' end, but her strong emotion is excitement and possibly a little fear at going out into the unknown. It's her first big concert without a parent. She is listening to the music to get her in an even more excited mood for the concert, and by the time her mum comes home she's absolutely buzzing about the night ahead. Maddy does see her mum when she comes out of the bathroom, but it hasn't even entered her head to ask her mum anything about her day and she's so excited to get to Aleisha's house and order the Uber to take them to the concert that, without thinking, she doesn't say 'Hi' to her mum and doesn't give her a second thought.

Maddy feels that her mum is making a big deal out of her not saying hello to her whereas, to Maddy, she's just in a rush to get to Aleisha's on time. Now her mum is starting to slow her down so she thinks it would be better just to get to her bedroom quickly and get out as soon as possible. When her mum bursts into her room she's really angry that she hasn't knocked and feels as if her mum is imposing her bad mood onto her, when she's done nothing wrong. In her head, she's got it all mapped out and she's madly excited, not just about the concert, but also about the journey there as they are going to play Billie Eilish music on the way and check out each other's makeup. Why can't her mum just be happy for her? This has got nothing to do with her, and what right has she got to spoil Maddy's longed-for evening out just because she had a rubbish day at work? Maddy thinks to herself her mum is probably jealous of her. When her mum says she's grounded, she feels completely mis-understood and explodes with anger as she feels she's being treated like her toddler sister, Molly.

Keep in mind . . .

- Remember that their brain is changing and still growing. It's harder for your tween or teen to understand other people's per-spectives, control their impulses, plan ahead and reflect accu-rately on themselves and others.
- Be actively attentive to what your teenager is thinking and feel-ing and try to listen more than you talk.
- Pause and reflect before you jump in to offer your opinion, and take time first to understand what their perspective is. Pay particular attention to what feels important to them, no matter what your opinion of this is.
- It's fine not to understand or know what your teenager thinks and feels and why. It's important not to pretend you understand or to offer an opinion when you don't understand their per-spective. It's okay to be unsure about what to say or to struggle to understand how they feel, but show that you are keen to try to understand.
- It's easier to lose control of your own feelings when your teen-ager behaves in ways you don't understand or that worry you. Start with using your Parent Map to mentalize yourself, regu-lating your feelings. Then choose a moment when you're clam to mentalize your teenager more effectively.
- Try to notice and be curious about what might be in your teen-ager's mind, but don't start off with too many intrusive ques-tions. I suggest starting with something they want to hear like, "Did you have a good time last night?" before asking any ques-tions that stem from your own concerns.
- Respect your teenager's need to have some autonomy. When you express curiosity about what they are thinking and feeling, gauge when it's the right time, and allow them some private thoughts that are theirs alone.
- Be aware of your tone and facial expression. Teenagers are sen-sitive to voices that sound patronising or judgemental. Speak to your teenager as you would want to be spoken to yourself. If you treat your teenager with respect, they will be more likely to give a thoughtful and more mature response.

- Help your teenager to problem-solve, knowing that this can be difficult during adolescence, when the brain acts more impulsively.

Looking ahead

I hope this book has given you lots of ideas to try out in your relationship with your child, but I'm sure that there are probably many more questions you will still have. I wouldn't see that as a negative, because if this book has prompted you to be more curious about what's going on in your child's mind, or to start to think about your tween, wondering what they are thinking and feeling, even if you don't know the answer, then that's great! Staying interested and curious is the key to good mentalizing, and not knowing is an inevitable part of trying to understand other people's minds. Do try giving it a go and know that it takes time and practice, but if you try modelling being reflective in front of your children you will start to see some real benefits. Your children love to feel your interest and curiosity in their world, and it will bring you closer together. I've noticed that with my own (now almost all adult) children, after a long time trying this approach out, they gradually started to make reflective, mind-minded comments about their friends and family members, and some of this has taken years. I hope it will get passed on to their relationships with their own children one day. For the families I've worked with, too, it's great to see that over time, helping parents and children to be more interested and curious about other people and what's going on in their minds has long-term benefits for children's behaviour, emotional development, mental health and their relationships with other people. It's also great to see how much happier these parents and caregivers feel in their relationships. Good luck with it all, and if you can, stay curious and!

REFERENCES

Introduction

1. Katsantonis, I., & Symonds, J.E. (2023, March). Population heterogeneity in developmental trajectories of internalising and externalising mental health symptoms in childhood: Differential effects of parenting styles. *Epidemiology and Psychiatric Sciences, 32.*
2. Fonagy, P., Steele, H., Steele, M., Leigh, T., Kennedy, R., Mattoon, G., & Target, M. (1995). Attachment, the reflective self, and borderline states: The predictive specificity of the Adult Attachment Interview and pathological emotional development. In S. Goldberg, R. Muir, & J. Kerr (Eds.), *Attachment Theory: Social, Developmental, and Clinical Perspectives* (pp. 233–278). New York: Analytic Press.
3. Fonagy, P., Steele, H., & Steele, M. (1991). Maternal representations of attachment during pregnancy predict the organisation of infant-mother attachment at one year of age. *Child Development, 62,* 891–905.
4. Bowlby, J. (1958). The nature of the child's tie to his mother. *International Journal of Psycho-Analysis, 39,* 350–373.
5. Ainsworth, M.D.S., &Witting, B.A. (1969). Attachment and exploratory behaviour of one-year-olds in a strange situation. In B.M. Foss (Ed.), *Determinants of Infant Behaviour* (Vol. 4., pp. 111–136). London: Metheuen.
6. Fonagy, P. (1989). On tolerating mental states: Theory of mind in borderline patients. *Bulletin of the Anna Freud Centre, 12,* 91–115.
7. Mansfield, R., Santos, J., Deighton, J., Hayes, D., Velikonja, T., Boehnke, J.R., & Patalay, P. (2022). The impact of the COVID-19 pandemic on adolescent mental health: A natural experiment. *Royal Society Open Science, 9* (4), 211114. doi: 10.1098/rsos.211114
8. Hogg, S., & Mayes, G. (2021). *Casting Long Shadows. The Ongoing Impact of the COVID-19 Pandemic on Babies, Their Families and the Services that Support Them.* The First 1001 Days Movement and Institute of Health Visiting.

9. Bronsard, G., Alessandrini, M., Fond, G., Loundou, A., Auquier, P., Tordjman, S., & Boyer, L. (2016). The prevalence of mental disorders among children and adolescents in the child welfare system: A systematic review and meta-analysis. *Medicine, 95* (7), e2622. doi: 10.1097/md.0000000000002622

10. Maslow, A. (1943). A theory of human motivation. *Psychological Review, 50* (4), 370–396. CiteSeerX 10.1.1.334.7586. doi: 10.1037/h0054346. hdl:10983/23610

Chapter 1 – The origins of Reflective Parenting

1. Fonagy, P., Steele, M., Steele, H., Moran, G., & Higgitt, A. (1991). The capacity for understanding mental states: The reflective self in parent and child and its significance for security of attachment. *Infant Mental Health Journal, 12*, 201–218.

2. Lecanuet, J.P., & Schaal, B. (1996). Fetal sensory competencies. *European Journal of Obstetrics & Gynecology and Reproductive Biology, 68*, 1–2.

3. Voegtline, K.M., Costigan, K.A., Pater, H.A., & DiPietro, J.A. (2013). Near-term fetal response to maternal spoken voice. *Infant Behavior and Development, 36*, 526–533.

4. Gerhardt, S. (2004). *Why Love Matters: How Affection Shapes a Baby's Brain.* Hove: Brunner-Routledge.

5. Schore, A.N. (2001). Effects of a secure attachment relationship on right brain development, affect regulation, and infant mental health. *Infant Mental Health Journal, 22* (1–2), 7–66.

6. Schore, A. (1994). *Affect Regulation and the Origin of the Self.* Hillsdale, NJ: Lawrence Erlbaum Associates Inc.

7. Thomas, D.G., Whitaker, E., Crow, C.D., Little, V., Love, L., Lykins, M.S., & Letterman, M. (1997). Event-related potential variability as a measure of information storage in infant development. *Developmental Neuropsychology, 13*, 205–232.

8. Fonagy, P., Target, M., Steele, H., & Steele, M. (1994). The Emmanuel Miller Memorial Lecture 1992. The theory and practice of resilience. *Journal of Child Psychology and Psychiatry, 35*, 231–257.

9. Meins, E., & Fernyhough, C. (1999). Linguistic acquisitional style and mentalizing development: The role of maternal mind-mindedness. *Cognitive Development, 14*, 363–380.

10. Trevarthen, C. (2010). What is it like to be a person who knows nothing? Defining the active intersubjective mind of a newborn human being. *Infant and Child Development, 20* (1), 119–135.

11. Nagy, E. (2010). The newborn infant: A missing stage in developmental psychology. *Infant and Child Development, 20* (1), 3–19.

12. Csibra, G., & Gergely, G. (2009). Natural pedagogy. *Trends in Cognitive Sciences, 13*, 148–153.

13. Grienenberger, J., Slade, A., & Kelly, K. (2005). Maternal reflective functioning, mother-infant affective communication, and infant attachment: Exploring the link between mental states and observed caregiving behavior in the intergenerational transmission of attachment. *Attachment and Human Development, 7* (3), 299–311.

Chapter 2 – The Parent Map

1. Kohn, A. (2005). *Unconditional Parenting: Moving from Rewards and Punishments to Love and Reason.* New York: Atria/Simon & Schuster.
2. Emde, R.N. (1983). The pre representational self and its affective core. *Psychoanalytic Study of the Child, 38,* 165–192.
3. Brown, G.W., & Harris, T.O. (1978). *The Social Origins of Depression: A Study of Psychiatric Disorder in Women.* London: Tavistock.

Chapter 3 – Managing your feelings

1. Kennedy, H., Landor, M., & Todd, L. (2011). *Video Interaction Guidance – A Relationship-Based Intervention to Promote Attunement, Empathy and Wellbeing.* London: Jessica Kingsley Publishers.

Chapter 4 – The 'Parent APP'

1. Fonagy, P., Redfern, S., & Charman, T. (1997). The relationship between belief-desire reasoning and a projective measure of attachment security (SAT). *British Journal of Developmental Psychology, 15,* 51–61.

Chapter 6 – Discipline: understanding misunderstandings

1. Doyle, A.B., & Moretti, M.M. (2000). *Attachment to Parents and Adjustment in Adolescence: Literature Review and Policy Implications.* CAT number 032ss. H5219-9-CYH7/001/SS. Ottawa: Health Canada, Child and Family Division.
2. Doyle, A.B., Moretti, M.M., Brendgen, M., & Bukowski, W. (2002). *Parent Child Relationships and Adjustment in Adolescence: Findings from the HSBC and NLSCY Cycle 2 Studies.* CAT number 032ss. H5219-00CYHS. Ottawa: Health Canada, Child and Family Division.
3. Moretti, M.M., & Holland, R. (2003). Navigating the journey of adolescence: Parental attachment and the self from a systemic perspective. In S. Johnson & V. Whiffen (Eds.), *Clinical Applications of Attachment Theory* (pp. 41–56). New York: Guildford.
4. Alessandri, S.M., & Lewis, M. (1993). Parental evaluation and its relation to shame and pride in young children. *Sex Roles, 29,* 335–343.

5. Alessandri, S.M., & Lewis, M. (1996). Differences in pride and shame in mal-treated and nonmal treated preschoolers. *Child Development, 67*, 1857–1869.
6. Hughes, D. (2006). *Building the Bonds of Attachment* (DVD). Produced by Sandra Webb & Lunchroom Production.
7. Fletcher, A., Steinberg, L., & Sellers, E. (1999). Adolescents' wellbeing as a function of perceived inter-parent inconsistency. *Journal of Marriage and the Family, 61*, 300–310.

Chapter 7 – Parenting around neurodivergence and trauma

1. Lobregt-van Buuren, E., Hoekert, M., & Sizoo, B. (2021, August 20). Autism, adverse events, and trauma. In A.M. Grabrucker (Ed.), *Autism Spectrum Disorders*. Brisbane: Exon Publications.
2. Roberts, L.A., Koenen, K.C., Lyall, K., Robinson, E.B., & Weisskopf, M.G. (2015). Association of autistic traits in adulthood with childhood abuse, interpersonal victimization and posttraumatic stress. *Child Abuse & Neglect, 45*, 135–142. doi: 10.1016/j.chiabu.2015.04.010. [PMC free article] [PubMed]
3. Wood, J.J., & Gadow, K.D. (2010). Exploring the nature and function of anxiety in youth with autism spectrum disorders. *Clinical Psychology: Science and Practice, 17*, 281–292. doi: 10.1111/j.1468-2850.2010.01220.x.
4. Frith, U., & Frith, C. (2009, November). The social brain: Allowing humans to boldly go where no other species has been. *Philosophical Transactions 12*, 165–173.
5. Feldman, E.K., & Matos, R. (2014). Training paraprofessionals to facilitate social interactions between children with autism and their typically developing peers. *Journal of Positive Behaviour Interventions, 15* (3), 169–179.
6. Baron-Cohen, S. (1995). *Mindblindness: An Essay on Autism and Theory of Mind*. Cambridge, MA: MIT Press.
7. Atwood, T. (2007). *The Complete Guide to Asperger's Syndrome*. London: Jessica Kingsley Publishers.
8. Siller, M., Swansonn, M., Gerber, A., Hutman, T., & Sigman, M. (2014). A Parent-Mediated Intervention that targets responsive parental behaviours increases attached behaviours in children with ASD: Results from a randomised clinical trial. *Journal of Autism and Developmental Disorders, July 44* (7) 1720–1732.
9. Steele, M.J., Kaniuk, J., Henderson, K., Hillman, S., & Asquith, K. (2008). Forecasting outcomes in previously maltreated children: The use of the AAI in a longitudinal adoption study. In H. Steele & M. Steele (Eds.), Guildford Press. 2008

10. Pollak, S.D., Chiccetti, D., Hornung, K., & Reed, A. (2000). Recognizing emotion in faces: Developmental effects of child abuse and neglect. *Developmental Psychology, 36,* 679–688.

11. Hughes, D., & Rothschild, B. (2013). *8 Keys to Building Your Best Relationships (8 Keys to Mental Health).* New York: W. W. Norton & Company.

Chapter 8 – Family, siblings and friends

1. Keavney, E., Midgley, N., Asen, E., Bevington, D., Fearon, P., Fonagy, P., Jennings-Hobbs, R., & Wood, S. (2012). Minding the family mind – The development and initial evaluation of mentalization-based treatment for families. In N. Midgley & I. Vrouva (Eds.), *Minding the Child – Mentalization Based Interventions with Children, Young Children and their Families.* (pp. 98–112). Routledge/Taylor & Francis Group, London

2. Rutter, M. (1981). *Maternal Deprivation Reassessed, Second Edition.* Harmondsworth: Penguin.

3. Rutter, M. (1971). Parent-child separation: Psychological effects on the children. *Journal of Child Psychology and Psychiatry, 12,* 233–260.

4. Asen, E., & Morris, E. (2020). *High-Conflict Parenting Post Separation. The Making and Breaking of Family Ties.* London: Routledge.

5. Fonagy, P., Gergely, G., Jurist, E., & Target, M. (2002). *Affect Regulation, Mentalization and the Development of the Self.* New York: Other Press.

6. McCrory, E., De Brito, S.A., & Viding, E. (2011, July 28). The impact of childhood maltreatment: A review of the neurobiological and genetic factors. *In Front Psychiatry, 2,* 48. doi: 10.3389/fpsyt.2011.00048

7. Dunn, J., Creps, C., & Brown, J. (1996). Children's family relationships between two and five: Developmental changes and individual differences. *Social Development, 5,* 230–250.

8. Bowes, L., Wolke, D., Joinson, C., Lereya, S.T., & Lewis, G. (2014). Sibling bullying and risk of depression, anxiety, and self-harm: A prospective cohort study. *Pediatrics, 134* (4), 1032–1039.

9. Perner, J., Ruffman, T., & Leekam, S.R. (1994). Theory of mind is contagious: You catch it from your sibs. *Child Development, 65* (4), 1228–1238.

10. Fonagy, P., Redfern, S., & Charman, T. (1997). The relationship between belief-desire reasoning and a projective measure of attachment security (SAT). *British Journal of Developmental Psychology, 15,* 51–61.

11. Slaughter, V., Dennis, M.J., & Pritchard, M., (2010). Theory of mind and peer acceptance in preschool children. *British Journal of Developmental Psychology, 20* (4), 545–564.

12. Redfern, S. (2011). *Social Cognition in Childhood: The Relationships between Attachment-Related Representations, Theory of Mind and Peer Popularity*. Institute of Psychiatry, King's College London. Doctoral Thesis.
13. Haidt, J. The Anxious Generation. How the Great Rewiring of Childhood Is Causing an Epidemic of Mental Illness 2024. Penguin Press

Chapter 9 – Mentalizing during good times

1. Ispa, J. (2015). Unpublished research from the Early Head Start Research and Evaluation Project *Social Development* (2015).
2. Youngblade, L.M., & Dunn, J. (1995). Individual differences in young children's pretend play with mother and sibling: Links to relationships and understanding of other people's feelings and beliefs. *Child Development, 66* (5), 1472–1492.

Chapter 10 – The transition from childhood to adolescence

1. Blakemore, S.-J. (2018). *Inventing Ourselves. The Secret Life of the Teenage Brain*. London: Penguin Random House.
2. Fonagy, P., & Luyten, P. (2018). Conduct problems in youth and the RDoC approach: A developmental, evolutionary-based view. *Clinical Psychology Review, 64*, 57–76. doi: 10.1016/j.cpr.2017.08.010

INDEX

For Product Safety Concerns and Information please contact our EU
representative GPSR@taylorandfrancis.com
Taylor & Francis Verlag GmbH, Kaufingerstraße 24, 80331 München, Germany

www.ingramcontent.com/pod-product-compliance
Lightning Source LLC
Chambersburg PA
CBHW050337270326
41926CB00016B/3497